Beyond Metaphor

The Theory of Tropes in Anthropology

Contributors

Hoyt Alverson
Benjamin N. Colby
Deborah Durham
James W. Fernandez
Paul Friedrich
Emiko Ohnuki-Tierney
Dale Pesmen
Naomi Quinn
Terence Turner

Beyond Metaphor

The Theory of Tropes
in Anthropology

Edited by
James W. Fernandez

Stanford University Press
Stanford, California

Stanford University Press
Stanford, California
© 1991 by the Board of Trustees of the
Leland Stanford Junior University
Printed in the United States of America

Original printing 1991
Last figure below indicates year of this printing:
04 03 02 01 00 99 98 97 96 95

Stanford University Press publications are distributed
exclusively by Stanford University Press within the
United States, Canada, and Mexico; they are distributed
exclusively by Cambridge University Press throughout
the rest of the world.

Preface

With two exceptions, the papers collected here were given the third week of November 1987 at the annual meetings of the American Anthropological Association in Chicago. Paul Friedrich's paper on "Polytropy" had been invited, but he could not present it at the colloquium; and the paper by Dale Pesmen on "Mixed Metaphor," which had been written before the meetings, was requested in revised version after them.

Naomi Quinn, one of our contributors, observed at the colloquium that it was a particularly "hot" moment, both literally and metaphorically. The meeting room in which the colloquium was held was tightly packed, with an audience that far exceeded seating capacity crowding the floor both before and behind the speakers, filling the doorway, and spilling out into the hall, making for a very hot and steamy room indeed. But one could also gather from the extraordinary attendance that the topic itself was a "hot" one. We would like to believe that the source of this heat was the promise, because of their previous contributions to metaphor theory, of the incandescence the colloquium participants might shed upon this "momentous" topic. And we do not think that the papers presented disappointed those who were in attendance. Nor are they, as revised and supplemented here, likely to disappoint those who were unable to gain entry at the time or who were there and wish to review in cooler circumstances the arguments made.

These papers, in any case, can stand as a record of the "state of the art" of trope theory in anthropology at the end of the 1980's; they will also, we hope, in their movement "beyond metaphor" to the interplay of all the tropes, stimulate work on that more complex dynamic in human affairs. Of course, interest in the tropes in human thought and action is an ancient one, not only in

Western thought but in other traditions as well. Anthropologists cannot pretend to an original subject matter here. But we can pretend to a particular perspective upon it, one derived from our field experience, cross-cultural for the most part, and our constant reflection on the ethnography of human thought in relation to action and as a shaping force—whether of facilitation or inhibition—in that action. The tropes, we know from our field experience, play an important role in human action and thus enter into any pragmatic understanding of things human. We hope to have communicated something of that notion here.

As editor of this volume, a task falling to me as convenor of the symposium, I wish first to thank the contributors for their prompt revision of these papers and for their dispatch in respect to the usual editorial requirements. Michael Silverstein and David Sapir made apposite and stimulating commentaries on the papers at the end of the symposium itself. We are all grateful for their participation and insights. I would like to thank Stanford Press, and especially our Stanford editors, William Carver and Ellen F. Smith, for their contribution to this volume. Lucille Allsen of the Institute for Advanced Study at Princeton provided efficient and accurate typing and editing of many of the revised papers, materially contributing to the consolidation of the final manuscript. Dale Pesmen has aided greatly in bibliographic matters, and Deborah Durham prepared the index.

J. W. F.

Contents

Part III. Metaphor and the Coherence of Culture

Contributors

Hoyt Alverson is Professor of Anthropology at Dartmouth College. He received his Ph.D. from Yale University and has worked on the economics of migration and industrialization and on cognitive and linguistic change in Southern Africa. He is currently working on problems in theoretical linguistics and on economic development.

Benjamin N. Colby is Professor of Anthropology at the University of California, Irvine. He received his Ph.D. in Social Relations at Harvard University. He has worked in Mexico, the United States, and Japan and is currently studying linkages among symbolic behavior, stress, and immunology in elderly Japanese and Anglo women.

Deborah Durham received her education at Smith College, Boston University, and the University of Chicago. She is currently completing her Ph.D. at Chicago on "Exile and the Historical Consciousness of Community Among the Herero of Botswana," based on fieldwork in Africa.

James W. Fernandez is Professor of Anthropology at the University of Chicago and was educated at Amherst College and Northwestern University. He has worked among Fang, Zulu, Ewe, and Fon in Africa and among cattle keepers and miners in Northern Spain. He is currently preparing an ethnography on the Spanish work.

Paul Friedrich is Professor of Anthropology, Linguistics, and Social Thought at the University of Chicago and was educated at Williams College, Harvard University, and Yale University. He has worked among the Tarascans in Mexico, the Nayars in India, and Russian dissidents. He is currently working on a book on Russian poetry and editing the Spanish translation of his book *The Princes of Naranja*.

Emiko Ohnuki-Tierney, a native of Japan, is Vilas Professor of Anthropology at the University of Wisconsin, where she received her Ph.D. She has worked among the Sakhalin Ainu and on the history and culture of contemporary Japan. Her current work examines the symbolism of rice in Japanese culture.

Dale Pesmen received her education at the University of Chicago. A painter who has collaborated on theater and conceptual art in the Chicago area, she is currently embarking on dissertation research on theater and culture in the Soviet Union.

Naomi Quinn is Associate Professor in the Department of Cultural Anthropology at Duke University and received her Ph.D. at Stanford University. She has worked in West Africa and is currently studying American cultural understandings of marriage. Her enduring interest is in the nature of culture and its relation to cognition.

Terence Turner is Professor of Anthropology at the University of Chicago. He received his Ph.D. from Harvard University. He has conducted fieldwork with the Kayapo of Brazil since 1962 and is currently involved with the making of documentary films about their resistance to Brazilian exploitation.

Beyond Metaphor

The Theory of Tropes in Anthropology

Introduction:

Confluents of Inquiry

James W. Fernandez

We are living at a very metaphorical moment in the human sciences in the several senses of that assertion. For one thing, there is just now an especially pronounced awareness that what is done in human affairs is not simply to be taken literally, at face value as it were, but that many such doings, like metaphor itself, stand for something else, so that our sober-sided constructions have obligatorily to be deconstructed. For another thing, we are living at a time when the referential value of language, its ability to provide us with an accurate, transparent view through to and mapping of the reality of things—an "immaculate perception," as it is called[1]—is profoundly questioned, and we have become acutely aware of the figurative devices that lie at the very heart of discourse, defining situations and grounding our sense of what is to be taken as real and objective and, therefore, entitled (by means of the figurative entitlements we employ)[2] to have real consequences. As a result and most obviously, we are living at a time when refer-

[1] One hears this play on fundamentalist thinking from a number of sources, but I owe it first to Donald T. Campbell in a talk on M. J. Herskovits's cultural relativism, delivered at the Philadelphia Anthropological Society in 1988.

[2] Kenneth Burke uses the term "entitlement" to conceptualize the capacity of symbolic action, including metaphoric predication, to give identity—that is, a title—to persons, situations, or things otherwise uncertainly conceived. See

ence to metaphor occurs with ever greater frequency in writings in the social sciences. Thus the fact that a collection of articles is oriented to the problem of metaphor and the other tropes in human thought and action will certainly have no surprise value to the reader at the present time.[3] What will be more interesting is the fact that these articles are written by anthropologists and are thus informed by anthropological, which is to say cross-cultural, perspectives, in which the pragmatic and coincidental work of figures of thought within social structures and cultural worldviews is the primary referent of theoretical understanding.

When we speak of a metaphorical moment, we mean it not only in the sense of the importance at the present conjuncture in the social sciences of a mode of understanding which focuses on the role of the figurative imagination and rhetorical forces in social life but also the moment at which these papers were given in that colloquium at the American Anthropological Convention in Chicago whose intensity and "incandescence" we have mentioned in the Preface. It was a moment within this larger moment in anthropology and the social sciences.

A Brief History of Associationist Principles and of the Vacancy of Human Understanding

In point of fact, anthropologists by profession can hardly be said to be strangers to the spirit of this metaphorical moment or dubious contributors to its elucidation in creating, in our case, a "moment" of our own. The experience of "crossing cultures" relativizes one's understanding, and even if it does not lead to a theory of the figuration of culture, it prepares one to recognize that the human capacity to define situations is very powerful and per-

---

"What Are the Signs of What? (A Theory of Entitlement)," *Anthropological Linguistics*, June 1962; collected in Burke 1966: 359–79.

[3] This was not always the case. When I began to speak and write about metaphor theory in the mid- to late 1960's (see Fernandez 1969), there was considerable feeling that the metaphor concept was essentially a literary device and of questionable relevance to anthropology, much less the social sciences in general.

suasive. In point of additional fact, anthropologists have long been interested in metaphor and alert to its presence in their materials. That awareness is directly present in the work of Franz Boas, as it is in that of Paul Radin.[4] And it is indirectly present in an earlier anthropology and particularly in the Frazerian corpus, which not only is rich in figurative argument but evokes in its theory of sympathetic magic, by contagion and imitation, the two axes of associationist thought, association by similarity and by contiguity. These axes have been, particularly as articulated by Ferdinand de Saussure, Roman Jakobson, Claude Lévi-Strauss, and Roland Barthes, of much subsequent importance in metaphoric analyses.[5] For trope theory in anthropology, the work of Lévi-Strauss, particularly his argument in *The Savage Mind* and its evocation of these associationist principles in addressing the workings of that mind, constitutes a central text.[6] Two other central texts of the late 1960's are Stanley Tambiah's "The Magical Power of Words" (1968), which reworks Malinowskian texts in a Jakobsonian–Lévi-Straussian vein, and his more directly Lévi-Straussian "Animals

[4] See Boas's "Introduction" to *The Handbook of American Indian Languages* (1914: part I, 5–75) and "Metaphorical Expression in the Language of the Kwakiutl Indians" (1982). There was an alertness to metaphor in Radin throughout his career, but see especially his comments on figurative devices in *The Culture of the Winnebago as Described by Themselves* (1949: General Introduction and chap. 3, "The Journey of the Ghost to Spiritland") and also *The Road of Life and Death* (1945).

[5] *The Golden Bough* chooses in its very title a metaphor (more properly a metonym) evoking the perpetual agonistic ritual quest for the prize of preeminence in human social relations. Frazer states his theory of magic, in associationist terms, in chap. 3 of his two-volume edition of *The Golden Bough* (1935). But see also the truly "short course" of the Frazerian argument: *Man, Gods, and Immortality* (1927). This associationist perspective is also seen in the work of E. B. Tylor, the founder of modern social and cultural anthropology, in, for example, *Primitive Culture* (1877: vol. 1, chaps. 4 and 10). For metaphor theory in the second half of the century, Roman Jakobson and Morris Halle's *Fundamentals of Language* (1956), which distinguishes the two aspects of language—metaphoric and metonymic or syntagmatic and paradigmatic—has become a classic source, particularly part II, "Two Aspects of Language and Two Types of Aphasic Disturbance." Jakobson's argument is fundamental in Barthes, *Elements of Semiology* (1964) and Lévi-Strauss, *The Savage Mind* (1966).

[6] See particularly chap. 3, "Systems of Transformation," and chap. 5, "Categories, Elements, Species, Number."

Are Good to Think and Good to Prohibit" (1969).[7] These various works were influential in the early 1970's in creating an increased sensitivity to metaphor and other figurative idioms in field data, a sensitivity seen particularly in the work of the period of James Fox (1971) and Michelle Rosaldo (1972), who were principally interested in structural problems of opposition and parallelism and the central role of metaphor in such cultural constructions.

In the 1970's there was, under the influence in part of these predecessors and in part of thinkers outside anthropology strictly considered, an important turn toward metaphor theory within anthropology. The rediscovered seventeenth-century Italian thinker Giambattista Vico was influential here, as was the American pragmatic philosophic tradition, which, like the Wittgensteinian tradition in England, focused attention on the "language games" of philosophers rather than on their metaphysical claims—and indeed at the expense of such claims![8] Vico had much earlier focused on the figurative "ingenuity," the "language games" in effect, that had been forced upon mankind by reason of the "indigence" and "vacancy" of human understanding. The Vichian catchphrase "Homo non intelligendo fit omnia" ("Man, in not understanding, makes his world") captures the weakness of human understanding relative to experience and the consequent dependence upon "vulgar reasoning," which is to say, upon reasoning that figuratively transfers meaning from that which is known most intimately, very domestic understandings as it were, to that which otherwise must remain unknown and not understood—in a word, vacant.[9] It

[7] For late 1960's works on metaphor see also R. Rosaldo (1968) and Fernandez (1969).

[8] The modern pragmatist Richard Rorty (1978 and other writings) captures the resurgent pragmatism of the 1970's. In less articulated form this pragmatism is also present among anthropologists as an awareness in them (partly a consequence of their own praxis) of the "constituted nature" of cultural realities whose instruments of constitution, it might well be deduced, are metaphors and the associated tropes. A historian and thinker of the 1970's of special importance both to metaphor theory and for the understanding of Vico was Hayden White; see especially "The Tropics of History: The Deep Structure of THE NEW SCIENCE" (in 1978: 197–217).

[9] See Vico 1976, esp. book II, 106–296. Most recently Michael Herzfeld (1987) has published an important critical study of the ethnography of Europe and more particularly of Greece. He makes the Vichian perspective and its in-

might be argued, as indeed it was by such philosophers as Locke and Hobbes, that the understanding thus achieved was inevitably a form of misunderstanding. But for Vico it was the best under- standing we could achieve—for, as Friedrich Max Müller (1873) would later argue, our language is inevitably diseased in this way— and the task of the New Science lay in understanding the origins and evolutionary vicissitudes of that language.

Vico's collocation of human consciousness and understanding in the vicissitudes of figurative argument is the main theme of the American philosopher Stephen Pepper's *World Hypotheses* (1942), a book influential in the turn toward metaphor theory of the 1970's. It is cited by both Sherry Ortner and Victor Turner in their pioneering work on "key symbols" or "key metaphors" (Ortner 1973) or "root metaphors" (V. Turner 1974) and by Dale Pesmen in this volume. Pepper's argument was that all enduring philosophic systems were grounded in "common sense," that is, in a "concrete evidential source of understanding." This is to say, our under- standing is grounded in one or another of six basic metaphors or world hypotheses: animism, participation, formism, mechanism, contextualism, organicism. This argument suggests the notion of "root metaphor" as basic not only to philosophy but to culture it- self. And both Ortner and Turner use this concept in their articles.[10]

These quasi-Platonic notions of an underlying figurative prem- ise, or set of premises in dialectical relation, upon which culture is built[11]—an old notion in anthropology after all, going back to Adolph Bastien's (1895) "elementary thoughts" (*Elementarge- danken*)—were, as "root metaphors" or "organizing metaphors," characteristic of much work of the 1970's.[12] But it would be more adequate to our understanding to distinguish several trends in that work, trends with which we are still contending. There is first

---

sistence on recognizing the metaphors upon which our analytic ideas are based fundamental to his argument—and fundamental to any adequate ethnography.

[10] I preferred the term "organizing metaphor" in my 1970's work on meta- phor (see Fernandez 1972; 1974).

[11] See also the argument for an underlying premise in Navajo culture (not specifically identified, however, with a metaphoric assertion or predication) in Witherspoon 1977.

[12] See various treatments of this "elementary metaphors" approach in, for example, J. Bastien 1978; and Armstrong 1975.

of all the Aristotelian-derived strain of metaphor theory, which, sharpened by a Saussurian interest in "differences that make a difference" in linguistic systems, focuses upon the transfer of features of meaning from one domain of understanding to another. In 1976 Keith Basso contributed an important paper arguing this position: because of lexical gaps in our vocabulary and a resultant weakness of understanding, we transfer features of meaning from domains of experience that we know well to domains that we do not understand.[13] There is, second, a strain, much influenced by the American critic and philosopher Kenneth Burke (1957; 1966), that concentrates on how experience in culture and position in society are constructed through metaphoric predication. This strain of metaphor theory in anthropology is primarily interested in the Social and Cultural Use of Metaphor, to paraphrase the title of a collection of anthropological essays of the period edited by David Sapir and Christopher Crocker (1977) focusing on the pragmatics of metaphor.[14]

This latter strain of metaphor theory, with its sense, on the one hand, of the diversity of the tropes and, on the other hand, of the transformative interaction of the various subtropes of which metaphor, as a generic term, is constituted—chiefly metaphor, metonym, synecdoche, and irony—has led to the contemporary notion of "the play of tropes"[15] (Durham and Fernandez, this volume) or "polytropy" as it is called in one of the foundational essays in this collection (Friedrich, this volume).[16] There was increasing realization in the 1970's that the challenge to our understanding lay not just in understanding metaphor—though in the

[13] The "feature transfer" position is presented with a concern for formal argument in Levin 1977.

[14] For an argument about the role of metaphoric predication in the "creation of culture" and the negotiation of social position, see Fernandez 1974 and Wagner 1975.

[15] A notion advanced in a collection of studies written mostly in the 1970's (Fernandez 1986).

[16] But see Friedrich's earlier essays, central to the poetics movement in anthropology, in which he seeks to give us a sense of the diverse shaping of—that is, the imaginative potentialities of—the tropes in poetic language; see particularly "Metaphor-like Relations in Referential Subsets" and "Poetic Language and the Imagination: A Reformulation of the Sapir Hypothesis" in Friedrich 1979.

philosophic and analytic sense that is challenge enough—but in understanding the creative interaction, the play, between the tropes. This interest, of course, is present in the work of Jakobson and Lévi-Strauss mentioned above and particularly in the dynamic, if more or less synchronic, relation between metaphor and metonym they contemplated.[17] But much earlier it is present in Vico's argument, which suggests a diachronic, figurative progression in the successive domination over historical time of the various tropes, beginning with vital and original metaphor and ending with the irony of "double entendres."

In any event, it is fair to say that the metaphor theory in anthropology of the 1980's has followed upon enduring pragmatic interests in human action in our discipline. It is, thus, focused more on the entirety of the tropes in dynamic relation as a congeries of figures with predicative and performative possibilities than upon the sole, so-called master trope of metaphor. It is a theory that has arisen much *before* the present remarkable interest in metaphor, and it is a theory that seeks to move *beyond* that interest. It is a theory that in Naomi Quinn's phrasing, we might also say, seeks to probe into the cultural foundations *behind* metaphor. This focus on the panoply of tropes as they interact in human life in culture is seen in practically all the papers here presented, though it is particularly persuasively argued in Emiko Ohnuki-Tierney's paper on the tropic dynamics over time of the monkey image in Japan.

Beyond Metaphor: Cognitive and Symbolic Perspectives

Of course, to play upon the locational phrasing "beyond" (both here and in our title) is to figuratively extol our various papers. It is to see in them an advance on previous discussion and hence as something at the very *forefront* of thinking. Though such figurative placement, such putting ahead and putting back, is a tried

[17] Of course, this interaction between metaphor and metonym is implicit in the preoccupation with the relation between similarity and contiguity relations in associationist psychology and in the dynamic relation between syntagmatic and paradigmatic relations in the Saussurian perspective.

and true figure of speech of frequent employ in agonistic moments in the intellectual life, we also seek to playfully evoke a debate that anthropologists have with cognitive linguists. This debate, centrally addressed in Hoyt Alverson's paper, concerns the pre-conceptual (pre-predicative) basis of metaphor, which is to say its universal origins in body-sense, body-image terms. In this context the phrase "Beyond Metaphor" evokes two notions. First, it suggests that reliance on metaphor to the exclusion of the other tropes and its universalization in experiential terms is an "obstacle" to understanding. Second, it suggests that the preoccupation with metaphor is a circuitous exercise in respect to a truly goal-oriented (or "source-path-goal"–oriented) thinking through of the roles of the imagination and the multiple paths they take in culture.

Bound up in the word "beyond," perhaps "behind" it, is the "life is a journey" metaphor at work. It is an organizing metaphor very familiar to us in the West. But we would insist that there are multiple, intertwined paths, and hence journeys, in the life "cycle"—and various tropes, quite beside metaphor, that animate and "organize" these journeys. And *beyond* that the question for an anthropologist is whether the notion of "beyond" and the "life is a journey" metaphor it implies are anchored in body images so pan-humanly experienced as to be universal. We anthropologists are bound to raise the question of cultural image reservoirs and of the culture shaping of such understandings as "beyond." We can easily imagine a secretive cultural tradition to which the title "Within Metaphor" would have been a more significant title than the one we provide.

In any event the entrance of cognitive linguists into metaphor studies in the 1980's has given a sign to this decade as regards the understanding of the figurative and has been also a "point de repère" for anthropologists committed to formal approaches. Here the work of George Lakoff and his associates at the Berkeley Program in Cognitive Linguistics has been central because of their effort, attractive to anthropologists, to ground argument in day-to-day experience (Lakoff and Johnson 1980a; 1980b). This fruitful work is now published in a series of books.[18] As is to be expected,

[18] This cognitive understanding of metaphor has, first of all, been worked out since 1980 in a series of reports and working papers published by the Berke-

and as indicated above, this cognitive approach to metaphor is an intellectual enterprise conducted under the sign of a more formal philosophy than anthropologists, given the thickness of the field experience and our commitment to it, could easily practice even should we wish to. The search by the cognitive linguists for universals of mental operations—such things as principles of metaphoric entailment or underlying image schemas that determine metaphoric choice—also enters in where most anthropologists are cautious to tread. For although they are sensitive to the possibilities of different metaphoric repertoires according to culture, the presence of culture in the argument of the cognitive linguists has been slighted by virtue of the fact that their data base has mainly been their own natural language, English, and their method has been mainly introspective inspection of the figurative content and schematic organization of purposefully selected (and sometimes denatured) utterances within that language. Hence the importance of "thick" natural contexts and cross-cultural perspectives, for these offer an important corrective to the possibility of culture-bound and/or overdetermined argument.

Two papers in this volume, those of Alverson and Quinn, are anthropological responses to the approach of the Lakoff group and use both natural discourse and cross-cultural data to offer such correctives. Naomi Quinn's paper, in its assessment of the cultural factors, the preexisting ideas presupposed in the figurative speech of natural discourse, has a particular virtue in view of her long-term participation, as an anthropologist, with the Lakoff group and her previous contributions to its body of argument.[19]

The contribution of anthropology to metaphor theory, then, lies first in its insistence upon the role of culture in the formation of metaphoric models with which various peoples reason—the central point of Quinn's argument, which is advanced from the perspective of cognitive anthropology—and second in its concern to avoid overconcentration on metaphor as the uniquely interesting trope but rather to see metaphors in their natural context in dy-

ley Cognitive Science Program, University of California Institute of Human Learning. The published results of this work may be seen in the following books: Johnson 1987; Kovecses 1986; Lakoff 1987b; and M. Turner 1987.

[19] See Quinn's early papers (1981a; 1981b) and the collection edited by Quinn with Dorothy Holland (1987).

namic relation to all the other tropes—the central point of Paul
Friedrich's argument, which is advanced from the point of view of
anthropological poetics.

The Sequence and Coherence of
This Collection of Papers

Since, as can be seen, metaphor theory in anthropology stretches
between cognitive concerns on the one hand and poetic perspectives on the other, it is fruitful to place in Part I as foundational
arguments to this collection the two basic statements on this
issue: Paul Friedrich on "Polytropy" and Naomi Quinn on "The
Cultural Basis of Metaphor." These are followed by Hoyt Alverson's closely reasoned reworking, in anthropological terms, of the
most recent Lakoff argument in respect to image schemas. Alverson's demonstration is appropriately anthropological, for he seeks
to retrieve these image schemas from what he regards as Lakoff's
overly philosophic or universalistic intent to give them primor-
diality—uninterpretability. Alverson employs cross-cultural linguistic data to illustrate the way in which the meaning of image
schemas are subject to the intentionality of pragmatic context—to
conventional, that is cultural, principles of use. So Alverson, in a
different way than Quinn, to be sure, is likewise arguing for the
cultural shaping of metaphor.

In Part II we find three papers directed to the play of tropes. The
first, by Terence Turner, treats a body of South American data on
the metaphor of the parrot—a metaphor previously much discussed (see esp. Crocker 1985) that has become something of a
classic reference among anthropologists interested in metaphor.
Turner brings together the fruit of his preeminence as a long-term
field researcher in this part of the world and a structural perspective—that is to say, a perspective that seeks to understand metaphor, or to "put it in its place" as Turner says, within the frame of
more long-term structures of meaningful relations, preeminently
relations of production, to which metaphor, among the other
tropes (Turner is adamant in questioning the tendency to focus on
metaphor alone), makes a dynamic and creative contribution.

Emiko Ohnuki-Tierney explores, in relation to the place of the monkey in Japanese culture, the semantic tensions that lie at the heart of the "play of tropes." In particular she reexamines the prevailing but overly formal biaxial analyses of the relation between metaphor and metonym conceived as intersecting planes of experience—essentially the experiences of contiguity on the one hand and similarity on the other. She enriches this strategy of analysis by pointing up the temporal movement of tropes and their interstitial quality as this is found in synecdoche. In addition to challenging this long-employed "elementary structure" of metaphor analysis—the two axes approach—Ohnuki-Tierney also brings into question the tendency, given the interstitial and transformative quality of all the tropes, to seek to identify a master trope, which is then usually argued to be metaphor.

In the third of these three papers, Deborah Durham and James Fernandez examine the play of tropes or, as otherwise formulated in their paper, the figurative "argument of images" involved in African struggles over social hierarchy and racial hegemony. The paper is essentially concerned with the dynamic of hierarchization and rehierarchization. Like Turner they insist upon the importance of understanding the subtle play of metaphor and metonymy in these figurative battles over placement in the social order and the structure of production.

In Part III are two papers that address one of the most important implications of the study of tropes in anthropology: that it can tell us something about the coherence and incoherence of culture. In the first paper Dale Pesmen examines the taboo—more than just a proscription of style—that has fallen on mixed metaphor in discourse and the possible source of that taboo in the "heterotopia," or confusion of possible worlds,[20] that such mixing suggests to the philosophically inclined. In point of fact, as Pesmen also points out, anthropologists who have studied the phenomenon of revival, or nativism, or any of the kinds of revitalization movements in culture find them to be built upon a congeries, a mixing, of meta-

[20] For the argument that a metaphoric assertion is always the creation of a new possible world see Levin 1977: chap. 5. For the argument that philosophically it is simply fruitless confusion to mix the metaphors upon which philosophical worlds are created, see Pepper 1942.

phors asserted and enacted. Anthropologists, unlike philosophers, find that cultural worlds are brought into being by the performance (enactment) of mixed metaphors. At the same time, whatever the actualities of the mixing of metaphor in culture creation, the impetus to assert and enact new cultural worlds may itself rest on a sense of unacceptable mixing of metaphor—as well as, undoubtedly, on the desire to counteract the inevitable dying away of the stimulating sense of coherence that original metaphor suggests as it expires and becomes conventional metaphor.

B. N. Colby addresses the degree to which cultures cohere in the imagination. At the heart of such imaginative integration, as we see in the Japanese tea ceremony, lie predicated relations, or linkages, between otherwise previously separated categories of experience. This sense of linkages—this ready crossing of boundaries—is precisely what metaphor accomplishes, and in that accomplishment it undoubtedly contributes to our sense of the coherence of cultures.

Colby's final chapter not only addresses the problem of cultural coherence in the light of what the study of metaphor can tell us about it, but also proposes a program of investigation that will link the study of metaphor and the symbolic anthropology in which it has been most often embedded to a larger culture theory and behavioral science anchored in processes of natural selection and aimed at understanding the adaptive potential of individuals and culture. In terms of such adaptive potential, he asks, what are the consequences of the coherence in human life and thought suggested by metaphor and the play of tropes? In part, Colby follows the lead of one of the leading symbolic anthropologists of the postwar period, Victor Turner, who also sought, toward the end of his career, the useful application of anthropological and, more particularly, symbolic understanding. This is not the first effort made by Colby and others to suggest the fruitfulness of interchange between symbolic anthropology and the more formal and scientifically constrained behavioral sciences, mainly cognitive anthropology and cognitive psychology (see Colby, Fernandez, and Kronenfeld 1981), and between the logic of the sciences and the logic of the humanities (see Northrup 1947).

But, of course, such efforts to assure or restore "coherence" in anthropology itself are challenged, as Colby recognizes, by the different discourses and the different objectives, these different logics, that prevail in the poetics approach on the one hand and in the cognitive approach on the other. Though these differences are a challenge to the coherence of anthropology as a discipline—a discipline, as we have remarked, that in its receptivity to all things human casts a very wide disciplinary net—they can also be fruitful differences. For, on the one hand, anthropological poetics challenges the dehumanization that lies in the reductionist tendencies of scientific formalization, while, on the other hand, scientific formalization forestalls the excessively extravagant and freewheeling intuitive interpretations that are a tendency in poetic approaches. Rather than producing "incoherence" within anthropology, therefore, the pronounced differences between symbolic or poetic approaches on the one hand and cognitive approaches on the other can—in just the kind of interaction we see in this collection of contemporary efforts to understand metaphor among the tropes and formulate a theory of the latter—be mutually enriching. It is anthropology's virtue, in short, not to be all things to all people but rather to recognize the great complexity of the human condition and to insist persistently on a continuing dialogue or dialectic within the discipline as regards what it is to be human. That dialogue or dialectic, motivated by the sense that no one method or point of view can embody all one needs to know about the human condition, is very fruitfully represented in the following essays.

Part I

*Trope as Cognition and
Poetic Discovery*

Polytropy

Paul Friedrich

> Mountain of Mountains it's called. Why so?
> The green of Chi and Lu is lost to view.
> Here Creation crystallizes grace.
> With northern and southern slopes defining dusk and dawn.
> Chest straining, where thick clouds grow.
> Eyes bursting to see returning birds.
> Shall I, one day, attain the final summit?
> All other mountains, at a glance, grown small?[1]

We might start by rereading this poem two or three times, because it is a made-to-order bit of "data" or "case" for illustrating and demonstrating the theory of plural figures presented here. "Gazing Toward 'Great Peak'" is by Tu Fu (712–70), who stands with Li Po and Wang Wei in the immortal trinity of the poetry of the T'ang dynasty (618–906). In fact, since he is felt to be the greatest of them all and since many regard this as his greatest poem, it is arguably "the world's greatest lyric poem"—for those of us given to such invidious comparisons. Be that as it may, "Gazing Toward

I am grateful to James Fernandez for having invited me to participate in the AAA colloquium on metaphor (Chicago, 1987); although I was unable to accept, the invitation spurred me to finish a paper I had been working on intermittently since 1984, and to offer it for this volume. For their perspicuous comments on parts or the whole of at least one of the drafts of this paper, I stand indebted to Hoyt Alverson, Tim Buckley, Cai Fang Pei, Lisa Crone, Deborah Durham, James Fernandez, Deborah Friedrich, Emiko Ohnuki-Tierney, Michael Puett, and Margaret Trawick.

[1] I begin with this translation—into English by D. A. L. Riggs and J. P. Seaton from the French of François Cheng—because this version is ensconced in Cheng's major interpretation of T'ang poetry, *Chinese Poetic Writing* (1982: 147), and because it offers a highly poetic reading that remains quite close to the original. Reprinted by permission of Indiana University Press.

'Great Peak'" is inscribed in huge Chinese ideographic characters on the face of the peak in question, so that it is readable at fifty yards to devoted pilgrims making the trek to share in Tu Fu's experience at various levels.

In what follows, the first, italicized line in each numbered group is a maximally "literal" translation of the Chinese character. Each of these italicized lines is followed in succession by (1) the still relatively literal running translation by David Hawkes, (2) the literary prose translation of William Hung, and (3) the highly literary, lyric translation by the superb team of American poet Witter Bynner (who, incidentally, delighted in writing parodies of Ezra Pound) and Kiang Kang-Hu, a Chinese sinologist and man of letters.[2] Such line-by-line juxtaposition of excellent but varied translations is usually more powerful than any one translation, partly because the variants suggest a quantum of ambiguities that, for richness, is analogous to that of the original. Let us now read through the four translations, either line by line or translation by translation, or both.

> Gazing Toward "Great Peak"
>
> (1) *Tai-Tsung then like-what?*
>   How is one to describe this king of mountains?
>   How becomes the Tai a worshipful mountain?
>   What shall I say of the Great Peak?
>
> (2) *Ch'i Lu green never ends*
>   Throughout the whole of Ch'i and Lu one never loses sight of
>   its greenness.
>   See how the greenness of the surrounding plains is never lost.
>   The ancient dukedoms are everywhere green.
>
> (3) *Creator concentrated divine beauty*
>   In it the creator has concentrated all that is numinous and
>   beautiful.

[2] Versions by Hawkes reprinted by permission from David Hawkes, *A Little Primer of Tu Fu*, Oxford, Oxford University Press, 1967, pp. 1–4. Version by Hung reprinted by permission of the publisher from *Tu Fu, China's Greatest Poet*, by William A. Hung, Cambridge, Mass., Harvard University Press, p. 30; copyright © 1952 by the President and Fellows of Harvard College. Version by Bynner and Kiang from *The Jade Mountain*, translated by Witter Bynner from the texts of Kiang Kang-Hu; copyright 1929 and renewed 1957 by Alfred A. Knopf, Inc.; reprinted by permission of the publisher.

Creation has lavished there its mysterious wonders.
Inspired and stirred by the breath of creation.

(4) *Northside (Yin) southside (Yang) cleave dark dawn*
The northern and southern slopes divide the dawn from
   the dark.
The sunny and shady sides fashion dawn and dusk at the same
   moment.
With the Twin Forces balancing day and night.

(5) *Heaving breast are born layered clouds*
The layered clouds begin at the climber's heaving chest
The growing layers of clouds might scour one's bosom of
   worldly thoughts.
. . . I bare my breast toward opening clouds.

(6) *Bursting eye-sockets enter returning birds*
and homing birds fly suddenly within the range of his
   straining eyes.
To follow those returning birds would strain my eyes.
I strain my sight after birds flying home.

(7) *Really must surmount extreme summit*
One day I must stand on top of its highest peak
One day I shall climb like Confucius to the top
When shall I reach the top and hold

(8) *Single-glance many mountain little*
and at a single glance see all the other mountains grown tiny
   beneath me.
to see how the surrounding hills dwarf into moles.
all mountains in a single glance?

We may now consider some of the figures of speech in this
poem and how they interact with each other, starting with five
dyads out of the possible total of ten made by the five classes of
tropes I propose.[3] The reader should perhaps be forewarned that in
the next few pages I will be discussing these tropes before the full
exposition of them that constitutes the body of the paper. I do this

---

[3] I could expatiate on the five remaining dyads (modal/analogical, analog-
ical/contiguous, modal/imagistic, imagistic/formal, contiguous/formal) to
complete the mathematically possible total of ten ($x = 5(5-1)/2$). And then
there are the triads and tetrads . . . But this would probably be redundant, because any line of poetry or even any sentence involves all five tropic levels. All
kinds of tropes interact with each other, reinforce each other, and feed into
each other to create insight, ambiguity, and richness of meaning.

in the confidence that practically all the readers who have come
this far will be familiar with ideas like imagistic, contiguity, figure
of mood, metonymy, etc.

1. The combination of metaphor (a kind of analogy) and purely
formal figures is illustrated in lines 5 and 6 by the pair "cloud" and
"bird." They belong to the same grammatical set ("numeral classi-
fier group"), which, if you will, reflects a grammaticalized dead
metaphor. The parallel between "heaving breast" and "bursting
eye-socket," on the contrary, is a brilliant and innovative metaphor.
More generally, the two lines are based on a parallelism that is to
be found in both the vocabulary and the syntax; for example, the
root for "burst" often functions verbally but in this case functions
as an adjective in the sequence adjective-noun-verb-adjective-noun.

2. The combination of a metaphorical figure and an imagistic
one is illustrated by the "green" of line 2; actually, the Chinese
color term means "blue-green," as is fairly widely known in anthropological (linguistic) circles. At one level this blue-green is an
"image that stands for itself" (Wagner 1986): blue-green is blue-
green is blue-green, stretching as far as the horizon and beyond
that as far as the eye can go. At another, perhaps shallower, level
this green-blueness is a metaphor alluding to other phenomena
such as growth, beauty, and the like, or passion, inspiration,
Federico García Lorca's Spanish *duende* (and his opening line to
one poem "Green, I want you, green, green")—and also to what
happens to the poet's mind when contemplating Tai Shan (Tai-
Tsung) or reaching its summit.

3. The figures of an image and of contiguity or juxtaposition
combine saliently in line 2, with the two abutting dukedoms between which the poet stands. Line 4 involves the same figures in a
more complex way. The term *Yin* refers to the northern, shadowy,
"dark" side of the mountain but also has the strong secondary association here of its often primary meaning of the female principle. *Yang* normally means the male principle and associated
things but here refers primarily to the light, sunny, southern side
of the mountain. Thus do the contiguous mountain slopes and
cliffs become "the opposite sides of the coin" of the basic Chinese
cosmological principle. The third unit in this line, incidentally,

means "cleave" ("knife" is part of the written character), and the cleaving of dawn from dark (also "murk," "chaos," and so forth) is frequent in Taoist, Chan, and other Chinese religious texts.

4. A similar figure of contiguity and a figure of mood (modality) are exemplified by the last couplet, lines 7 and 8. The understood subject of the poem—the author or the reader—has to pass through some sort of boundary, reaches the top, and then goes beyond it. All the other mountains collapse to "little," contained in a glance. More generally, the poem and its title are also related by a transformation in relations through space: first some subject is gazing *up* *at* the mountain, then *down* *from* it. All these metonymies contribute to the moods of awe and wonder (reminding me of Wallace Stevens's "There it was, word for word, the poem that took the place of a mountain"). Yet more generally, there is an enormous condensation of space into time and of time into space as the poet and reader gaze at and then (mentally) ascend the mountain.

5. The modal and formal figures are best illustrated by lines 5 and 6. The strong syntactic rule of order in both spoken and written poetic Chinese is subject-object; the line "ought" to mean "The bursting eyes enter returning birds." This may in fact be a possible reading if in early Chinese optics, as in early Greek optics, the rays go *out* from the eyes to engage with what is seen. But all authorities and translations seem to agree that the line "really" means that the image of the birds enters the eyes, so that the effect of this almost agrammatical inversion is "daring and bizarre" (Hawkes 1967: 3–4). Actually both readings are possible, and their combination, as the reader mentally races up and down the line, contributes to a powerful ambiguity.

With this review of the translations and a partial tropic analysis, let us turn to a relatively literal translation (synthesized by myself) with the radical elements and the original order, which the reader is now more prepared to appreciate. (This is also an exercise demonstration in the "impossibility of translation," partly because of the salience of what is probably the main problem in Chinese translation, that is, the disambiguation of what is [and often is meant to be] ambiguous: singular/plural, present/past, definite/indefinite, proximal/distal, and so forth.)

Tai-Shan then what-like?
Ch'i Lu NEG end
Create-change(r) concentrate divine beauty
Northside (Yin) southside (Yang) cleave dark/chaos dawn
Heave breast birth / give birth layer cloud
burst eye-socket enter return bird
must really surmount top summit
once glance many mountain little

This pentasyllabic (also pentamorphemic, penta-ideographic, and pentalexical) poem of eight lines is an example of the so-called "Chinese sonnet," and, with its realization of complex additional rules for tones and rhyme—not easily dealt with here—exemplifies the so-called "Regulated Verse" that was instituted by the Empress Wu (684–704) and stunningly exemplified during the T'ang dynasty, which lasted until 906. The first half of the T'ang (until 757) was marked by economic welfare, social order, and general cultural efflorescence, of which poetry, painting, and calligraphy were the most outstanding examples.

Let us not take leave of the wondrous Tu Fu without a biographical *nota bene*. Tu Fu, the scion of a clan with many learned officials and squires in its genealogy, had because of politics failed the main exams (which were mainly literary). At the time of the composition of this poem he was in his early twenties, living on a generous allowance that allowed him to travel "in the grand style. He wore fine furs and rode fine horses. He spent most of his time sightseeing and hunting but also worrying about not attaining the peaks of government service. It is quite possible that he never actually climbed T'ai Shan Mountain" (Hung 1952: 29–30). Yet the counterpoint between readings—youthful adventurer / frustrated scholar / government savant / inspired sage—contributes to the play of intentionality that marks many of these Chinese poems of the T'ang.

Polytropy: An Overview

In what follows I will be setting forth a theory, not just of polytropy, but, more specifically, of five classes of tropes that actually comprehend a great deal of what is normally understood to be "the poetry of language and of speech." Singly or in combinations, they are the focus of aesthetic positions: the imagist, the emotive and expressive, the formalist and "new critical," the semiotic and symbolic, and the interpretivist and hermeneutic (the first three of these foci correspond, roughly and respectively, to the image, modal, and formal macrotropes to be dealt with below). All five are involved in the problems of ambiguity and translation.

The major tropes and many other specific tropes could be stated as a long inventory, with working definitions, as was done in classical, Renaissance, and some recent theory (Turco 1973). I have taken some of these rich schemes into account but have tried to go further by constructing an all-encompassing system of interrelated macrotropes. These sets of tropes, or macrotropes, are as follows: imagistic, modal, formal, contiguity-based, and analogical.

The polytropic theory is not a hierarchy, for at least five reasons. First, none of the macrotropes is a subtype of any other: none can be derived from any other. Second, none of the five is logically derivable from some yet more comprehensive supertrope or "unique beginner." Third, the more specific subcategories of trope that are grouped under the head of one of the major categories cannot, in general, be ordered into a hierarchy in terms of explicit dimensions. Fourth, the macrotropes are not, in fact, related to each other in a highly organized or rule-governed and definable way. Their categories constitute a theoretically open-ended and constantly changing set, and, consequently, the ways in which they interact are infinite and characterizable to only a limited degree. This is another reflection of the role of chaos as an element in linguistic creativity (Friedrich 1986: 135–52). The ingredient of chaos becomes experience in the peculiar psychic state catalyzed by the beginning or, sometimes, the entire duration of a poem—an intriguing analog to the "onset of turbulence" that is being explored in the so-called "chaos theory" of physics today (Gleick 1988: 123; Friedrich 1988).

Fifth, the macrotropes are not exclusive of each other; on the contrary, every poem and conversation depends—at least implicitly—on the collaboration of all of them in a synergistic, simultaneous intertwining within every sentence and every line. In other words, though it is true that "All language is metaphorical" (except, for some, mathematics), it is far more true that all language is necessarily modal, formal, imagistic, and implicated in tropes of contiguity and analogy. All language is always totally tropological. One result of this synergistic process is that all tropes contribute to both ambiguity and disambiguation. Stephen Tyler's fine formulation can be paraphrased as follows: a trope may mislead in exact proportion to the amount it reveals, but that is the price of any revelation (1978: 336).

All troped also interact constantly with social situation, cultural values, the poetic tradition, and so forth. These multiple context-dependencies increase with the size and complexity of the unit, from a simple phrase to the implicitly galactic dimensions of a long poem. They are deepened yet further by the multimedia potential of the foregoing scheme of five macrotropes, which could be used, analogically, for a new theory of music, or culture, or a musical theory of culture, or for semantic reconstruction, or for conversation and other kinds of "ordinary language"—and for interrelating these and yet other universes of symbolism (e.g., Tedlock and Tedlock 1985; Ohnuki-Tierney 1987). The scheme could form the basis for new approaches and even new fields.

I shall finish this section with an important qualification and one overarching generalization. To begin with the former, the set of five macrotropes, while certainly comprehensive, does not pretend to be exhaustive. Among some of the figures and devices that do not fit into it—or at least could be made to fit only with difficulty—is one that is becoming more and more common in film and, to a lesser extent, in verbal art. At the very close of the given work, a short span of a few words of text or a few seconds of time categorically transforms an enormous chain of values that has just been elaborated. This fragment of words or time is akin in function to the denouement in a mystery novel or a detective story but is more complicated and pervasive, because it not only solves a question of plot structure but commutes a great number of specific values, meanings, and symbols that have been developed up to that point; a good example is the finale of the recent cinematic thriller *No Way Out*, where the American naval officer-hero turns out to have been a Russian spy all along and a hero of the Soviet Union to boot! I am in the habit of calling this the "comprehensive, terminal commutation-of-values trope"; it could also be called the "terminal redefinition of subtext." In any case, it syncretizes all the tropes, notably the formal and the analogical.

The overarching generalization to be made here is that there are two types of tropes in terms of scope—and an indeterminate number of subtypes ranged in between. To begin, any of the five macrotropes can have relatively restricted scope over a sentence, a clause, a line, even a word; for example, a single adjective and noun combination such as "brilliant opacity" can (but need not) constitute an oxymoron; this sort of thing can be called a local trope. On the other hand, as already noted, the scope of any one of the macrotropes may include an entire poem or article or conversation; for example, the key vowel in a poem, a pervasive mood of outrage in an article, or a set of interlocking metaphors in a complex riddle all instance macrotropes with what could be called total scope. A purely formal trope can structure an entire epic, as in the case of chiasmus in *The Iliad* (see below) or the Chinese-boxes structure of some novels and poems or the parallelism in many epic songs. Let us call these tropes global. Basically, any of the types of macrotrope can operate or even dominate either locally or globally, and by the same token there is enormous variation in the role, the communicative freight, that is carried by a single subtype of trope such as the metaphor and in the way local and global tropes interact to produce complex structures.

A major problem for the anthropological poetics of the future is to work out the differential globalness and localness of tropes. A second, related problem is to describe and better understand how the combinations of tropes interact with each other. The aesthetically powerful ethnography *Bwiti*, by James Fernandez (1982), is explicitly organized in terms of the macrometaphor of "The Pleasure Dome" (with references to Coleridge and to Coleridge scholarship). But equally powerful is the partly implicit global metaphor of the hunter on a path or trail (e.g., as distilled in the Fang proverb, "The hunter is the father of the thinker"). Just how do these metaphorical global tropes relate to each other? How is each related to all the other formal, imagistic, analogical, contiguity-based, condensation/expansion, and yet other figures in Fang religious experience and Fang culture more generally? Fernandez's work is replete with all the figures I have set forth above, and they are all frequent and functionally effective. How, then, do all the constellations of subtropes, tropes, and macro- tropes in the culture of the Fang or any other people impinge on or at least comment on the subtropes, tropes, and macrotropes in the mother culture of the author and his readers? And vice versa? In particular, what is the differential role, the differential rhetoric of the various figures? These are questions that cannot be answered fully, but that can be revealingly explored. The most fruitful and constructive way to explore them is not through the sort of hit- and-run deconstruction that has become an anthropological fash- ion, nor by writing a volume of quasi-literary criticism. The most fruitful and constructive route is to extend the insights and crafts- manship in Fernandez's magnum opus into the ethnography, his- toriography, and biography of other areas on the map of the world. In this spirit, let us turn now to a specific consideration of tropes.

The Field of Tropes:
The Horizontal Continua

Our immediate situation is the whole field of tropes. Admit- tedly, the old word "trope" and the somewhat better-known "fig- ure" are barnacled over with connotations from classical rhetoric and recent literary criticism. And they are limiting in the sense that they tend to trigger instant, prefabricated associations with the most obvious trope: metaphor. In what follows, on the contrary, trope or figure means anything that a poet, politician, pundit, or Everyman uses or employs—whether intentionally or uninten- tionally—to create poetic texture and effect, poetic meanings, and poetic integration. This approach follows both ordinary (literate) language and traditional literary criticism, where irony, apos- trophe, chiasmus, dialectal marking, and vivid images are spoken of as figures of language. The full multitude of tropes and the feed- back between them should be recognized, as should their partial independence and their partial interdependence. By thinking in terms of the whole field of tropes we are closer to being Everyman or a poet; that is, someone using language in a fairly natural, fa- miliar way (or the poet's recovered naturalness).

Image Tropes
"Ch'i Lu [blue-] green . . ."

This first and seemingly most simple trope appears to describe
and represent various kinds of perceptual images that "stand for
themselves." Epistemologically, these tropes depend on the experience or feeling of qualities that are in some sense primary or irreducible. Image, in this sense, corresponds roughly to what C. S.
Peirce (building on Emerson) called "Firstness," or, in the East Indian tradition, "suchness." In his words, "there are certain qualities
of feeling such as the color of magenta, the odor of attar, the sound
of a railway whistle, the taste of quinine, the quality of the emotion upon contemplating a fine mathematical demonstration, the
quality of feeling of love, etc. . . . the qualities themselves which,
in themselves, are mere may-bes, not necessarily realized . . . the
vividness of a feeling . . . a psychic feeling of red without us which
arouses a sympathetic feeling of red in our senses . . . red, sour,
toothache are each sui generis . . . the quality in its monadic aspect" (1940: 80–87).
A famous example of the image trope is the programmatically
imagistic poem by William Carlos Williams called "The Red
Wheelbarrow":[4]

> So much depends
> upon
>
> a red wheel
> barrow
>
> glazed with rain
> water
>
> beside the white
> chickens.

This poem was intended to demonstrate the imagistic—or, more
precisely, objectivistic—thesis that a poem should involve "not
words, but things."

[4]William Carlos Williams, *Collected Poems, 1939–1962*, vol. 2, copright
1939 by New Directions Publishing Corporation and Carcanet Press Ltd.;
reprinted by permission.

From a second look at this exemplar of objectivism, an extreme form of imagism, we see that "The Red Wheelbarrow," though ostensibly about "things," is contextualized in the rhetorical assertion just named above. Later, the main "thing," that is, the wheelbarrow, is foregrounded by juxtaposition, that is, a kind of metonymy which, by its sheer vividness, suggests metaphorical relations of diverse kinds (for me, the red wheelbarrow and the white chickens suggest a brightly painted red tractor in a snow-covered field). As Robert Duncan (1973) has astutely noted, the entire image set of the poem is cast in syllabically and rhythmically measured lines. There are in fact so many other tropes at work here that the poem defeats or at least heavily qualifies its own theoretical message: it is not wheelbarrows that matter as much as, for example, poems about them and how to write such poems.

The imagery of other poems involves secondary and tertiary iconicities between vision and sound: the sound texture of the poem is somehow analogous to the visual images it evokes; the textures in such cases resemble the tone poems of Romantic music but are combined with a screen of images that simply lie beyond the power of program music. Take William Carlos Williams's marvelous "The Dance," where a dance rhythm (poetically, in amphibrachic meter) is combined with Breughel's view of peasants rollicking at harvest time. Or the Russian Futurist experiments: poems constructed out of syllables on the basis of euphony and the vague etymological meanings of Russian (or Common Slavic) roots. Or H.D.'s final lines to "Epitaph": "Greek flower; Greek ecstasy / reclaims forever / one who died / following / intricate song's lost measure," where, at least to my ear, the phonic decrescendo is iconic with a particular meaning of dying away.

Of a different order is the iconicity achieved in Carl Sandburg's ten-minute-long rendition of his "one-liner": "My name is John Johnson, / And I come from Wisconsin" (the name is pronounced Yon Yonson). I think of this as a sort of phonic analog to the wall of a house covered with rows and columns of the word "RED." Yet another iconicity is achieved by, for example, a poem about a swan or a cat with the constituent words arranged on the page in the shape of the animal in question. Both the highly repetitive and the "concrete" forms of iconicity partly or gradually erase or suppress and replace the original meaning (reference, signification, connotation) until the hearer (and the declaimer of "John Johnson") is mainly aware of the sign—sounds, shapes—as they themselves take over as signifiers. These are, admittedly, extreme variants of the image trope.

Musical images condense musical potentials of the language. Musical imagery may govern not only an entire poem but the entire work of a poet—and be the main issue in his theory: Thomas Campion and the early Heinrich Heine, some of the major Russians, and many of the French Symbolists took it as axiomatic that poetry should be melodious or musical—if not above all, then to a major degree. Certain aspects of the musical images in question can be precisely scored, like the intonations of a conversation (Bolinger 1980; Urciuoli 1985). Others are as refractory to explicit analysis by linguistics and poetics as melody and tone color are to musicology. Image tropes of all kinds vary enormously in the degree to which they lend themselves to explicit analysis or any sort of formalization.

Together with their illusory autonomy, image tropes are highly interdependent on other tropes. Visual image and metaphor, in fact, are used almost synonymously or at least as mutually implicatory in many sophisticated discussions, especially of Chinese poetry (e.g., Cheng 1982; Liu 1983). Image interdepends as much, if perhaps less obviously, with such other tropes as metonymy and the modal tropes that will be dealt with in the next section. Correspondingly, an image trope of some kind is always present to some degree in all uses of language, whatever the perceptual faculty or theoretical dependency—be it staccato syllables or images of a holocaust or beads of sweat on the biceps of a worker.

What makes the image trope pervasive is its relation to mimesis and description, and there is no sharp line between (1) a visual image-trope, (2) an effective description, or (3) any old description. What starts as one may end up as another as description is metamorphosed into an image trope: as it dawns in our imaginations that the bomb-transporting munitions-train locomotive bearing down on and then reaching peace activist Bryan Wilson as he stands his ground . . . Giving these diverse images the status of tropes means that the diverse theories that are based heavily on imagery—ranging from the musical theories of Edgar Allan Poe to mimetic theories in naturalism—all have cogency and relevance for the poetics of lyric poetry, and for anthropological poetics.

— Modal Tropes
"Really must surmount extreme summit . . ."

A second group of tropes includes expressions of mood that run from emphatic assertion to passivity to outrage to joy to command to sarcasm to threat to pathos to assertion to question to perhaps the most intriguing of all, irony. All these moods can interact and combine with each other, and each one is distinct only as a matter of degree.

Mood is conveyed through diverse resources of vocabulary and syntax, most obviously through one-word exclamations ("Christ!") or expletives and interjections ("Oops!"). A similar overt modal is apostrophe, where the poet turns aside from the main discourse to address someone real or imagined. Apostrophe may be peaceful and meditative, as when Wallace Stevens turns to "Pale Ramon" (that is, the critic Ramon Ramírez) near the end of his philosophical poem "The Idea of Order at Key West." It is often combined with interjection, as in William Blake's "O Rose, thou art sick!" Related forms of address may be violent, like the blinding scene in *King Lear*: "Out, vile jelly!" where an adverb is used expressively to address the eyeball of the victim. The same word was used over three centuries later by Robert Frost in a starkly realistic poem about a farm boy who loses his arm in a sawing accident and then dies of shock: "Out, Out—" (but alluding to Macbeth's "Out, out, brief candle"). Thus direct address, invocation, exclamation, apostrophe, and the like are among our most powerful figures—be the addressee an imagined skylark, an imaginary tiger, a jilted lover, or the whole polluted world.

More, perhaps, than the image or the metaphor, the tropes of mood can dominate, and function, as deep, organizing principles of an entire poem or corpus of poems, or of a conversation or all the conversations of an individual. They can do this because the modal tropes in their full philosophical and psychological implications are rooted in a speaker's underlying emotions, affects, and feelings. This rootedness is particularly true of poets—take, for example, the pervasive but markedly distinct skepticism of Brecht and Heine, or of Frost and Stevens. Some poets stand out for the way they have elaborated the potentials of a mood—rhetorical exclamation from religious poetry, for instance. Or Stevens's uncannily evocative use of the simple declarative in "The Planet on the Table": "Ariel was glad he had written his poems. / They were of a remembered time / Or of something seen that he liked."

The modal tropes do vary greatly in their analytical accessibility, the degree to which they lend themselves to formalization. The strictly syntactic moods—declarative, imperative, interrogative, and so forth—can be formalized to a large degree via the many methods and concepts of linguistics and sociolinguistics (these moods are so entangled with tense and aspect as to have justified the technical term TAM—for "tense-aspect-mood"); the syntactic moods, then, resemble chiasmus and metaphor in suggesting formal analysis.

Pervasive moods such as skepticism and shame, on the other hand, are egregiously difficult to analyze with our existing formal tools. Irony, for example, has been defined, vaguely, as where "what is said is not what is meant." More rigorously, irony has been defined as a subtype of modal trope and subdivided into eighteen varieties, including romantic irony, four kinds of dramatic irony, and irony of fate: the contrast between the individual's mainly conscious aspirations and what the society—by processes of which the individual is largely unaware—eventually makes of him or her (this irony motivates most Marxist criticism). Irony, in short, runs the gamut from Socrates's pedantries to Shakespeare's playful sonnet that begins, "When my love swears that she is made of truth, / I do believe her though I know she lies." Irony is so embedded in—but not equatable with—context, scene, drama, motives, paradox, mendacity, idealism, disillusion, and social ambiguity that it is surely the most powerful and pervasive of all the tropes. It positively enjoins an approach that is not only synthetic, pluralistic, and eclectic, but also specifically pragmatic in emphasis. Irony could be called the pragmatic trope, the figure of pragmatism—and neo-Peircean pragmatism at that.

The modal tropes, with their component of emotional and perceptual response, correspond roughly to C. S. Peirce's category of "Secondness" (1940: 76, 87). Secondness involves awareness of difference, of a second reality, with its action and reaction, effect and resistance, ego and non-ego, "the element of struggle . . . mutual action between two things" (1940: 89). Secondness is particularly experienced in the sudden *shock* of a change of perception, as in the lowering of a train whistle just when the train passes.

Giving the status of macrotrope to mood implies that the so-called expressive and emotive theories of poetics should be regarded as among the most valid and revealing.

Formal Tropes
"Bursting eye-sockets enter returning birds . . ."

The third set of tropes is formal and entails operations such as addition and deletion—for example, the many kinds of ellipsis (of pronouns, adverbs, and so forth) that perhaps constitute the main figure in T'ang poetry (Cheng 1982: chap. 1). Equally vital are the patterns of commutation where, for example, the normal or unmarked order is commuted with various aesthetic effects: Keats's key line, "Yet did I never breathe its pure serene." But the formalness of formal tropes is only relative, partly because of the potential or underlying form of all tropes (as Brecht says, "The antiformalists are the real formalists"), partly because many of the other subtypes not only lend themselves to formal treatment but actually suggest such treatment. This is notably true of metaphor and some of the metonymic tropes.

At the phonic level a good example of formal trope would be the so-called reversed second foot in a metrical line, particularly an iambic one: because of the norm that a second foot should be regularly metered or at least more regularly than the others, and the statistical fact that it is so, the reversal (to a trochee in this case) creates considerable emphasis and marks the syllable or word in question. Reversed second feet are relatively rare in English poetry, but one example, from Frost, where we might expect to find them, is, "And he likes having thought of it so well," where the stress on "likes" underscores the ornery, oppositional, contrastive feel of the whole poem, "Mending Wall," and leads into the last line: "He says again, 'Good fences make good neighbors'" (which, as if for closure, is insistently iambic). A second good example of a phonic formal trope would involve the third foot of a four-foot iambic line in many Russian poems. Here omission of stress was so common that, depending on the poet or the poem, either the stress or its omission could have subtle tropic functions. I cannot overemphasize the degree to which formal tropes and their meanings and functions are pegged into the particularities of a given tradition. Most of metrical poetry in English is iambic, whereas a great deal of Russian poetry, including many of the best poems, is in other feet: trochaic, anapest, dactylic, even amphibrachic. Sappho used ten kinds of feet in six "principal meters." Similarly, "the meter" of conversation would reveal enormous, albeit mainly quantitative, differences from one (sub)culture to another.

The formal tropes that I have discussed so far—addition, deletion, and commutation—may involve a sound system or a morphosyntactic one or structures in between. A poet such as e. e. cummings deliberately uses totally unexpected and unexpectable and often ungrammatical orders and wild degrees of their synthesis in a personal but generally intelligible and appreciated universe where "love is more thicker than forget" and "anyone lived in a pretty how town." These reorderings are often combined with other syntactic and grammatical alterations. The highly marked surface textures of cummings, Dylan Thomas, Poe, Stéphane Mallarmé, and others exude linguistic energies—Wilhelm von Humboldt's *energeia*—even when, as so often in cummings, they also function to impart a false sense of profundity or originality to underlying meanings that may be truisms, and trite ones at that (i.e., the formal trope is fresh but the underlying meaning is trite).

Just what is the relation of these formal tropes to metaphor? It is true that in Chinese, traditional Western, and many other traditions, the integration of such formal tropes with metaphor may produce exceptional poems, as when, for example, the image-bearing words also rhyme: in a notable case, Marina Tsvetaeva rhymed the famed Carrara marble (from which she was metaphorically fashioned) with the (street)wares (*tovar*) of the street-

walker for whom she had been jilted (Carrara, incidentally, refers
to the quarry from which Michelangelo got his marble).[5] These
synaesthetic feats, here of synthesizing phonic and semantic contrasts and complementarities, are typically overlooked, or at least
neglected, by literary critics and literary-criticism-oriented anthropologists, most of whom tend to deal with metaphor outside its formal matrices or without attention to the formal figures
with which it interdepends. It is the enormous number of formal
tropes—or better, the formal potential for tropes—in a natural
language which, when actualized in poetic discourse, do much or
even most of the poetic work. What makes a good line in English
always depends heavily on form and usually depends more on
form than metaphor, and this is truer in traditions like the Eskimo
one and, I am told, most Native American ones, where "how it
sounds" outranks analogical figures. At a higher, more inclusive level the formal figures integrate long stretches, as in Iliadic
chiasmus (see below), or in the principle of ring composition in the
poetry of Alexander Blok and others, or the principle of recur-
siveness or looping backward that we find in Eliot or Stevens
(where, albeit irregularly, lines allude to or loop back to earlier
lines, with much forward and backward anaphora hooking the
ends of lines together). But whatever the level of poetic form, from
surface sound to the semantic depths, the poetic strategies and
creative processes that draw on these potentials must be seen as
an integral part of any poetics: while rejecting the extremes of
Russian formalism or the assertion that poetics should be a sub-
field of linguistics, we stress the primacy of formal figures and of
their analysis in any adequate poetics.

Contiguity Tropes
"Northside (Yin) southside (Yang) cleave dark dawn . . ."

The fourth class of trope includes the many kinds of aesthetically effective juxtaposition, collocation, or, more simply, contiguity in time, space, and other dimensions such as social and

[5] The forms in the poem are actually *Carrary* (genitive singular) and *tovarom*
(instrumental singular), making for a deliberately imperfect rhyme.

textual context. Of these tropes of contiguity, at least four call for
some definition and discussion.

The first main variant includes the huge class of deictics or
"pointers," such as demonstrative pronouns: as Zukofsky quipped,
a poet is someone who loses sleep over whether to use the definite
or the indefinite article (assuming that the language, unlike Latin,
has articles);[6] by the same token, shifting or omitting articles
can play a crucial, if subtle, role. In addition to the many sets of
deictics for space and time (the "here-and-now" deictics; Hanks
1990), there are many kinds of pronominal or other person-referring
systems. Again, switching pronouns (e.g., from formal to infor-
mal), what I call "pronominal breakthrough" (1979) or, more generally, dialogic breakthrough (Attinasi and Friedrich 1990), is often
crucial in the construction of dramatic and, to a far lesser extent,
lyric poetry. Such switching and breakthrough become particularly informative in the many languages where elaborated pronominal systems and related indexical systems match up with and
in some sense symbolize enormously elaborated and hierarchized
systems of class and caste (Friedrich 1979; Errington 1985). Such
deictic tropes saliently illustrate the second main type of sign in
Peircean semiotics: the index, which, figuratively speaking, points
at something (Peirce 1940: 102, 107–11).

A second variety of the contiguity trope is the inventory, where
symbols of the same class are juxtaposed in a string. Inventories
involve, however, not just syntactic juxtaposition, but the association of the referents in terms of space, time, function, and so forth:
plow, harrow, seeder, weeder, and combine are here ordered in
terms of their successive use in the agricultural cycle. Inventory,
very widespread as a trope in primitive and archaic societies, was
conspicuous in Old Russian saints' lives, often with, for instance,
an ascending order of partial synonyms approximating the true
name of the saint. But inventory was exploited most often and
most originally by Walt Whitman, "the poet of inventories": states

---

[6]Deictics are a subtype of "shifter" (Jakobson 1957), along with tense, and
so forth. The poet referred to is Louis Zukofsky (1904–78), the American master who coined the term "objectivism," and who was a leading modernist and a
fine translator of Catullus.

of the Union, American rivers, sets of farm implements, human types, and so on are reeled off in rich profusion. Inventories as trope continue strong in American poetry today, much of which is rooted in Whitman in any case. Gary Snyder's poem "Hunting 13," for example, starts out, "Now I'll tell you what food we lived on: mescal, yucca fruit . . ." and so on through 47 other nature foods of sorts. The inventory is relatively favored not only by American poets, but also by American ethnographers.

A third variant of the contiguity trope is anatomical relations. Anatomies always imply analogies: the part of the body, the house, the car, the natural landscape (foot, footstool, foot pedal, foothill, and so forth). Body parts are primary in many ways (Friedrich 1979: chaps. 10, 11). The imaginative patterns by which they are extended or projected onto social, technological, political, and intellectual fields of meaning is surely one of the most powerful and universal forms of metaphor.[7]

Anatomies, in turn, are but a subset of the fourth, more general, set of all part-whole and whole-part relations—traditional synecdoche. The roles of synecdoche are multitudinous at the formal level of paradigm and of other geometrical symmetries and asymmetries—as formal poetics has amply shown. The form of synecdoche may be reductionist (scapegoating) or expansionist ("collective guilt"). In terms of social context, its destructive force has often been seen to break out when, for example, entire populations, allegorized as individuals and frozen in the formulas of racist ideologies, are held up as collectively responsible for misdeeds in which only a small fraction was engaged and which a large or at least significant fraction opposed: "the Russians" and "the Americans," in specific historical contexts, dramatically exemplify such synecdochically miscoded information.

Many relations of contiguity involve time or space (Bühler 1982): the president and/or the entire staff and retinue are alluded

---

[7]By "primary" I mean that, in any set of sets that includes the parts of a biological (e.g., human) body, these body-part names will have been learned earlier in life, will be psychologically more basic, and will more often be the point of departure in new metaphors, and so forth; all such "primacies" are highly relative and probabilistic. For my own basic research on the central role of the body in metaphorical and other symbolism, see Friedrich 1978.

to as "The White House." Such relations of contiguity are of enormous scope and frequency because all of language is as metonymic
as it is metaphoric. Metonymy is omnipresent in conversation, in
particular, both in the rates of forms as they are spoken and as a
constantly present potential. Metonymy is more typical of prose
than of poetry, at least in most traditions. Yet poetry is often
marked by metonymy, and many poets such as Pushkin, Whitman,
and Tu Fu, the greatest, respectively, in the Russian, American,
and Chinese traditions, are heavily metonymic in their figures—
although in the case of Tu Fu, owing in part to the nature of Chinese poetic writing, it is often impossible, in a given case, to say
which type is dominant. The major fact about the contiguity
tropes is that every poem—just as it or its content is a metaphor of
something—is also contiguously part of a large context, be this
the plains of Nebraska at sundown or the venue of an East Village
poetry reading or simply the bracketing silences from which the
poem arises or is declaimed.

The degree to which metonymy and other contiguity tropes
lend themselves to analysis varies greatly. At one extreme there
may be a clear, obvious, and easily explicated taxonomic or serial
order of some sort. At the other extreme, there may be diffuse and
irregular universes where different, select parts of an ill-defined
whole are playing different aesthetic roles in a larger design.

Analogical Tropes
"Layered clouds . . . the returning birds . . ."

The fifth macrotrope is based partly on the fact that any one
thing in the universe resembles any other thing in more than one
way: a sweater and a socket both produce electricity. This fact of
universal interresemblances supports the metaphysical position
of the universal interconnectedness of things and elaborates the
pragmatic position that the meaning of any idea is the sum of
all its conceivable consequences. Yet the metaphor in the more
useful, relevant, and tropological sense does not include *all* logical and realistic similarities, but only those that are aesthetically
effective and culturally appropriate. It is these poetic and cultural

values that determine what degree of novelty and semantic distance is right: that a woman under a roof means happiness, as the Chinese ideogram has it. To take a more complex example, that a small-town boy is "made of different cloth," like the tweed of the high school English teacher he admires, provides a metaphorical synapsis for a sudden shift of scene where the boy from Minnesota suddenly IS Garrison Keillor, now in a white suit, speaking to YOU directly from a staging of "The Prairie Home Companion" in New York City, and then that scene as a whole—the faces in the crowd as violets on the wallpaper, the microphone as the handle of a Hoover vacuum cleaner, and so forth—is a gestalt metaphor of that same Garrison Keillor, back, in his memory, in his room in Minnesota, staring at the wallpaper, leaning on the vacuum cleaner in his room, being scolded by his mother for not practicing his high school speech so that he will "amount to something in life." As Keillor's only real precedent, Mark Twain, would put it, metaphors work "with the right amount of stretching." As we move away from well-stretched metaphors, whether in complex stories or atomic dyads, we enter the mixed, confused, or far-fetched types. In other words, fire across the synapses of metaphor should reflect, not things too far apart, nor near identities (which takes us into polysemy or tautology), but a sort of metaphorical golden middle-ground.

Metaphor raises acute problems of scope. If we stay within the grandiose model of metaphor that began with Aristotle, then we will include any transfer of names (1) along a series or class inclusion, (2) involving any sort of analogy, (3) or any substance or quality, cause or effect, synecdoche or other metonymy; indeed, metaphor in this sense would also include analogous moods or shapes relatable by any formal operation, although even extreme metaphorphiles and metaphor-maniacs do not as a rule try to subsume irony, apostrophe, chiasmus, or dialectical polyphony. It is my conviction that a category so comprehensive is almost equivalent to thought, mind, or imagination; for example, Hume repeatedly equated the imagination and thought with "RESEMBLANCE, CONTIGUITY in time and place, and CAUSE AND EFFECT" (1927: 13, 88, and *passim*). In the same category of "too inclusive" belong such definitions as "a miniature poem," or "a theoretical model that can reveal new relations," as in the adage "every model is a metaphor of reality."

The workable or useful meanings of metaphor are more constrained, as is shown by the empirical discussions carried on by the same persons who quote the grandiose definitions. Such more workable definitions include "a figure of speech in which one thing is likened to another by being spoken of as if it were the same," or "implicitly and novelly equating things that are just different enough" (Goodman 1978). More comprehensive and sensitive, but still workable, is W. K. Wimsatt's "two clearly and substantially named objects (denotation) are brought into such a context that they face each other with fullest relevance and illumination (connotation). . . . Truth of reference or correspondence reaches a maximum degree of fusion with truth of coherence. . . . External and internal relation are intimately mutual reflections" (1954: 149).

Metaphor in the usual sense suggests some sort of formal semantic, syntactic, or pragmatic analysis (e.g., into constituent semantic features) and has indeed inspired just such analysis by a long series of schools, including Russian Formalism, descriptive linguistics, the New Criticism, transformational linguistics, recent semiotics, and various congeries of posttransformational linguists and semiotic anthropologists. The vulnerability of metaphor to formal approaches accounts in part for the way it has been favored over modal tropes such as irony or what were above called image tropes. By the same token, though, our inclusion of metaphor and other analogical figures as one of the five macrotropes reflects the opinion that most metaphor theories must form an essential part of a general theory of figures.

Vertical Analogy

The horizontal continua whereby metaphorical and other analogical tropes shade into or interlock with other coordinate tropes are balanced or crisscrossed by the vertical continua whereby within the same analogical parameters we range up toward, for example, greater abstraction and scope or greater diffuseness and suggestiveness, and downward toward greater concreteness or condensation. The vertical continua consist of many interacting and more or less parallel dimensions. There are of course interacting vertical dimensions for all the (macro)tropes.

Let me put this more explicitly and specifically. The vertical dimension of degrees of similarity, for instance, can run through at least the following gamut:

1. Tautology, where X = X, yellow is yellow, and so forth.

2. So-called significant tautology, where the second element is actually a subset of the first: "Business is business" means that the second "business" is a subtype of the first; another significant type is Yogi Berra's "It ain't over till it's over."

3. Synonyms, which really means near-synonyms, since pure ones are hypothetical only; even "gorse" and "furze" are never used in identical contexts and at the same frequencies.

4. Polysemy, where the two or more terms are relatively close by some combination of etymological, semantic, and pragmatic senses; polysemously related terms often figure in poetic rhetoric as a kind of semantic texture, as in the speeches of Jesse Jackson; or think of the polysemous meanings of "mouth" and other body parts.

5. Metaphor itself falls into various kinds of apt metaphor such as "honey/dew" and other examples sprinkled through this essay, where the similitude is neither too great nor too small (as determined by cultural attitudes).

6. Metaphors that stretch the culturally conditioned analogical sense, leading to problematical, inept, or outlandish comparisons.

7. Sets of things that might lend themselves to comparison under the special circumstances provided by surrealist poetry or an article on poetics (e.g., lawnmower/moon, related to a scythe/gibbous moon).

8. Any two things, since any two things, acts, words, or whatever in the universe will share features. The inevitable comparability of any two things is an interesting complement to the categorical, overall nonidentity of any two things (outside mathematics).

A critical implication of this set of degrees on the analogical continuum, incidentally, is that metaphor and its aptness are quintessentially embedded in social situation, cultural context, and textual traditions. Two areas of language study that are sometimes seen as alien, poetics and pragmatics, are in fact or at least potentially mutually implicatory.

Vertical analogy is given added power through its continuous interaction with other tropes on the horizontal continua. And the other tropes also have vertical dimensions, as illustrated, for example, by the degrees of intensity of a modal trope or the many layers of derivation in syntactic trees (i.e., tree diagrams). In a mathematical (e.g., topological) sense, it is the interaction between these vertical and horizontal levels that gives the tropes their imagination-boggling combinatory power. The vertical continua, incidentally, require us to take some account of information theory, problems of redundancy and entropy, various kinds of mathematics, and some as yet unformulated theory of self-similarity between things of different sizes; all these could be components in a future poetics.

Condensation and Expansion

There is a second way of looking at the vertical continua, and that is in terms of two fundamental processes and the problems of creativity that they pose: the two poles here are extraction of gist and maximization of suggestiveness.

The strength of many poems and conversations results from their having extracted the gist or the essence of meaning: Stevens's "the act of finding what will suffice" (in "Of Modern Poetry"). This extracted gist is often cryptic or paradoxical; that is, in terms of information, redundancy has been reduced, the text has been cut, and, as one consequence, ambiguity has been piled on ambiguity. Good examples of gist are the final couplets in many a sonnet and the exploitation, at key points, of proverbs and similar gnomic expressions; Frost's "Nothing gold can stay" (in his poem of the same name) is gnomic, and sounds proverbial, but actually involves a (truthful) reversal of the commonplace that gold endures unchanged. Entire poems that exemplify the extraction of

gist are the Middle English lyric "Oh Western Wind," and the
William Carlos Williams poem "El Hombre":[8]

> It's a strange courage
> you give me ancient star:
>
> Shine alone in the sunrise
> toward which you lend no part!

Condensation, or the extraction of gist, is dominant in entire traditions characterized by enigma, paradox, and riddling, such as the
Skaldic verse of Iceland, and in what Karl Kroeber (1983) calls
the "mnemonic summary" of much Native American poetry. The
extraction of gist in vertical metaphor is also curiously analogous,
incidentally, to what goes on when a linguist (notably a phonologist) practices "the criterion of economy."

The closely related trope of expansion makes a poem or other
statement open out, suggest, and yield many intimations: "like
ripples in a pool or like echoes" are clichés for this quality. Or, to
paraphrase some Chan and Zen aesthetics, a poem is drawn to the
point where the reader wants to complete it, to fashion one of the
many suggested completions. The types of suggestiveness and
opening-out ambiguity in question can be created by anything
from an unfamiliar word order or end rhyme to the omission of a
particle for prosodic reasons to the deliberate conflation of contrastive information. The expansion trope, although a hallmark of
Symbolism and traditionally associated with metaphor, may be
achieved through any other figure and has been the dominant concern in, for example, Japanese and contemporary American haiku
(Henderson 1958).

The figures of condensation and expansion are of course logically interrelated—are in fact mirror images of each other: an
aptly stated gist will give off many reverberations, whereas rich
suggestiveness necessarily implies a deep core. Condensation and
expansion are also implicitly chaotic. There is more chaos and turbulence in a realized poem than in such phenomena as a forming
drop of water, an eddying river, or a snow crystallization—things

---

[8] William Carlos Williams, *Selected Poems*, copyright 1963 by New Directions Publishing Corporation; reprinted by permission.

that have recently come within the scope of "the new mathematics." In fact, the twin tropes of distillation and gist cannot be defined explicitly and strictly—they flout formal definition. And yet . . . and yet a great deal of verbal art has been directly or indirectly, explicitly or implicitly, concerned with the elaboration of gist and suggestiveness, and a great deal of the finest criticism, particularly criticism by poets, has been concerned with giving some intimation of these things: Plato, Coleridge, and, above all, Wallace Stevens.

This essentially concludes my discussion of the system of interacting tropes, with continuous back-reference to the poem by Tu Fu. I will now turn to variations and enlargements on problems that have arisen, under the following basic rubrics: "Minimizing Metaphor," "Relativizing Metaphor," "Contextualizing Metaphor," "Maximizing Metaphor," "The Power of Metaphor," "Initial Conclusions," "Wider Implications" (which consist of "Tropes and the Real World"), and "Polytropy and Anthropology."

Polytropy and/versus "Metaphor Theory": Minimizing Metaphor

The foregoing point of view is basically of someone, particularly a poet, constructing language, combining sounds into words and words into sentences, or conceiving of paragraphs and putting them into sounds, as the case may be—rather than of someone who has decided ahead of time that metaphor is primary and that language is primarily an object of analysis. One necessary structural consequence of this "poetical" point of view is that the specific trope of metaphor is only one subtype of one of five or more major classes of trope; as such, it constitutes only a small fraction of the total tropological *system* in any given case. A second, sociolinguistic consequence is that metaphor constitutes only a fraction of the total *repertoire* of tropes and subtropes and of their potential combinations. A third, dialogic *and* speech act consequence is that metaphor is only a small fraction of what is actually put together by the speaker and apprehended by the hearer—be they conversationalists, poets, or scientists. From certain points of view overlapping with that taken in this essay, the metaphor, and even analogy, can be viewed as a subset of formal tropes or of the modal tropes, particularly irony (Brooks 1949). In short and in sum, metaphor is only a (small) fraction of "the poetic," be this poetic in something as strictly poetic as a sestina, or the undercurrents of routine chitchat.

Relativizing Metaphor:
Roman Jakobson

The ardent advocacy of some of Roman Jakobson's more superficial goals has obscured the more central thrust of his better-known papers and articles such as "Two Aspects of Language" (1956) and "Concluding Statement: Linguistics and Poetics" (1960).

In the first of these, Jakobson took Bühler's crucial (1982 [1934]) discovery of the axiom that contiguity and similarity constitute the two fundamental dimensions of meaning. Jakobson generalized this by relating it to the Saussurian dichotomy between the syntagmatic (relations of alignment in terms of contiguity) and the paradigmatic (relations of substitution in terms of similarity). Indeed, he extended the relation beyond language proper and suggested that the two traditional classes of magic are dependent either on contiguity (casting spells over someone's nail clippings) or on similarity (sticking pins into someone's carved image). Within the domains of poetry and poetic language, the two dimensions are reflected in the metonymy (the part/whole relation between "fleet-footed" and Achilles) and the metaphor (the substitution/similarity relation between Aphrodite and her incarnation, Helen of Troy). Both the syntagmatic and the paradigmatic axes are involved in what is the crucial poetic process: symbols on the axis of substitution such as color words or words beginning with a vowel are "projected" onto a line that involves, as the case may be, chromatic antithesis or vowel alliteration. But the basic point (sometimes de-emphasized by Jakobson) is that the metaphoric and the metonymic tropes, the paradigmatic and the syntagmatic tropes, are structurally coordinate, equally frequent, and have topologically comparable spread. In these essentially polemical statements, Jakobson was trying to correct the focus on the metaphor as the master trope or, in some usages, a virtual synonym of trope. As he put it, with characteristic incisiveness, "nothing comparable to the rich literature on metaphor can be cited for the theory of metonymy. . . . The actual bipolarity has been artificially replaced in these studies by an amputated, unipolar scheme" (1956b: 82). Jakobson showed that metaphor theory can be strengthened by taking account of metonymy as a coordinate trope, and his other work often deals saliently with modal tropes such as irony and with many formal tropes. But he was careful not to demote metaphor or in any sense to qualify natural wonder at the power of metaphorical language or at the magical power of a new and effective metaphor. Like the poet Richard Lovelace, who "could not love thee, dear, so much, / Lov'd I not honour more," Jakobson is suggesting that we can appreciate and create metaphors even more if we take account of the form of their production, and of their horizontal relations with coordinate tropes such as metonyms and their vertical relations to more or less powerful metaphors—what I call the dual metaphor continua.

Contextualizing Metaphor in Poetry and Poetics: Individual Talent and the Tradition

We can further limit "metaphor theory" by grounding it in poets' practice and in the patterns of actual traditions (Eliot 1975). Let us begin with a range or continuum of metaphor-like figures as they have emerged in "The West." In Homer the numerous and far-ranging similes are all complex metaphors, many of them contrasting war and peace. In the Renaissance there was a preference for studied, artful metaphors that compare specific terms within a line. Petrarch and Thomas Wyatt may have one or more fresh metaphors per line, as well as governing conceits: "Shall I compare thee to a summer's day?" is a typical first line by Shakespeare, and it is followed by numerous comparisons. Then consider the far-reaching metaphors of the surrealists of our own century, as in Pablo Neruda's "Brussels": "among the frightening bodies, / like a tooth made of whitish wood, / coming and going under the stubborn acid, / close to the substances of agony, between men and knives, dying at night." Thus Homer, Wyatt, and Neruda, and many others in world poetry, illustrate a conspicuous or highly cultivated metaphor tradition.

Moving away from these metaphor-motivated extremes, we find many poets and poetic traditions where metaphors of the usual sort—metaphors by some strict or narrow definition—are replaced by masked metaphors, or delicate, implicit, and more distantly and deviously connected analogies of various kinds. In poets such as Tu Fu and Wang Wei (701–61), writing eight-line "Chinese sonnets" of the sort analyzed above, we find scores of subtle, metaphorical echoes or suggestions, partly motivated by the rules of "regulated verse" and its requirements of grammatical and lexical parallelism in adjacent lines, but also interacting with Wang's Buddhist outlook and his personal response to the mist-hung mountains around his rural home. Sometimes all four of the constituent couplets in a Chinese sonnet are imagistically and metaphorically integrated by alluding to the same underlying (shape) category: the nouns in the second position in each line in one poem by Li Po (701–62) all allude to the same image or shape that underlies a new moon, a half ring, an old fort's wall, the edge of some clouds, the Milky Way, a mountain pass, a courtyard, and (the edge of the petals of) a carnation; the poem is rooted in the cross-linguistic, universal value of the crescentic shape (Friedrich 1979: 351–56).

Let us move further along the continuum of concern with metaphor. Considerably less metaphorical, both in practice and precept, is the looser, rambling parallelism of Whitman: a web of connections, often fragile and obscure, is elaborated and contextualized in numerous nonmetaphorical figures. Many of the greatest poets, notably Sappho, Pushkin, Constantine Cavafy, and Stevens, have at least at times striven to avoid the looseness or potential sentimentality of metaphor (e.g., the pathetic fallacy). They preferred clear images, crackling wit, emotional confrontation, or the convolutions of extended paradox. Yet further removed is the poetry of the imagists and hard-core objectivists. Or of the realists and naturalists who try to write *about* working-class poverty or war, famine, and disease—with the least possible comparison, connotation, or analogy of any sort. And finally there are the explicitly, theoretically antimetaphorical poets and "antipoets" such as Nícanor Parra (1960), whose self-conscious tough stuff and natural language become a trope in their own right.

There are poetic and linguistic traditions that highly value some sort of descriptivism or even literalism, and where metaphor and similar analogical figures are actually avoided or at least neglected in favor of such alternatives as formal deconventionalization, telegraphic condensation, or the sustained expression of moods through exclamations, repetition, and the like.

Along our continuum of metaphorical preference and constraint, then, we run from (1) luxurious, clause-by-clause exploitation to (2) many kinds of indirect or secondary metaphor to (3) a limited and supplementary use of analogies to (4) various shades of qualified, would-be literalism to (5) hard-core objectivism. In terms of the foregoing theory, this would be one vertical continuum intersecting one of the analogical (i.e., metaphorical) continua on the horizontal axis.

The Renaissance, Romantic, Symbolist, and generally Western predilection for the metaphor does not hold even for many poets within those sets, such as Whitman, and can by no means be extended to the world at large. Indeed, to such masters of the arts of Euterpe as Wang Wei, Pope, Pushkin, the desert bards of the Old Testament, and the Eskimo bards recorded by Knud Rasmussen, it would seem weirdly trivializing to contend that metaphor is the master trope in some class by itself or that the ability to metaphorize is *the* hallmark of great poetry—as Aristotle and many contemporary theorists of poetry would have it.

Maximizing Metaphor

The idea that metaphor is primus inter pares has a long and venerable history that probably began with Aristotle's implicitly

rationalist claim that the ability to coin metaphor is the touchstone of the poet and, although a matter of degree, the index of poetic quality. Complex ideas about metaphor are also rooted in
early Indic and Chinese poetics (e.g., Cheng 1982: chap. 3), although the trope is not accorded the primacy to which we have
become habituated in the West. Down through the centuries the
focus on metaphor has remained strong among us despite oscilla-
tions and the *relative* silence from persons from whom one might
have expected more, such as Peirce, Saussure, and Edward Sapir.
The foci have increased in number and been sharpened in recent
decades in the work of linguistic structuralists such as David
Sapir, transformationalists such as Samuel Levin, social anthropologists such as Stanley Tambiah, philosophers such as Max
Black, literary critics such as Philip Wheelwright, and a host of
others. Recently J.-P. Noppen published a bibliography of metaphor studies that runs to 484 pages, although it *starts* at 1970!
Much of this recent work has been brilliant, or at least needed, but
some has veered into uncritical or totalizing metaphorphilia or
metaphormania. By 1978 the noted critic Wayne Booth, faced by
the flood of publications, could semiseriously call for a mora-
torium on the whole subject.

The Power of Metaphor

Having played the devil's advocate, I shall loop back to a duly
appreciative, even affectionate, consideration of some of the bases
of metaphor's power. First, there is Roman Jakobson's "beautiful
formula" for the essence of the poetic process: the poetic process
projects symbols from the vertical axis of substitution to the
horizontal axis of selection. For example, the t's in "truth" and
"terrible" are substitutes and "terrible truth," like "truthful ter-
ror," is ipso facto a poetic phrase; the shared feature of mercy and
dew makes poetic the line that equates them. Jakobson's formula
leaves much unaccounted for—for example, it generally leaves us
without criteria or even intimations of criteria for differentiating
between a line of Coleridge and a Coca-Cola jingle. But there is
considerable truth to it also, and it has generated myriad fruitful

research questions. This formula is a formula for the metaphor in particular (and thus its role in Jakobson's poetics partly, implicitly, contradicts his goal of relativizing metaphor).

Second, metaphor is an aesthetically specific subtype of the powerful and creative processes of analogy. Analogy, of course, figures in mathematical argumentation, in the social and natural sciences, and in cultural and psychological phenomena generally. But analogy is no more powerful than the emotions of the modal tropes or the form of the formal ones. And analogy should not be confused—or worse, identified—with metaphor, its subtype in the present universe of discourse, which is mainly the language of poetry and the poetry of language.

Third, if we draw together what has been said above, metaphor exemplifies all three types of Peircean sign. First, it characteristically involves vivid and concrete image ("The world is my oyster," "The man is a toad"); the so-called "magic" of metaphor typically involves this conversion into Firstness. Second, metaphor strongly entails the actor-reactant, ego–non-ego counterpoint and dialectic, the interaction between "reality and fancy"—in short, a Peircean Secondness. Third, metaphor forces the interpretant to (re)evaluate the relation between the sign and the things it refers or alludes to; it, like the syllogism, is a little law, an exemplar of Peircean Thirdness. I hasten to add that the other figures also can exemplify all three types of Peircean sign.

These three reasons—that metaphor motivates Jakobson's formula for the poetic, that it is a type of analogy, and that it synthesizes all three kinds of Peircean sign—account, if not for a putative rule of metaphor or a putative status as first among equals, then at least for the fact that its power is coordinate with that of such figures as irony and synecdoche. On this fairly authoritative (Jakobsonian and Peircean) plane and the gut feeling that metaphor *is* also miraculous, as in Tu Fu's "Great Peak," I have tried to give a new turn to the entire subject, starting with a consideration of the image tropes and seeing metaphor as part of fields of tropes, macrotropes, tropological continua, and so forth. The situation of metaphor theory perhaps resembles Homeric scholarship: although graduate students are traditionally directed away from it

"because everything has been said," the fact is that an infinitude
has *not* been said, and much of what has been said is wrong-
headed, or at least dated.

Initial Conclusions:
The Poetic Is Not Just in the Message

One general implication of the foregoing theory is that specific
figures vary enormously in the degree to which they are related to
or determine the message. This implication is crucial, because
in structuralist and formalist terms the essential poetic function
is to highlight or foreground the form of the message through,
for example, rhyme, unusual word order, and the like (Jakobson
1960: 356).

Two nonobvious examples of tropes as they (negatively) illumi-
nate this problem are global chiasmus and individuation through
dialect.

To start with chiasmus, this extraordinarily effectual formal
figure entails "crossing over," in the sense that a sequence of
words or lines or other units runs in the order a-b-c-d and then
comes out again in the reverse order d-c-b-a, in the manner of a
palindrome, whose spelling is the same backward or forward: the
names of the Mam language and of the Malayalam language. But
chiasmus also provides a deep and pervasive structure to the *Iliad*:
the internal structure of Book 1 corresponds to the internal structure of Book 24, that of Book 2 corresponds to that of Book 23,
and so forth until the battle-scene books 7–8 (Whitman 1965:
chap. 11). This overall gestalt-level structure is essential to the
work, but it does not serve to forefront the message in the sense of
the constituent sounds, lines, and so forth, or even sentences and
paragraph-type units of meaning. Chiasmus in this global sense
therefore varies independently of the structuralist and formalist
definitions of poetry, or, more precisely, of the poetic function.

The second tropic practice is individuation through dialect. Although dialects can, of course, serve to foreground the message, in
fact they do so rarely in the conventional and/or high lyric poetry

of the Western world, where hardly any such lyric poems counter-point three or more dialects. Even dialect poets such as Robert Burns tend to stay within one or two dialects, and the overwhelm-ing majority of lyric poems in English, T'ang Chinese, Italian, and other great traditions are monodialectal—usually the dialect of the aristocratic upper class, or at least the highly educated. Many critics would go so far as to argue that a touchstone of *prosaic* quality is the extraordinary dialectal heteroglossia (Bakhtin 1981) found in *The Sun Also Rises* or *Huckleberry Finn*—the latter with its seven specified Missouri dialects, including the "ordinary" one of Pike County. (The dialectal marking in these illustrious cases is achieved not so much through spellings of the segmental phonetic features as through suggested rhythms and contours of intonation.)

By an inverse of the preceding situation of global chiasmus, therefore, the trope of individuation through dialect does forefront the forms of the message but, far from illustrating the "poetic function" as a structuralist aesthetics would have it, actually con-tributes to the *prosaic* character of the work in question. Speaking more generally, there is, in fact, considerable independence be-tween the underlyingly tropological (and otherwise poetic) and, in contrast, whatever is tropological (and otherwise poetic) in the surface message of the text. All five of the macrotropes can enter into a structural definition and analysis of myth, which, in struc-turalist terms, is independent of the surface (e.g., phonetic) forms of the messages in which the myth is cast.

The conflicted relations between the lyric and the dialectal may be one reason why Mikhail Bakhtin, Georg Lukács, Raymond Williams, and other Marxist critics have had little or nothing to say about lyric poetry; the first of these authorities simply be-lieved that lyric poetry was monological. This Marxist silence on lyric contrasts with the rich output on drama, satire, and the realistic, psychological, or historical novel, or even the realistic-historical long poem or epic; Stephen Vincent Benét's epic *John Brown's Body*, for example, has a wide gamut of finely marked dialectal inflections that could provide much grist for a conven-tional Marxist critique. Two apparent exceptions to the Marxist silence or incoherence on lyric poetry would seem to be Walter

Benjamin (1979) and Julia Kristeva (e.g., 1984), but they have nothing to say about dialects in lyric poetry and how they might reflect the class struggle; in fact, their preferred poets, whether Mallarmé or Baudelaire, are singularly monodialectal.

And yet the lyric poet, the lyric poem, and individual figures in a lyric poem are also of necessity part of an encompassing and partly determining culture and political economy—whether this is a question of Eskimo sealing poems, or Nuer cattle songs, or, by way of antithesis, the many political and economic allusions in Tu Fu, the obstetrical subtexts in the poetry of "Doc" William Carlos Williams, or even the Gallic dandyism of Harvard aesthete cum wealthy corporate executive Wallace Stevens. Some lyric poets are highly sensitive to class conflict, and the correlated clash of dialects figures in their work: D. H. Lawrence and Robert Frost in English, for instance; Alexander Pushkin and Nikolay Nekrasov in Russian. And there is Josephine Miles's masterpiece, "Reason," about an exchange between a chauffeur, a trucker, and a valet. In Thomas Hardy's "The Ruined Maid," the then aristocratic word "aint" functions to mark off the new, achieved status of the gentleman's mistress and to contrast her with her more virtuous, that is, unruined, interlocutor (with a neat if unintended irony, since almost all readers today would take the same diagnostic word to be substandard, reflecting the courtesan's farm-girl origins). A relentless analysis and synthesis of the relation between lyric poetry and figures involving such factors as class conflict, as they work *within* the poem, remains one of the major goals of tropological analysis—as would a comparable study of such things as political economy working as a context *outside* the poem; the poetry of Tu Fu would lend itself to such approaches.

Wider Implications: Tropes and the Real (External) World

All the major tropes and subcategories of trope involve or imply engagement of various kinds, entanglement with worlds that are relatively external to or independent of language. Let us recur to the above scheme of tropes and its implications.

1. Image tropes work in part to the degree to which they resonate with, say, the perceptual reality of red and the optical-psychological facts of advancing red and retreating blue.

2. Tropes of mood work in part to the degree to which they are involved and engaged in fear, sympathy, and other primary emotions that in one shape or another are primary facts of life in all cultures.

3. Formal tropes are entangled in the real world of mathematics, be this the deductions of Euclidean geometry, the statistical bases of information theory, or the beauty of fractal geometry.

4. Metonymic tropes such as anatomy and synecdoche correspond to various kinds of part-whole relations in nature and culture, often serving to mask or distort them.

5. Metaphor and other analogical tropes, when they compare aptly, create new synapses in the mind and new relations between language, thought, and reality.

6. The very idea of gist and of ever-widening allusiveness arises from a dialectic relation between language and a real if not always material world.

Polytropy and Anthropology

By a strange and productive turn of fate, all of the problems just discussed, originally the domain of poets, have become relevant to anthropology and linguistics today.

1. Poetic language in the sense given above intersects in revealing and indispensable ways with all natural, ordinary, conversational language, and it is a moot question whether poetic language is a subset of ordinary language or vice versa.

2. The sheer multitude of and complex interrelationships between specific tropes such as inventory, irony, and commutation and macrotropes such as analogy constitute an expressive and denotative system of unimaginable power; a full explication of all the tropes in terms of Peircean categories is an urgent job for the future.

3. The system of five (or more?) macrotropes is an integral part of the linguistic system and process at all levels; for example, hun-

dreds of figures of irony and synecdoche intersect with the phonic and syntactic levels of language in terms of which they are variously coded. A language consists of myriad tropes that have passed into its structure and content; but they are only playing possum and can be brought to life at any time.

4. Language, with its dozens of levels and substructures, is interdependent with the natural world, including environmental problems, and with the sociocultural world, including social problems such as racism and exploitation, and it is the dozens of types of figures, which are part of language, that also mediate between language and all these relatively nonlinguistic worlds or universes.

5. The metaphorical continua—metaphor related to many coordinate tropes and the metaphor-internal levels—synthesize and synergize between, on the one hand, subjective and egocentric consciousness and, on the other hand, the society-based, sociocentric consciousness. As Voloshinov put it, "Between psyche and ideology there exists a continuous dialectical interplay" (1986: 39), which we can paraphrase, "Between the psyche of the unique individual, whether Poet or Everyman, and a society's ideologies and myths there exists a continuous, dialectical interplay via the mediation, among other things, of figures such as irony, metaphor, and synecdoche."

A focus on tropes could be the beginning of a totally formal, linguistic, and nominalistic theory of art. But a focus on tropes as practiced here can also mark a more natural and logical path of engagement with empirical facts of perception, with nuts-and-bolts experience, with mystic and scientific insight, with the relation between metaphor and scientific reasoning, and with yet other dimensions of experience, including the relatively word-free aspects of the world. Neither this relatively word-free world nor the relatively language-bound world are intelligible without each other, and it is tropes—irony, synecdoche, metaphor, vivid image—that help us to relate the two, to create the theoretically infinite number of little connections between the two, the tropic synapses. In terms of most language use most of the time, tropes are the great and little prepatterns that variously channel, influence, and determine how the speaker interrelates elements of language to each other and interrelates language itself and the rest of the world. In terms of the creative individual or any individual in a creative moment—of which phenomena Tu Fu is an extreme example—tropes are a basic means for synthesizing with language and for relating language to experience and practice.

The Cultural Basis of Metaphor

Naomi Quinn

It is only natural that practitioners of any discipline should tend to claim a large amount of explanatory territory for the phenomenon they study. Recent theory in cognitive semantics has put a heavy explanatory burden on metaphor, positing that it structures and indeed constrains human understanding and reasoning. Although I am in strong sympathy with the general approach these fellow cognitive scientists take to metaphor and although my own work owes an enormous debt to their thinking on this subject, I would like to try in this paper to retake some of the territory cognitive semanticists have claimed for metaphor and claim it instead for the phenomenon I study—culture. I do not mean by my own metaphor of imperialist conquest to suggest that culture and metaphor are directly opposing theoretical terms or to propose that the former supplant the latter. Instead, I will be arguing that cultural

With the usual caveat about authorial resistance to some of their suggestions, I would like to thank Paul Friedrich, Joel Robbins, and Claudia Strauss for their extremely helpful comments on drafts of this paper. I also want to acknowledge exchanges with George Lakoff and Mark Johnson that, although they did not result in our agreement, were certainly invaluable in clarifying, for me, the issue I try to address in this paper. I hope the paper will contribute to a more general clarification.

understanding underlies metaphor use, and I hope to show that there is more to culture than just metaphor. I will base my argument on work of my own in reconstructing Americans' understandings of marriage from their discourse on the subject, including the metaphors for marriage that appear in this discourse.

By culture I mean the shared understandings that people hold and that are sometimes, but not always, realized, stored, and transmitted in their language. Unfortunately, the case of metaphor illustrates a uniform tendency for linguists and other cognitive scientists outside of anthropology to neglect altogether the organizing role of culture in human thought, or to grant culture, at best, a residual or epiphenomenal place in their accounts. That, on the contrary, culture plays a central, profound role in human understanding is a conclusion of much recent research in cognitive anthropology (see D'Andrade 1989).

The approach to metaphor to which I refer is most fully represented in two recent books, one by the philosopher Mark Johnson, called *The Body in the Mind: The Bodily Basis of Meaning, Imagination, and Reason* (1987), and another by the linguist George Lakoff, called *Women, Fire, and Dangerous Things: What Categories Reveal About the Mind* (1987b). The treatment of metaphor in these works develops further a view first set forth by Lakoff and Johnson in their earlier and influential book, *Metaphors We Live By* (1980b).

In this view, metaphor is a mapping from some source domain to some target domain. Target domains are best thought of as "abstract" conceptual domains, often of the internal mental or emotional world, sometimes of the social world, occasionally unseen and unknown domains of the physical world as, for example, the world of molecular action (Quinn and Holland 1987: 28–94; see also Sweetser 1990: 28–32). Source domains are familiar ones, most often of the physical world; these are easy to think with, in the sense that the thinker can readily conceptualize the relations among elements in such domains and changes in these relations that result when these elements are set in motion conceptually. My last clause can serve as a convenient illustration of the postulated relationship between source and target domains. To speak of change among related elements of a domain in terms of entities in motion, arriving at spatial positions vis-à-vis one another different than the positions they took at the start, is more than a colorful turn of phrase. It is, as Lakoff and Johnson emphasize, conceptual. This transformation of abstract change into movement in space, or mapping of the latter onto the former, actually helps me imagine what a complex notion such as "changes in the relations between elements of a domain" could possibly mean.

Johnson and Lakoff argue that a small number of schemas of physical-world relations, which they call *image schemas*, underlie metaphors and are themselves based on fundamental bodily experiences in the world. For example, says Johnson, our understanding of containment is based on our experiences of looking into and taking things out of containers such as bowls, going in and out of containers such as rooms, and comprehending our bodies themselves as containers of, for example, blood and sensation. Our understanding of pathways is founded on our experiences, beginning as soon as we are able to crawl, of determining where we want to go and progressing along a chosen trajectory to reach that place. Although this is not one of Johnson's examples, it would be consonant with his argument to suppose that our understanding of relatedness is based on our experiences of our spatial position vis-à-vis other reference points—people, animals, things—in our immediate environment. Metaphors take this image-schematic understanding of the physical world and map it onto abstract concepts so that, for example, theoretical arguments can be understood as containers, full of inconsistencies or empty of data, human purposes can be understood as physical destinations that we strive to reach or from which we can be sidetracked, human social relationships can be conceptualized as points in space, perhaps close together, sometimes moving apart, and so forth.

This conception of metaphor has some important implications for the way humans understand. As Johnson (1987) points out, his and Lakoff's view of metaphor suggests a central role for what he calls *embodiment*, or bodily experience, in the development of individual understanding and in the evolution of human intellective capacities. More germane to the issue I will raise in this paper is the implication of one of these capacities in particular—reasoning—in a view of metaphor as mapping from one domain of experience to another. Gentner and Gentner (1983) have shown that naive subjects required to explain how electricity works were able to reason about this unknown domain by analogy, mapping the structure of relations among elements in a familiar domain (in their experiment, either the flow of water through a channel or the advance of crowds of "lemmings" through a chute) and reasoning from these relations. (That subjects using one or the other of these analogies consistently made different "mistakes" in their explanations of electrical phenomena was traceable to the fact that each of the two analog domains contained different, and differently misleading, mismatches to the scientific theory of electricity.) Metaphorical mappings of all kinds[1] might be presumed to facilitate reasoning in the same way. That reasoning about complex logical problems taking the form *modus tollens* is aided significantly by translation of the reasoning problem into familiar terms has been shown independently of metaphor or analogy in work by D'Andrade (1982; n.d.).

For Johnson and Lakoff, mapping one domain into another by means of metaphor not only plays a role in human understanding but is a central process in that understanding. Their argument sometimes takes the form of a seemingly unqualified claim that metaphor underlies and constitutes understanding. To say that metaphor constitutes all or most understanding may be too broad a construction of the intended argument.[2] Yet it is important to put to rest this most general and extreme position if only because other readers of Lakoff's and Johnson's published works are likely to go away, as I did after what I thought was a careful reading, with

[1] A distinction between "metaphor" and "analogy," the term preferred by the Gentners, would seem to have no significance in the context of the present discussion.

[2] Lakoff's writings, in particular, do not bear this interpretation unequivocally. Compare, for example, some of the assertions from *Women, Fire, and Dangerous Things* to be quoted below with other assertions, also quoted, from the same source and with a more recent statement in the foreword to Mark Turner's *Death Is the Mother of Beauty* (Lakoff 1987a). According to Lakoff (personal communication), he does not now and has not ever intended to make the claim that metaphor alone structures understanding. A more accurate representation of his current view, to be addressed in this paper, is that metaphor is partly constitutive of understanding.

a sweeping interpretation of their claim or at least with some confusion about how sweeping their theory of metaphor is meant to be.

A narrower claim, that metaphors partly constitute understanding, can be distinguished from the broader one. This claim amounts to the position that metaphors when used do not merely recast existing understanding in new terms, but supply the understander with heretofore unconsidered entailments drawn from the metaphorical source domain. This alleged productivity of metaphors has implications for reasoning—what many might assume to be the least metaphorical of intellective tasks, because of metaphor's association with imagination and creativity, and the dichotomy between these and rationality in Western thought. Johnson, in particular, argues that metaphor governs (and not merely facilitates) reasoning—that new metaphorical entailments allow new inferences that would not have been otherwise reached.

I will take up each of these claims in turn, addressing each with findings from my own research.[3] I will be arguing that metaphors, far from constituting understanding, are ordinarily selected to fit a preexisting and culturally shared model. And I will conclude that metaphors do not typically give rise to new, previously unrecognized entailments, although they may well help the reasoner to follow out entailments of the preexisting cultural model and thereby arrive at complex inferences. I do not want to suggest that metaphors never reorganize thinking, supply new entailments, and permit new inferences; but my analysis will argue that such cases are exceptional rather than ordinary.

Does Metaphor Constitute Understanding?

Johnson (1987: 104–5) offers the example of a metaphor that, as Lakoff and he (1980b) previously demonstrated, unifies a large

[3] The initial research on which this paper draws was funded in 1979–80 by National Institute of Mental Health research grant No. 1 RO1 MH330370-01. Analysis and write-up of the research findings have been pursued under National Science Foundation research grant No. BNS-8205739, a stipend from the Institute for Advanced Study in Princeton, New Jersey, where I spent a year as a

number of otherwise anomalous ways of talking about theory construction in American English, such as "Quantum theory needs more *support*"; "You'll never *construct* a *strong* theory on those assumptions"; "I haven't figured out yet what *form* our theory will take"; "Here are some more facts to *shore up* your theory"; "Evolutionary theory won't *stand* or *fall* on the *strength* of that argument"; "So far we have only put together the *framework* of the theory"; "He *buttressed* his theory with *solid* arguments"; and "Is that the *foundation* for your theory?" (All these examples are theirs.) Johnson reminds us:

> Lakoff and I argued that all of these (and other) conventional expressions cluster together under one basic metaphorical system of understanding: THEORIES ARE BUILDINGS. We examined several other important metaphors for the concept of ARGUMENT or THEORY CONSTRUCTION, such metaphors as ARGUMENT IS WAR, ARGUMENT IS A JOURNEY, AN ARGUMENT IS A CONTAINER, and so forth. Our central point was that metaphors of this sort are a chief means for understanding. . . . They organize our conventional language about arguments and theories because they constitute our understanding of argument, including how we will experience and carry on rational argument.

The main example of this constitutive role of metaphor in Lakoff's volume is his case analysis of the word *anger* in American English. Lakoff (1987b: 380–415) shows how a "central metaphor" for anger as HEATED FLUID IN A CONTAINER[4] provides "detailed correspondences between the source domain and the target domain," such as the fact that anger, like heating fluid, will increase pressure on its container (in the case of anger, the body) un-

visiting member, several grants from the Duke University Research Council at my home institution, and, most recently, a National Science Foundation Visiting Professorship for Women, grant No. RII-8620166, hosted by the University of California, San Diego. The research project has been an ambitious and lengthy one, and all these diverse sources of support have been essential to its completion.

[4] In paraphrasing his argument, I observe Lakoff's convention of representing metaphors in capital letters. In discussing my own findings, later in this paper, I revert to my own practice of referring to particular metaphors in lower case, and whenever helpful setting off the labels I give these metaphors in quotation marks.

til some limit at which it explodes, injuring bystanders, and the fact that this explosion can be prevented, either by exerting sufficient counterforce to keep the fluid (anger) from erupting out of the container or by releasing fluid (anger) to lower the pressure in the container. This "extremely productive" (ibid.: 384) metaphor accounts for expressions such as "I had reached the *boiling point*"; "His *pent-up* anger *welled up* inside him"; "She *blew up* at me"; "I *went through the roof*"; "He managed to keep his anger *bottled up* inside him"; "I *gave vent* to my anger"; and many more. (Again, all these examples and those to follow are supplied by Lakoff.)

Lakoff identifies several other "principal" and "minor" metaphors of anger in American English, metaphors that relate more or less loosely to the central one just described. For example, in the HEATED FLUID metaphor, the physical agitation of anger corresponds to the agitation of hot fluid under pressure. Agitation, Lakoff argues, is also an important part of our folk model of insanity, and this lays the basis for the metaphor ANGER IS INSANITY (e.g., "I'm *mad*"; "You're *driving me nuts*"). Anger is understood in our folk model of physiological response to produce undesirable bodily reactions, to interfere with normal functioning, and to eventuate in total loss of control that can be dangerous to others, from all of which follow the metaphors ANGER IS AN OPPONENT ("She *fought back* her anger"; "Her anger has been *appeased*") and ANGER IS A WILD ANIMAL ("He has a *ferocious temper*"; "He *unleashed* his anger"). Two other metaphors, in which THE CAUSE OF ANGER IS A PHYSICAL ANNOYANCE ("He's a *pain in the neck*"; "Don't be a *pest*") and THE CAUSE OF ANGER IS TRESPASSING ("This is where I *draw the line*"; "Don't *step on my toes*") suggest to Lakoff that anger is further conceptualized as the response to an injustice. A final metaphor, ANGER IS A BURDEN ("*Unburdening himself* of his anger gave him a sense of *relief*"), tells Lakoff that anger incurs responsibility—the dual responsibility of controlling one's anger and seeking retributive justice for the offense that provoked it in the first place.

Lakoff delineates "a certain prototypical cognitive model of anger" or "prototypical scenario" on which all these metaphors converge, each mapping onto a part of this model. This is a scenario of offense, anger in response to the offense, attempt at control of the anger, ultimate loss of control, and finally the act of retribution that restores balance and dispels anger. The central metaphor of anger as HEATED FLUID characterizes the physiological effects that figure in this scenario, while other metaphors such as that of anger as a WILD ANIMAL or a BURDEN characterize angry behaviors or the social responsibilities engendered by the emotion. Lakoff shows, lastly, that other recognized but nonprototypical scenarios can be understood as variants of this prototypical one.

In this analysis Lakoff has used metaphorical clues together with his own competence as a member of American culture to reconstruct Americans' "cognitive model" of the emotion of anger and its physiological, psychological, and social consequences. His reconstruction—and his frequent reference to the "folk theory" that "provides the basis for" given metaphors (ibid.: 388) and the "folk model of anger that has emerged" (ibid.: 396) from his analysis—would seem to assume that such a folk model—or what Holland and I (Quinn and Holland 1987) elsewhere call a "cultural model"—underlies and gives coherence to the various metaphors for anger. This assumption is entirely consonant with my own theory of the relation between metaphor and culture.

Yet, elsewhere in the same analysis, Lakoff seems to reject such a conclusion. In a final section (1987b: 405–6), he opposes his own stance to "a certain traditional view of metaphor" that would treat the concept of anger and the elements of what he calls the "anger ontology" as literally existing, and as being understood, independently of any metaphors. This is simply not the case, he asserts. Rather, "the anger ontology is largely constituted by metaphor."

In making this argument, he distinguishes between *basic-level metaphors* and *constitutive metaphors*. The latter, which include ENTITY, INTENSITY, LIMIT, FORCE, CONTROL, and BALANCE, "provide the bulk of the anger ontology," he says. Thus, in this ontology, ANGER IS AN ENTITY; "it does not really, literally exist as an independent entity, though we do comprehend it metaphorically as such" (ibid.: 405–6).[5] Basic-level metaphors are what

[5] We also understand anger to vary in intensity, which is oriented upward in accordance with the metaphor MORE IS UP and which has a limit. We further

we have become accustomed, in the course of Lakoff's analysis, to think of as the metaphors for anger: HOT FLUID, INSANITY, and so forth. These "allow us to comprehend and draw inferences about anger, using our knowledge of familiar, well-structured domains" (ibid.: 406). From these basic-level metaphors derives most of our understanding of anger; the HOT FLUID metaphor, for example, gives us an understanding of what kind of entity anger is. By contrast to these, then, ENTITY and other such metaphors are abstract, superordinate concepts. Constitutive metaphors appear to be the same as what Johnson, and Lakoff elsewhere in the same book, have classed as image schemas. In an earlier section of his book (ibid.: 282) that develops his key concept of an *idealized cognitive model*, or "ICM," Lakoff declares that it is image schemas that "provide the structures used" in complex cognitive models.[6]

While I certainly agree that metaphors play some role in the way we comprehend and draw inferences about abstract concepts,

---

understand anger to be capable of exerting force and of taking control of a person. The ontology of retributive justice contributes to that of anger the elements of offense and retribution, which exemplify both intensity and balance. These are the metaphors that are said (Lakoff 1987b) to constitute anger.

[6] For example the *scenario*, one kind of ICM, is structured in relation to its elements by a PART-WHOLE schema and temporally by a SOURCE-PATH-GOAL schema, while relations among elements in the scenario are structured by LINK schemas (the elements presumably themselves LINKED ENTITIES) and human purposes that figure in the scenario are, once again, structured by the SOURCE-PATH-GOAL schema. Of the other kinds of idealized cognitive models that Lakoff enumerates, the *propositional* ICM at first seems to be an exception in that it is one "that does not use *imaginative devices*, i.e., metaphor, metonymy, or mental imagery" (1987b: 285; italics in original) but is instead formed out of propositions, themselves consisting of arguments and their predicates. In describing the proposition, however, Lakoff observes that *its* overall structure is characterized by a PART-WHOLE schema, while semantic relations holding among the arguments (agent, patient, instrument, and so forth) are represented structurally by LINK schemas. In any case, it would seem to be a scenario structure that Lakoff has in mind when he describes the model of anger as a "prototypical scenario" of offense, anger, unsuccessful attempt at control, and so forth. I read him to be saying that our understanding of anger is constituted by image schemas, both those he mentions as specifically pertaining to the anger ontology, such as INTENSITY and CONTROL, and those he identifies as general to prototypical scenarios, such as the SOURCE-PATH-GOAL and LINK image schemas.

I take issue with the claim that they or the schemas on which they are said to be founded actually constitute the concepts. I will argue that this conclusion, or the tendency to talk as if it were so, is helped by a missing level in Lakoff's and Johnson's analyses—that of culture. This is not to say that Lakoff and Johnson are unaware that culture plays some role in understanding: Lakoff, as we have already seen, introduces assorted "folk theories" and "folk models" into his analysis, and although Johnson's concern is with "embodied" meaning, he takes care to include "cultural traditions," along with language, values, institutions, and history, in a list of factors that he repeatedly reminds his readers are part of the environment in which meaning is embedded. But culturally constituted meaning has no place of its own beside embodied meaning in Johnson's analysis and no systematically developed or well-articulated place in that of Lakoff.

I want to argue further, and I think quite contrary to what Johnson and Lakoff seem to be saying, that metaphorical systems or productive metaphors typically do not structure understandings de novo. Rather, particular metaphors are selected by speakers, and are favored by these speakers, just because they provide satisfying mappings onto already existing cultural understandings— that is, because elements and relations between elements in the source domain make a good match with elements and relations among them in the cultural model.[7] Selection of a particular metaphor for use in ordinary speech seems to depend upon its aptness for the conceptual task at hand—sometimes, as we shall see, a reasoning task.

Here I will turn away from metaphors for anger or for theory construction in American English to my own cultural analysis of the metaphors Americans use to talk about marriage,[8] in order to

[7] These latter, cultural understandings cannot be reduced to image-schematic structures, I will argue, because far from taking unique image schemas, these understandings can be recast, and constantly are recast by speakers, into different metaphors resting on different schemas.

[8] The body of discourse on which this analysis has been performed is a set of interviews about their marriages collected in 1979 and 1980 from 22 husbands and wives in 11 marriages. Each individual was interviewed separately, for an average of 15–16 hours. All interviewees were residents of the same middle-sized southern city; all were native-born Americans who spoke English as a

bring evidence against the view that metaphor constitutes understanding. Elsewhere (Quinn 1987; in progress) I have shown that, in hundreds of hours of analyzed discourse on the topic, only eight classes of metaphor for marriage recur. These are the following: metaphors of *sharedness*, such as "I felt like a marriage was just a partnership" or "We're together in this"; metaphors of *lastingness*, such as "It was stuck together pretty good" or "It's that feeling of confidence we have about each other that's going to keep us going"; metaphors of *mutual benefit*, such as "That was really something that we got out of marriage" or "Our marriage is a very good thing for both of us"; metaphors of *compatibility*, such as "The best thing about Bill is that he fits me so well" or "Both of our weaknesses were such that the other person could fill in"; metaphors of *difficulty*, such as "That was one of the hard barriers to get over" or "The first year we were married was really a trial"; metaphors of *effort*, such as "She works harder at our marriage than I do" or "We had to fight our way back almost to the beginning"; metaphors of *success or failure*, such as "We knew that it was working" or, conversely, "The marriage may be doomed"; and metaphors of *risk*, such as "There're so many odds against marriage" or "The marriage was in trouble."

This striking finding, that the superficially varied metaphors people use to talk about marriage are reducible to a very small number of classes, suggests that metaphor, far from being productive of understanding, is actually highly constrained by understanding. I have postulated that the metaphors for marriage make sense in terms of an underlying model shared by my interviewees, the eight classes of metaphor reflecting the conceptual elements that together, and in interaction, define this model. Here I certainly do not have space to describe this cultural model of marriage fully or to demonstrate the analysis on which its description rests convincingly; I will only summarize my findings.

In Americans' model of it, marriage is expected to be shared, mutually beneficial, and lasting. I argue elsewhere (Quinn 1988;

---

first language. All were married during the period of their interviews, all in first marriages. Beyond these commonalities, they were selected to maximize diversity with regard to such obvious differences as their geographic origins, religious affiliations and ethnic and racial identities, their occupations and educational backgrounds, and the age of their marriages.

in progress) that this particular constellation of expectations derives from the mapping of our cultural conception of love onto the
institution of marriage and the consequent structuring of marital
expectations in terms of the motivational structure of love. Because people want to be with the person they love, they want and
expect marriage to be shared; because they want to fulfill the
loved person's needs and have their own needs fulfilled by that
person, they want and expect marriage to be beneficial to both
spouses in the sense of mutually fulfilling; and because they do
not want to lose the person they love, but want that person to go
on loving them forever, people want and expect their marriages to
be lasting.

I speculate that the motivational constellation that is part of
our understanding of love and that provides marriage with its
structure itself makes sense in psychoanalytic terms. Psycho-
analysts since Freud, who characterized adult love as a "re-finding"
of infantile love for the first caretaker, have theorized about the
relation between the two. My claim is that Americans' distinctive
conception of marriage takes the particular shape it does and has
the force it does for us because of the cultural model of love mapped
onto marriage and, thus, indirectly because of an infantile experience that Americans have shared and that underpins our conception of adult love.

The remainder of the cultural model of marriage reflected in
the metaphors for marital compatibility, difficulty, effort, success
or failure, and risk, derives from a contradiction that arises inevitably between the expectation of mutual benefit and that of
lastingness. Fulfillment of spouses' needs, the expected benefit of
marriage, is understood in terms of the mutual benefit expected
of all voluntary relationships. Just as in other such relationships, if
one individual or the other is not benefiting from this one—not
experiencing fulfillment—he or she is free to leave it. However,
another understanding already described, one special to marriage,
is that it is not supposed to end. A variety of situations can initiate
a felt contradiction between the expectation of marital fulfillment
and that of a lasting marriage.

Many of these situations have to do with incompatibility between one spouse's needs and the other's capabilities to meet these
needs, as when, for instance, the two are mismatched in this re-

gard from the beginning or when one or the other or both change, in the course of a marriage, in unexpected ways that render one incapable of filling the other's needs any longer. The further expectation that marriage be shared is implicated in another, slightly different, marital dilemma, because sharedness can affect fulfillment. A couple must share common goals and interests, joint activities, and interpersonal intimacy to some degree in order to be in position to fulfill each other's needs, for instance, yet too close a marriage may threaten the ability of each individual spouse to meet his or her autonomous needs. Americans treat all such contradictory marital situations as difficulties to be overcome so that needs can be fulfilled and a lasting, successful marriage achieved. To overcome difficulty requires effort and entails risk of failure as well as the possibility of success.

I argue that my interviewees' understanding of this story about marriage exists, for them, independently of the metaphors they use to talk about marriage. Earlier I gave just two common examples of each class of metaphors for marriage, but it is essential to my argument to emphasize that each element in the reconstructed cultural model of marriage—lastingness, marital difficulty, and so forth—can be and is instantiated by a wide variety of metaphors. Thus, while speakers frequently cast marital lastingness in a metaphor of a manufactured product—one that is well-made ("stuck together pretty good" in my earlier example) and has a solid foundation, a sound framework, and good, well-fitting parts—this is far from the only metaphor that conveys this expectation. Another very common metaphor for a lasting marriage, for example, is that of an ongoing journey that the married people undertake together ("that's going to keep us going" in the other example given earlier). Somewhat less frequently but not less consistently, speakers use still other metaphors of marriage as two inseparable objects ("We knew we were going to stay together"), an unbreakable bond between them ("That just kind of cements the bond"), a permanent location ("I was able to stay in the marriage"), an indestructible natural object ("the everlasting Gibraltar nature of the thing"), a secure possession ("We got it"), or a convenant with God (a "sacrament"), for example, to convey the expectation of its lastingness. None of those metaphors is more "central" than the others to Americans' understanding of marriage. All capture the prototypically enduring in Americans' experience, and all are selected by speakers, we may suppose, for precisely this reason.

Notice that not only are these different metaphors for marital lastingness, but they derive from different schemas. The "well-made product," "indestructible natural object," and "secure possession" metaphors can be considered to instantiate an ENTITY schema, the "ongoing journey" metaphor a TRAJECTORY schema, the "inseparable objects, "unbreakable bond" and "covenant with God" metaphors a RELATION schema, and the "permanent location" metaphor a CONTAINER schema.[9] These four schemas are

[9]Although I have adopted their habit of setting off references to these schemes in capital letters, my constructs here resemble but are not exactly the same as what Lakoff and Johnson mean by image schemas and should not be mistaken for the latter—clarification of which distinction I owe to George Lakoff (personal communication). The difference revolves around the point that, in line with their commitment to the origins of understanding in embodied experience, Lakoff and Johnson intend image schemas to have unique imageable realizations. My four schemas, and particularly the RELATION schema, which subsumes such Johnson-Lakoff candidates for image schemas as LINK, CONTACT, MERGING, SPLITTING, and NEAR-FAR, are more abstract. My reasons for preferring my classification scheme are two.

First, even in the limited context of metaphors for the marital dyad, the number of possible instantiations of the RELATION schema is arbitrarily large, making for potentially endless additions to Johnson's (1987: 126) list of 27 candidates for image schemas. To appreciate this observation we need consider just one example of a metaphorical description of a marriage relationship: "I can almost think back to those particular things with a certain amount of nostalgia and say, 'That was a time when we did something and it was just the two of us,' and, you know, 'we weren't just staring at each other through the event,' you know" (4H-1). Detachment gives way here to a sense of joint participation. To handle this husband's perception of the shift in his marriage, an image schema for something like JOINT ACTION, perhaps conjoined with another image schema, ISOLATED DYAD, would have to be introduced. Yet other image schemas—perhaps SEPARATENESS (not precisely the same as either FAR or SPLITTING) and MUTUAL ORIENTATION TOWARD—would have to be added to describe the earlier situation when they were "just staring at each other through the event." These novel candidates are not just subtypes or more elaborated instances of those Johnson gives, but appear to match the level of abstraction of his selections. They make his claim that his list, while admittedly selective, "includes what I take to be most of the more important image schemas" seem quite optimistic. Analytic recognition of all the varied metaphors for relations between spouses as instantiations of a common RELATION schema effectively eliminates this problem of proliferation. Recognition of a more general and abstract schema also accommodates metaphors such as the

the bases for all the metaphors for marriage in the talk I have analyzed.[10] I could, given space, illustrate this same range of metaphors across schemas with each of the other terms of the cultural
model I have described. The point these examples make is that not
only does there exist no one central metaphor for marriage, as
Lakoff claims there to be for anger, but neither are the metaphors
that do occur reducible to a central schema, or a single stable assemblage of schemas, of the sort Lakoff posits for anger. The cultural model of marriage can take expression in variant schematic
or "ontological" terms.[11]

---

one considered here in which "staring at each other through the event," despite some physical correlates, cannot be understood without recourse to substantial social knowledge hardly captured in, say, MUTUAL ORIENTATION
TOWARD.

Second, in talking about their marital relationships, speakers readily ac-
complish transformations and comparisons between different metaphorical instantiations of the RELATION schema, as in this example. A schema at this
level of abstraction would seem to be justified not merely on grounds of analytic convenience or parsimony but as an accurate representation of how
speakers themselves conceptualize the dynamics of marital relationships and
the differences across them. Although metaphors of marital relationship offer
an especially rich illustration of the analytic utility of a RELATION schema,
the same argument can be made from my interview material for treating such
proposed image schemas as PART-WHOLE and CENTER-PERIPHERY as metaphorical instantiations of a more abstract ENTITY schema; for treating FULL-
EMPTY, another of Johnson's candidate image schemas, as an instantiation of
the CONTAINER schema; and for treating others such as CYCLE, ITERA-
TION, SCALE, as instantiations of the TRAJECTORY schema. Of course, my
argument for non-imagic schemas at the level of abstraction of the RELATION
schema and the others I have posited raises yet another doubt, not to be resolved here, about whether image schemas as Johnson and Lakoff define them
play the fundamental role in human understanding that these authors claim
for them.

[10] Particular schemas appear sometimes to be adopted deliberately by speakers in order to foreground different aspects of the experience of marriage (as the
ENTITY schema objectifies the marital experience while the TRAJECTORY
schema highlights change in this experience, for example [Quinn in progress]),
although schemas are at other times simply functions of the metaphors speakers have chosen to elaborate on them.

[11] This is not to say that given metaphors may not conjoin two or more schemas; indeed, metaphors frequently do so (Quinn in progress). Thus, for example, marriage in the "manufactured product" metaphor of "It was stuck together pretty good" and other similar remarks, such as "It was going to be a

A key proof for Johnson that understanding is structured *by* metaphor is his and Lakoff's identification of "clusters of conventional expressions under one metaphorical system" (Johnson 1987: 105) as, for example, when a marriage or (in his example) a theory is characterized as a building that may be well- or ill-constructed, out of good materials or not, and so forth. What Lakoff and Johnson have failed to note is that the clusterings of metaphorical entailments they identify do not exhaust the systematicity in metaphor usage. With regard to metaphors for marriage, I find *different* "metaphorical systems," each with its distinctive "clusters of expressions," are alternative instantiations of the same underlying concept. A lasting marriage can be both a

---

solid thing" or "You have to start out with something that's strong if it's going to last," might be said to be the product of an implicit process of manufacture. I would characterize these last metaphors as instantiating the ENTITY schema because they leave this production process implicit while highlighting the durability of the thing produced or the quality of the materials out of which this thing has been made. However, other metaphors, such as "Never having learned what you need to learn and work through to make the first marriage stick," or "It was made as we went along," explicitly highlight the making and, in so doing, instantiate a TRAJECTORY schema in which the marriage ENTITY is the end point. Equally, of course, marriage may be an ENTITY that follows some TRAJECTORY in the "ongoing journey" metaphor, as in "We take a lot of credit for the direction it went in"; or it may be a CONTAINER of the married people on this TRAJECTORY, as in "I'd have to say, 'Stop the boat, I want to get out.'" Metaphors such as "We wanted to continue together" or "We might come to a place where we have to separate" rest on a joining of the TRAJECTORY schema with the RELATION schema. The last example, indeed, instantiates three schemas conjoined: the place where the married people have to separate is a CONTAINER of the RELATION on the TRAJECTORY. In "You can go to some place that you'd like to be at or you can not," the place reached is a CONTAINER of a different sort, this time of marital benefit. To provide one last, and different, example, "We got it," a metaphor of marriage as an ENTITY firmly in possession, might be said to invoke as well the hand or other CONTAINER in which it is kept, the TRAJECTORY of its acquisition (made more explicit in the metaphor "The marriage was up for grabs"), or the RELATION of ownership. Whether a metaphor makes a given metaphorical entailment explicit or leaves it implicit, or focuses on one entailment or another, almost any such metaphor for marriage has conceivable entailments that may invoke multiple schemas. However, these schematic potentialities of the metaphors for marriage, although they enlist the same four schemas in different combination, do not reduce to a stable assemblage of schemas that could be said to constitute a single distinctive ontology of marriage.

well-made product and an ongoing journey, as well as a firmly held
possession, a secure bond, and a permanent location, and that this
is so can only be made explicable in terms of the underlying concept, independent of any of these metaphors, of marriage as lasting.

Does the Metaphor Give Rise
to the Entailments?

Lakoff (1987b: 384), writing of the central metaphor of anger as
HEATED FLUID IN A CONTAINER, suggests that it is the extreme productivity of the metaphor that "gives rise" to a "rich system of metaphorical entailments":

> Let us refer to the HEAT OF FLUID IN A CONTAINER as the source do-
> main of the central metaphor and to ANGER as the target domain. We usu-
> ally have extensive knowledge about source domains. A second way in
> which a conceptual metaphor can be productive is that it can carry over
> details of that knowledge from the source domain to the target domain.
> We will refer to such carryovers as metaphorical entailments. Such entail-
> ments are part of our conceptual system. They constitute elaborations of
> conceptual metaphors. The central metaphor has a rich system of meta-
> phorical entailments. For example, one thing we know about hot fluids is
> that, when they start to boil, the fluid goes upward. This gives rise to the
> entailment:
> When the intensity of anger increases, the fluid rises.

Other metaphorical elaborations such as "Anger *welled up* inside
him" or "We got a *rise* out of him" give rise to a series of further
metaphorical entailments. These entailments, and those of other
"basic level" metaphors, carried over into the target domain, then
allow us to draw inferences about anger.

Lakoff brings this argument to my analysis of American marriage. While granting that there is a cultural model of marriage
that is not metaphorically constituted, he deems this to be

> a fairly impoverished model, one not rich enough to live by. What people
> do is extend this model via metaphor, e.g., they view marriage as a PART-
> NERSHIP, a HAVEN, a STRUGGLE, a DIFFICULT JOURNEY THROUGH
> LIFE TOGETHER, etc. Each of these concepts maps partly onto the im-
> poverished shared model, elaborating it, adding inferences about what to
> expect, what constitutes a difficulty, etc. (personal communication)

According to Lakoff, metaphors such as the above do more than "name parts of the cultural model" as I claim; they give rise to inferences of their own. In my analysis I "did not attribute inferences to those basic-level conceptual metaphors but only to the central model," and hence I fail to account for inferences that can arise from the metaphors. For example, he says, "in the partnership metaphor, the main problems are internal (the other partner not doing his job, the lack of benefits); while in the journey-through-life the problems tend to be external obstacles" (personal communication).

The following two excerpts illustrate that, as an empirical matter, this internal-external distinction does not hold up too well.[12] The first of these passages shows that the "difficult journey" metaphor can be and is used freely to talk about difficulties that are interpersonal in nature (and hence, Lakoff would presumably agree, "internal" to the marriage). In the second case, the "partnership" metaphor is used to point up the need to assist one's spouse in resolving unspecified problems in life—problems that may be individual as well as mutual (including, presumably, ones derived from circumstances "external" to the marriage).

4H-7: Accepting the differences that were there and that were going to—you know, and that I would have to put up with some of the situations that I didn't like and continue to until we had worked it out. But that however long and stony a road it was, we had agreed to set out on it and meet each small situation as it came.

3H-2: Life is not a bed of roses. And we really prove to the other person—you prove to your partner in life that you're worth living with. You're worth having around and sharing your life with. You prove your worth by how you react to these kinds of situations where it takes some kind of

[12] In reproducing interview segments in this and other publications, I use the following format. The code at the beginning of an interview segment contains, in order, an interviewee identification number, an H to indicate that the speaker is a husband or a W to indicate a wife, and the number of the interview from which that segment was drawn in the sequence of interviews with that person. Comments or questions interjected by the interviewer (of which there is one in this paper) are prefaced by an I, and resumption of the interviewee's part of the conversation is indicated, in this case, by an H. For ease of reading comprehension, all interview segments have been regularized for stammers, stutters, elisions, and slips of the tongue; paralinguistic phenomena such as hesitations, laughter, or throat-clearing have been omitted.

perception or extraordinary type of, you know, action. Each of—you know, to resolve a problem, help your partner out. Or help the both of you out of your—it's a mutual concern. You know if one—sometimes one partner takes the initiative or knows what to do instinctively and things work out. Then everyone's grateful. Or sometimes it's a shared thing where, you know, you actually work it out. That's the best of all.

In line with my analysis, the "long and stony road" metaphor in the first passage expresses the difficulty of marriage and also its lastingness; the "partners in life" metaphor expresses the sharedness of marriage and, again, its lastingness.

More generally, Lakoff is correct to point out that given metaphors may reflect "enrichments" or "elaborations" of the cultural model. He is wrong to suppose that the metaphors themselves "give rise to" the embellishments. As the two excerpts also illustrate, each of the metaphors used, far from raising previously unconsidered entailments, iterates, and lends emphasis to, a point being made in the discussion into which it is introduced. The first metaphor emphasizes the point under discussion, that not only is marriage difficult and lasting, but (like a long, stony road) its difficulties may be long-lasting. The second metaphor is also introduced in the context of a larger argument, that one has to prove one's worth to one's spouse by helping that other person resolve problems as these arise. The metaphor of partnership would seem to be well-suited to the theme of such mutual assistance. In recognizing, emphasizing, and elaborating upon marital experiences such as occasions that call for mutual help or commitments to work out persistent differences, people live their marriages and make them uniquely theirs. While a newly considered metaphor might conceivably become part of this process of interpreting experience, it is surely not the central way, nor even a common way, in which people arrive at understandings of their marital experience as this unfolds. Rather, metaphor typically captures existing understandings.

Metaphors of marital sharedness like that of "partnership" often provide especially good examples of how metaphor is selected to fit a point. Marital sharedness involves a global assumption that married people will share their lives with each other, made explicit in the last passage above. To suggest that this general assumption is part of an "impoverished model" of marriage not rich enough to live by is to miss the enormous force of this and other elements of that cultural model for the way in which people live their lives. There are few Americans who do not expect some kind of life together as a condition of marriage, and who do not strive to satisfy this condition, according to their own lights, in their own married lives. But what constitutes "a life together" is multiplex. Such a life almost always assumes co-residence, time spent together, common activities, and shared thoughts and feelings. To lead this life together people must agree on common values and interests and confront the world as a social unit. They endure a common fate, finding it necessary to plan for the future together, and, as the "partnership" metaphor highlights, they work toward common goals. Because of the complexity of this part of the cultural model of marriage, speakers often attempt to clarify the aspect of marital sharedness a particular metaphor is intended to point up, by commentary on that metaphor.[13] This commentary normally occurs immediately following the metaphor itself, as in these examples:

11W-11: Only thing I could see in our marriage is—that I had imagined is just like I said, that we would be just sitting around now just like—I guess like two love birds, heh, you know. Just taking up the time with me and I with him and all that, which it just didn't materialize exactly like that and it still doesn't.

1H-1: And then I see marriages where it's just like they are brother and sister, they cross paths occasionally. They don't have anything in common or they don't ever do anything together.

3H-4: We present a front of sorts together. Not a couple front, but a united front. A common value system that we share and things that we want to show to other people. Where we're at.

8H-4: And another thing we've got into problems of, you know, "Who am I? What do I want to be? Who are you? Where are you going? What do you want to be? And how do we both get there?" Being that we're sort of tied

[13] Of course, metaphors other than those of marital sharedness may take commentary and do so, whenever the speaker is unsure that the metaphorical point will be taken unambiguously.

together, you know, like a three-legged race, this kind of thing, in terms of,
you know, handling an issue of, suppose someone gets offered a job in
Alaska or something?

As the commentary on them clarifies, the metaphors in these
successive passages represent marital sharedness, respectively, as
time spent together, common interests and activities, a common
value system, and a shared fate. The commentary on the heels
of the metaphor shows quite unmistakably that the speaker has
adopted this metaphor to make a point already in mind, rather
than being led to this point by a previously unrealized entailment
of the metaphor. This demonstration is particularly compelling in
the middle two examples. In the second passage, far from the point
about a lack of common interests and activities arising as the entailment of some metaphor, two different metaphors, one of the
married couple as brother and sister, the other picturing them on
"paths" that only "cross occasionally," are concatenated to reinforce this point. In the third passage, the metaphor itself is
amended, and then commented upon, to clarify the intended point
that the married people do not merely confront the world as a social unit but that they exemplify common values to other people.

Do Metaphorical Entailments
Provide Inferences?

For Johnson, another crucial piece of evidence that metaphors
constitute understanding is their role in reasoning. Metaphors, he
argues, govern reasoning by allowing only those inferences that
follow from relations between entities in the metaphorical source
domain. These metaphorical entailments constitute a grasp of the
situation to be reasoned about (1987: 130).

I would like to suggest that the metaphor appears to structure
inferences in the target domain, carrying these inferences over
from entailments in the source domain, only if it be supposed that
the selection of this metaphor is unconstrained. Once it is recognized that choice of metaphor is itself highly constrained by the
structure of cultural understanding, then it can be seen that reasoners ordinarily select from possible metaphors those that provide them with a felicitous physical-world mapping of the parts

of the cultural model—the elements and relations between elements—about which they are intent on reasoning. The idea of such selection assumes, of course, that unlike the subjects who were purposely asked to reason about a phenomenon (electricity) that they did not understand very well (Gentner and Gentner 1983), thinkers ordinarily do already know the structure of the domain that is the target of their metaphor.

This view of the role of metaphor in complex reasoning about familiar but abstract domains such as marriage does not suppose that the metaphors "constitute" a grasp of the situation to be reasoned about, only that they render this situation more amenable to the simultaneous apprehension of multiple relations and the manipulation of these relations. It does not say that the metaphors give rise to the inferences reasoned to, only that they help the reasoner to follow out the chain of entailments to these inferences. It is not the metaphors they use for marriage, I will try to show next, but the cultural model they have of it, that constitutes the dilemmas people reason about and frames the solutions they reason to.

This is not to deny that metaphors that have become usual or conventional may direct our attention away from features of the target domain that have no structural match or a poorly delineated match in the source domain in favor of elements that are well delineated in the source domain. As Johnson (1987: 127–37) illustrates with the story of physician Hans Selye's discovery of the stress syndrome, there may be occasions when a previously unconsidered metaphor leads the thinker to reorganize a target domain in its terms and to reason to new conclusions by following out the entailments of the new metaphor. As the Gentners (1983) demonstrate with the example of electricity, metaphor is especially likely to organize experience and guide reasoning in just those domains for which there is no other available model. Metaphor may play this role in life as in science, outside the psychologist's experiment just as in it. My argument will be that this is simply not how people ordinarily use metaphors in everyday reasoning. Reasoning about marriage, I will illustrate, follows the well-worn tracks of quandaries posed by the cultural model of marriage. It would be surprising to find that other everyday topics of reasoning were any different.

A metaphor for marriage may isolate a single element of the cultural model—as, for example, "There are so many odds against marriage" seems to capture just the riskiness of marriage, or "The first year we were married was really a trial" appears to highlight just its difficulty. But such pure cases are in the minority. Instead, those metaphors are favored that capture two or more related elements in the cultural model. Sharedness may be captured in a metaphor such as "We decided to stay together," and lastingness in a metaphor such as "If ever a marriage was nailed in cement, that was the one." Favorite metaphors, however, are ones that combine these two concepts—for example, by casting marriage in terms of some durable link between spouses, such as the comment introduced earlier "That just kind of cements the bond" or the similar "We're more tied to each other now than we were then." Some metaphors, judiciously chosen, bear still a third element. Thus the concept of difficulty is added to those of sharedness and lastingness in the following example: "That was a point of contention really driving a wedge between people." Similarly, the concepts of sharedness, lastingness, and effort are all conflated in these metaphors: "Those two couples did hang together—are still together"; and "We're sort of tied together, you know, like a three-legged race." Metaphors of marriage as an "ongoing journey" or as a "manufactured product" are among those favored just because they can so readily accommodate, at once, multiple elements of the cultural model. Travelers can keep going (that is, their journey is a lasting one) together (and shared) over routes that may take them to places they might like to stay (that are mutually beneficial) and uphill or through rocky terrain (difficulties) over which they must struggle (make effort) to meet unknown dangers (risk). Manufactured products can be made to last (are lasting) with care and hard work (effort), and they will fill the uses for which they were intended (be beneficial) if the parts out of which they are built are good ones that fit together well (are compatible), in which case they are said to work (succeed). All these entailments of the journey metaphor and the manufactured product metaphor are used in discourse on marriage.

It would be a mistake to assume, then, that given metaphors recur in talk about a domain like this one simply because the metaphors themselves have become "conventional"—in the term

used by both Lakoff (1987b: 380) and Johnson (1987: 106). It may
be closer to the case to say that metaphors are reintroduced over
and over again because they are satisfying instantiations of a "conventional" or culturally shared model, capturing multiple elements
of that model. The invention of new metaphorical expressions is
constrained, not by a necessity to stay within the entailments of
particular conventional metaphors, as Johnson (1987: 106–7) argues (although new metaphors may certainly play out previously
unexplored entailments of these conventional ones), but by the
necessity of finding metaphors that make sense in terms of the
cultural model and by preference for metaphors that do a particularly good job of this.[14]

Why do speakers favor metaphors that map onto multiple ele-

[14] Lakoff and Johnson have rightly observed that some metaphors appear to
be more widespread than others, recurring in many different domains of experience. They conclude that such metaphors have a very general cultural significance. For example the metaphors "LABOR IS A RESOURCE and TIME IS A
RESOURCE are by no means universal. They emerged naturally in our culture
because of the way we view work, our passion for quantification, and our obsession with purposeful ends. These metaphors highlight those aspects of labor
and time that are centrally important in our culture" (1980b: 67). Might not
some of the metaphors used to talk about marriage be of this sort? The "manufactured product" metaphor, for example, would seem to be a likely candidate.
Perhaps, just as they are said to think of labor and time as resources, Americans
tend to think not just about marriage but of many matters, social, intellectual,
and affective as well as physical, in terms of manufacture. It seems reasonable
to suppose, as Lakoff and Johnson do, that the recurrence of such metaphors
across multiple domains is diagnostic of major themes in a culture. Notice that
even if this proved to be true of, say, the "manufactured product" metaphor,
this metaphorical source domain would not necessarily represent the original
or primary experience around which the theme or set of themes reflected in
this metaphor has been elaborated. The metaphor may have come to be widespread across domains for the same reason that it is common within the domain of marriage: because it captures a set of American preoccupations about
mastery of the natural and social worlds and redirection of natural phenomena
and social institutions, as Lakoff and Johnson put it, to purposeful ends. The
metaphor may even come, ultimately, to stand as a symbol for that constellation of themes. Indeed, Lakoff and Johnson, in the passage just quoted from
their earlier book, appear to be arguing for just such an origin for the two related "resource" metaphors, said to have emerged because they highlight a
cluster of underlying cultural themes. Note that this position would seem at
odds with any claim that metaphor constitutes understanding, including, presumably, these thematic understandings.

ments of the cultural model these metaphors target? This preference may simply reflect the fact that such metaphors allow this
model to be apprehended in its entirety, as an "experiential gestalt"
(Lakoff and Johnson 1980b: 77–86). This capability of metaphor to
present experience holistically may have a further, special import
for reasoning. For aptly chosen metaphors for marriage do not
merely map two or more elements of the source domain onto the
domain of marriage; in doing so they map the relationship between or among these elements as well. Journeys are not just
made over rocky roads to distant destinations; they are parables
teaching that one must overcome difficulties in order to reach
one's goal. Manufactured products are not just well made or badly
made, and prone to last or break down; they are physical realizations of the lesson that something made well is made to last.

Gentner and Gentner (1983) showed that their subjects were
aided by analogy to a familiar source domain in reasoning about
a target domain, electricity, of unfamiliar structure. Even if the
structure of the target domain is well understood, as I argue the
relations among elements of the cultural model of marriage are
understood by interviewees in my study and by other Americans,
complex reasoning about these relations may still pose a mental
challenge. Reasoners may find it easier to transpose the reasoning
problem, or parts of it, into the terms and relations provided by
metaphor. How would this reconceptualization aid reasoning? Toward the beginning of this paper I suggested that metaphorical
source domains were typically familiar domains of the physical
world and that these were "easy to think with, in the sense that
the thinker can readily conceptualize the relations among elements in such domains and changes in these relations that result
when these elements are set in motion conceptually."[15] In the par-

---

[15] Indeed, the vast majority of metaphors do draw, for their sources, on
physical experiences (as, in the case of metaphors for marriage, the experience
of traveling, or that of making something). Yet there are other metaphors that
draw on experiences like possession (for instance, the "We got it" example and
others such as "We have a very good thing" or "The marriage was up for grabs")
or economic exchange (for example, "When you realize how much you're trad-
ing off" or "When the cost is more than the reward, maybe it's time to get out"
or "You shouldn't feel that you're being short-changed"), no less socially constructed than marriage itself. Why should such domains be easier to think

ticular case of reasoning, it may well be easier to trace a chain of causality across a set of hypothetical relations when these relations can be envisioned as unfolding in the physical-world domain that metaphor provides. A metaphor might fix in mind a particularly lengthy, complex causal sequence or preserve a piece of a longer, more complex one, so that that piece can be retrieved and fit into the rest of the causal chain. The examples to follow in the next section will suggest how metaphors might aid reasoning in this way, and at the same time they contest the alternative view, that metaphors constitute the situation reasoned about.

A Close Examination of Metaphor in Reasoning

As noted, a central contradiction in the model of marriage I described earlier is achievement of a lasting and successful marriage in the face of the formidable difficulties of fulfilling one's own and one's spouse's needs. This is a clear intellectual preoccupation of interviewees, who are frequently motivated to explain why, or infer whether, given marriages—their own actual and potential marriages, those of other people they know, marriage nowadays in contrast to the past, or American marriages compared to marriage in other societies—do or do not, might or might not last. These inferences and explanations often make explicit the causal relations interviewees entertain among marital benefit in the form

---

with? Even the largely socially constructed domains of these last examples are physically realized, in relations between people or between people and things. It seems plausible to suppose that these domains, like those of more purely physical experience, provide ready images of a schematic sort. From such images complex relations among elements can be held in mind, and from their mental manipulation changes in these relations can be tracked. Marriage, indeed, may supply one such schematic image for other domains. For marriage itself sometimes figures as a source domain, in metaphors such as "It was a marriage of minds" or "The dish marries those flavors perfectly." The entailment invoked by these metaphors is marital sharedness, extreme among relationships, and the image seems to be one of two (or more?) entities merging to create a single new one. But taken as a whole, marriage is apparently too abstract an experience to be understood always in its own terms, let alone to provide metaphors for other experience on a regular basis.

of mutual fulfillment, marital lastingness, sharedness, difficulty, effort, and so forth. The analysis of reasoning in these passages supports my original, metaphor-based reconstruction of the American cultural model of marriage, specifying the causal interaction among its terms and, at the same time, filling in pieces of the model. It also provides a close, revealing look at the use of metaphor in natural reasoning.

The recurrent dilemma that I will use for illustration arises from my interviewees' recognition that for various possible reasons the two people in a marriage may be incompatible, in which case the marriage will not be mutually beneficial, and therefore will not last. Interviewees worry over the circumstances under which incompatibility arises and puzzle about how compatibility can be achieved.

Consider first the following example, in which the possibility of a certain kind of marriage is rejected on the grounds of incompatibility:

4H-11: I couldn't see myself marrying another suburbanite who was as vulnerable to the world as I am. And the two of us holding on to each other, through hostile situations, you know. 'Cause I think we would—I think our vulnerabilities would complement each other, you know, and we would go down together.

What "complement each other" are the vulnerabilities of two suburbanites; the context makes clear that the speaker really means to say that these vulnerabilities do not complement but match each other. The vulnerabilities have to do, as this speaker elaborates elsewhere in the course of his interviews, with what he perceives as his own rootlessness, a product of growing up in a family transplanted to California from the East. He eventually married, instead of another suburbanite like himself, a woman from a small rural eastern town who, in his eyes, had "roots," and through whom he gained a sense of being rooted.

That he and the other suburbanite would have been "holding on to each other, through hostile situations," rather than meeting these situations separately and individually, follows from the understanding that marriage is shared. A conjunction of circumstances surrounds this imagined marriage, then: that the external

world is hostile, that married people must face this world together, and that these particular married people, having the same
vulnerabilities, would not be equipped to do so. This set of circumstances frames the argument to follow, about what would necessarily happen to such a marriage.

In the metaphor of "vulnerabilities" that "complement each
other," two such people would be incompatible. Their incompatibility consists in a *non*-complementarity of defensive capabilities,
as it were, leaving the two of them unable to meet their common
need for protection against a hostile world. Not all interviewees
are as preoccupied with the hostility of this outside world as is
this man. However, the larger body of discourse from which this
passage is excerpted makes clear that for other interviewees, as for
this one, spouses' support of each other in their individual endeavors and in attainment of their common goals is an expected benefit
of marriage. This support is understood to include protection of
each other from outside perils and exigencies, in the interests of
their individual well-being and common good. Incompatibility
of the sort described by this husband leaves spouses unable to provide each other this crucial benefit of marriage. Without this mutual protection, the couple fails to survive, and by implication, the
unbeneficial marriage, too, fails.

The metaphor of two married people vulnerable to a hostile
world sustains this sequence of reasoning. To survive, people must
defend themselves against hostile situations. But people who both
lack the same defenses cannot compensate for each other and
hence cannot help each other to insure their mutual protection.
They can only hold on to each other while they "go down together" to defeat. An unsuccessful marriage is one that has not
lasted, and this implicit understanding helps us to interpret the
metaphorical defeat of this couple as the failure of their marriage
to last. In the view I have argued, the metaphor of vulnerabilities
to hostile attack, failed common defense, and ultimate defeat
allows the speaker to pursue to its end what is a fairly complex
line of reasoning without losing track of its logic. Johnson and
Lakoff would find support in this use of metaphor for a more extreme position. It would seem to exemplify exactly the kind of
mapping of the structure of a source domain onto a target domain

that they have in mind when they argue that the metaphor drawn from the former "gives rise" to entailments about the latter and hence "constitutes" a grasp of the situation to be reasoned about.

I will demonstrate, however, that the connections made in this passage between spouses' incompatibility, represented metaphorically by their corresponding vulnerabilities, and lack of mutual benefit to them, represented by their consequent inability to mount a joint defense, and between this lack of mutual benefit and marital failure, represented by their resulting defeat, correspond to a set of shared understandings more general than the metaphor used to capture these entailments in this instance. That incompatibility leads to lack of mutual benefit, which leads in turn to a failed marriage or, to put it conversely, that compatibility leads to mutual benefit and mutual benefit to a lasting marriage is a matter of broad agreement among these interviewees. If this is so, as I intend to show it is, then the case before us poses a challenge to Johnson and Lakoff's position.

While the last man speculated about the probable adverse effect of incompatibility on a marriage he did not make, the next one reflects on the role of compatibility in explaining why the marriage he made has been a lasting one. This piece of reasoning employs different metaphors and exhibits a less perfect fit of metaphorical entailments to the set of relations being reasoned about than the one above.

6H-4: But it could be that situation when we got married, that it was such that we had lots of room to adjust. Because we didn't have any idea what we were getting into. That gave us a lot of room to adjust. And by the time we had been through the first year we realized, you know, there would have to be adjustments made. And a few years afterwards when things really got serious we were—you know, when the marriage was strong, it was very strong because it was made as we went along—it was sort of a do-it-yourself project.

This husband considers that initial incompatibilities, at least of the kind his wife and he encountered, need not spell marital failure, but can be eliminated by subsequent efforts of each spouse to be more compatible with the other. He argues that their lack of preconceived expectations allowed his wife and him to make such adjustments and that these adjustments ultimately made their

marriage a strong one. Lack of prior expectations is captured in a
CONTAINER metaphor, a very common one in talk about marrying, in the remark, "We had no idea what we were getting into."
Then this concept is recast in a new metaphor, in "that gave us a
lot of room to adjust." The positive side of not knowing what they
were getting into is that neither of them were locked into pre-
determined attitudes or behaviors. This "room to adjust" made
it possible for them to do so—to make the changes both had to
make in order to "adjust" themselves to each other. That is, their
lack of preconceived expectations enabled them to attain mutual
compatibility.

The next assertion, that "it was made as we went along," at
once refers back to this process of making adjustments and carries
the sense of mutual compatibility achieved in the "adjustment"
metaphor forward into the final metaphor of the passage, recasting
it in these new terms. As one does a "do-it-yourself project," this
man and his wife could tailor the marriage to their specifications—that is, make it fit their needs—as they came to realize
what these were. Compatibility leads to mutual benefit. Implicit
in this last metaphor, also, is the knowledge that a do-it-yourself
project is likely to be crafted with more care, and hence be stronger,
than something factory-made. Compatibility leads to a lasting marriage. We can follow this conclusion because we insert an assumption left implicit by the speaker. This is the understanding carried
by the metaphor of defeat due to matching vulnerabilities in the
previous excerpt, and frequently made explicit elsewhere in these
interviews about marriage—that a mutually beneficial marriage
will be a lasting one. Lack of preconceived expectations, then,
allows a couple to attain a compatible relationship, which in turn
causes them to experience benefit in the marriage, which in turn
makes the marriage last.

But mark two points about this example. First, this chain of reasoning, taken in its entirety, depends upon an overlapping entailment of the two metaphors. "It was made as we went along" refers
to the "adjustments" that were made, and both stand for the compatibility achieved in the marriage. It is by means of this overlap,
by translating this term from one metaphor into the next, that the
piece of reasoning achieved with the first metaphor is connected
with the reasoning embodied in the second. For the proposition

that lack of prior expectations leads to compatibility is not an obvious entailment of a do-it-yourself project; and lack of prior expectations does not entail either the strength or the functional design of such a project. In fact, not having a detailed plan worked out for it in advance might well be considered a liability to the outcome of the undertaking. The connection imported from the earlier, "adjustment" metaphor is necessary to the conclusion that in marriage, unlike in, say, cabinetmaking, lack of preconceived expectations leads to mutual benefit and hence to lastingness. It is as if the speaker, running out of metaphor to extend his argument where he wants it to go, finds another one and cleverly patches it to the first. Each of these metaphors appears to do its work by facilitating a different part of the reasoning sequence.

This case also bears out a second point. Mutual benefit and lastingness are co-entailments of this final "do-it-yourself project" metaphor: compared to a store-bought, factory-made version, we have noted, something that you make yourself will ordinarily be both more functional, because made to your specifications, and stronger, because made well. However, these two entailments are not related to each other in the metaphor in the way they are in marriage. Because the marriage "was made as we went along," or tailored to their emerging needs, it ended up filling these needs and hence it lasted. It is not because it is tailored to one's own specifications and hence suitable to one's needs that a do-it-yourself project is strong, but because, presumably, it is made with special care and quality materials. Functionality and strength are both attributes of a successful do-it-yourself project, but the latter cannot be interpreted as resulting from the former. Less successful projects, in fact, have been known to be sturdy but impractical, or structurally unsound and hence of short-lived, if marvelous, utility. The speaker's claim "When the marriage was strong, it was very strong because we made it as we went along" makes perfect marital sense, but it only makes metaphorical sense if we interpret "we made it as we went along" as referring, not to the tailoring that was done in the course of the do-it-yourself project, but to something else about the way it was made—the fact that it was homemade in contrast to ready-made, hence well built rather than poorly so.

What this last example demonstrates is that to be used, and presumably useful, in reasoning, a metaphor need neither do the reasoning task alone nor match that task exactly. Both the speaker's resort to a second metaphor to complete his argument and the inexact fit of this new metaphor to this argument support the interpretation I have put forward: that the speaker has the reasoning he wants to do in mind independently of the metaphors in which he casts it. If there were any doubt of this interpretation of the last example, it should be laid to rest by comparison with other explanations of marital compatibility and incompatibility, like that given by the previous husband. The chain of reasoning pursued is the same in both excerpts, but the metaphors are entirely different ones. The entailments reasoned to arise from none of these metaphors, but from the cultural model that motivates all of them and that both these men share.

To reinforce the claim that this model is indeed shared and to illustrate yet another style of reasoning about the relations in this model among compatibility, mutual benefit, and marital lastingness, I introduce one last example, from an interview with a third husband. This case is particularly telling in that various terms of the argument are cast in a series of disconnected metaphors. While a metaphor of "fit" once again, as in the previous excerpt, carries the relation between a compatible marriage and a mutually beneficial one (or, in this case, one that is incompatible and not beneficial), the remainder of what is a highly complex causal structure in this passage is reasoned out and conveyed independent of its metaphor.

2H-2: I don't feel like you can really rest assured that it's go—that anything can last forever and forever. But I feel like it's possible that one person may reach a really different height of maturity and realize that a lot of things that they're doing now and wanting and all their desires are elementary, you know. Whatever, you know, and like their change may be so much of a change that, you know, you don't really fit into their life anymore. I think it's possible. I can't say that it will happen, you know. I'm not living on—well I'm—today I'm saying it looks like we will be able to stay together and stay together, you know. But, you know, I have to be honest and say that, you know, there are things that I've thought would continue before in my life, you know.
    I: That didn't?
    H: That didn't.

While the other two men were concerned with past and present circumstances, this last man thinks ahead and expresses uncertainty about whether his marriage will last, given the possibility of future incompatibility. That he cannot "rest assured" that his marriage will be permanent is expressed in three different metaphors: one, at the beginning of the passage, in which marriage is an ENTITY, perhaps a manufactured one, that cannot "last forever"; then a RELATION metaphor, toward the end of the passage, in which the married couple is together but may not "be able to stay together"; and a final TRAJECTORY metaphor, in which the marriage, like other things that he "thought would continue before in my life," may not in fact do so.

The explanation this man gives for why his marriage may not last forever is easy to follow. He is puzzling over a different set of circumstances that can affect the compatibility of two people and hence their marriage: not their initial mismatch to one another or their subsequent ability to improve this match by adjusting it, but change that occurs later in a marriage. This change relates to a folk model of personhood in which, in some respects, individuals continue to mature into adulthood. In a metaphor for this maturation process, one person may mature to a "different height," realizing from this new perspective that former wants and desires were "elementary" and no longer reflective of his or her mature needs. This is "so much of a change that," presumably because the other person cannot keep up with it, the first person doesn't "fit into their life anymore"; the two have become incompatible. The consequences of this incompatibility are implied by the nature of the change that leads up to it: now the other person, we may suppose, is no longer able to meet these new wants and desires. Incompatibility results in unfulfilled needs, a lack of benefit. The metaphor here, of misfit between the other person and the first one's life, reinforces this connection between incompatibility and unfulfilled needs: like a misfitting machine part, the second person is useless to the first. That this eventuality, in turn, results in the marriage not lasting is a conclusion made explicit in the two final metaphors in the passage, which refer to "it will happen" and tell that what will happen is that the married people might not "be able to stay together" and the marriage itself might not "continue"—

might not last. The "it," in turn, refers to not fitting into the changed person's life anymore, so that the possibility of the marriage not lasting is understood to be the ultimate consequence of this misfit.

That we make sense of this speaker's explanation, and do so readily, is partly attributable to the ways in which he ties this explanation together. One, but only one, of the ways he accomplishes this is in the metaphor of "fit" that suggests the analogy between a misfitting, and hence useless, machine part and an incompatible, and hence unfulfilling, spouse. In common with other speakers, he resorts to several other devices that structure the remainder of this passage. For example, he sets out his premise at the beginning and repeats it at the end so that we are sure to identify it as his conclusion. Besides assisting us to follow his argument, this explicit restatement may help the speaker himself to keep track of where he wants this argument to lead. Perhaps, indeed, the passage represents a style of reasoning alternative to that exemplified by the other two husbands quoted above, who rely instead on metaphors that carry multiple entailments of the argument being developed.

As do those men and other reasoners, this third husband also uses syntactic order to convey causality. As Linde (1987: 347) has pointed out, speakers of English recognize the "narrative presupposition": that the order of a sequence of sentences and main clauses matches the order of events. And this presupposition about temporal order allows inferences about causation, events represented by earlier sentences or clauses being inferred to be causes of those represented by subsequent ones. One person may mature *and* realize that former wants and desires are elementary, *and* this change may be so great that he or she is no longer compatible with the other person. That is, maturation causes wants and desires to alter; greatly increased maturity produces radically different wants and desires. When you don't fit into the other person's life anymore, it may happen that the two of you will not be able to stay together (no matter how confident you are at present that you will be able to do so), that the marriage will not continue. That is, incompatibility leads to a marriage not lasting. As do other reasoners, this one sometimes also employs special syntactic markers of causation: "Their change may be *so* much of a change *that* you don't really fit into their life anymore": X *so that* Y. Radically altered wants and desires on the part of one person cause incompatibility with the other.

But the rest—the exact nature of the process by which incompatibility follows from maturation and prevents the new needs from being fulfilled, the understanding that the benefit of marriage is fulfillment of these needs, the causal relation between cessation of this benefit and discontinuance of a marriage—is left unspoken or only hinted by this speaker as by other interviewees. We are able to fill in these links, of course, because we too share the cultural model of marriage, and other cultural models such as those of need fulfillment and maturation, on which this argument relies.

Conclusions

At the beginning of this paper I suggested facetiously that what is at issue here is a territorial squabble between anthropologists and linguists. (If metaphor has been our subject as long as it has been theirs,[16] it is perhaps more closely associated with their discipline—probably because of the very tendency Lakoff and Johnson deplore, of treating metaphor as a mere matter of language.) But there are other, deeper reasons why cognitive semanticists may have accorded too much explanatory power to metaphor. An important part of Lakoff's and Johnson's joint project is to refute a so-called "objectivist" view of the world. Metaphor is the quintessential challenge to the objectivist account, according to which only literal concepts and propositions can describe the real world—the "traditional" account by which, in Lakoff's characterization, "the

---

[16] Although metaphor is certainly an old topic in anthropology, today a distinctive tradition of metaphor study, grown up over the last twenty or so years, exists in American anthropology. This tradition is well represented by other papers in this volume and by such works as Sapir and Crocker (1977) and Fernandez (1986) and is concerned as I am (although I have not been a part of it) with the relation of metaphor to cultural understanding. For example, Fernandez (1986: 55–57) provides a discussion of "latent factors" or "latent intentions" lying behind metaphors that anticipates my argument for cultural models underlying and constraining metaphor use.

concept of anger literally exists and is understood independently of any metaphor." In this ascendant, objectivist view of cognition, "metaphors do no more than provide ways of talking" (Lakoff 1987b: 405); metaphor is treated as a mere "literary device" and thereby denied any serious place (Johnson 1987: 65–72). Johnson and Lakoff counter that rational thought is bound up with metaphorical reasoning and hence defies analysis in these objectivist terms (Lakoff 1987b: 303). To place metaphor in the center of his own scheme as Johnson does is a bold stroke. Yet the reinterpretation I am offering does not undermine this important part of his and Lakoff's project. On the contrary, mine is also a "non-objectivist," constitutive view of understanding. I am simply claiming that metaphor plays a comparatively minor role in constituting our understanding of our world, and that a relatively major role in constituting this understanding is played by cultural models of that world.

It is worth adding that the cultural view I propose has an important piece to contribute to the philosophical puzzle of relativism that Johnson (1987: 194–96) addresses: how can knowledge be the construct of individual minds, yet public and shared? There is a vast amount of understanding that is relative to given cultures and *not* universal, but that is still *shared* by individual members of a culture. If, as Johnson argues, our common human experience of ourselves in the world gives rise to universally shared understandings, culturally received models of the world best account for this other kind of understanding that is shared across individual minds, but not universally so.

In part, also, the failure to grant culture its own place in the linguistic analysis of metaphor may be an artifact of method. Lakoff and Johnson pursue a methodology, time-honored in the discipline of linguistics, that relies on idealized cases, disconnected from the context of actual use in natural discourse. Applied to metaphor, this method precludes verification of an account based on analysis of a corpus of such idealized, decontextualized metaphors against other kinds of evidence speakers provide in the discourse in which metaphors are ordinarily embedded. The danger of such unverified interpretation can be seen, in this paper, in Lakoff's attempt to impute entailments to the PARTNERSHIP and DIFFICULT JOUR-

NEY metaphors without examining the contexts of their use. The rich interview material only sparingly introduced in this paper allows a cultural analysis of discourse that goes beyond metaphor analysis, permitting me to draw upon other, convergent evidence for the model of marriage Americans share. One kind of independent linguistic evidence comes from the analysis of usages of key words, such as *love, fulfillment,* and *commitment,* that recur in discourse about marriage. Such an analysis of usages of *love,* for example, supports the description of its role in marriage that was summarized early in this paper, revealing a precise mapping of the concept of love onto that of marriage and detailed correspondences between the motivational structure of the former and the expectational structure of the latter (Quinn 1988; in progress). Other kinds of evidence, the utility of which has only been suggested here, come from the explicit statements interviewees make about marriage, the commentaries they offer on the metaphors they use for marriage, and the reasoning they do about marital problems (Quinn 1987; in progress).[17]

What the underlying structure of cultural models is, if not

[17] It is all the more important that this contrast between methodologies be appreciated in light of the following comment by Lakoff (1986), in his regular column, "Metametaphorical Issues" in the journal *Metaphor and Symbolic Activity,* in which he himself seems to misconstrue the intent and dismiss the potential of my approach to the cultural analysis of metaphor: "Quinn's techniques of discourse analysis can show, in some cases, which metaphors a particular speaker is using in everyday reasoning (see Holland and Quinn, in press). But Quinn's techniques, though extremely elegant, are difficult to apply and are not universally applicable. Like syntactic analysis, metaphorical analysis is not very good at studying individual variation and works best for idealized speakers." I do not see why analysis of natural discourse could not, in principle, be applied to the study of individual variation in the pattern of metaphor use. However, far from aiming to be such a study, my approach—in the paper referred to by Lakoff (now Quinn 1987) and elsewhere—is explicitly directed at reconstructing, from metaphor and other evidence, the culturally shared framework on which varied individual understandings are elaborated. For the reasons discussed in the text of this paper, the fiction of the idealized speaker seems a misleading one for such an investigation of metaphors; analysis of actual discourse discovers regularity across the utterances of real speakers. As for the feasibility and applicability of my techniques, the reader of my work can judge.

metaphoric or image-schematic, I am not prepared to say. Perhaps there is no one kind of structure more fundamental than any other,[18] but a variety of alternative transformations of our understanding, instated for different purposes, in the way that, we have argued, metaphor is invoked to reason with. What these transformations might be, if such exist, and their possible roles in human understanding pose a challenging set of empirical questions that will only be settled eventually on the basis of new evidence. I have presented some evidence that I believe argues against the position that metaphor constitutes (in any of several senses of that term) everyday understanding, while it suggests, at the same time, how culturally given this understanding is. What is important is that we not commit ourselves prematurely to one theoretical scheme of things. For if we do, we will not be in a position to interpret, or even recognize, new evidence.

[18] As indeed Lakoff's characterization of the scenario as one of a family of idealized cognitive models suggests (see footnote 6, above).

Metaphor and Experience:
Looking Over the Notion of Image Schema

Hoyt Alverson

Two missions of any linguistically adequate theory of meaning are
to account for "meaning invariance"—how it is possible that
terms or sentences in different languages, cultures, or theories can
be said to have the same meaning—and for the semantic/pragmatic
linkage—the relationship of linguistic knowledge to the rest of experience. Any such theory of meaning will also have to be consistent with two well-justified background assumptions: that all
known natural languages are to an extraordinary degree mutually
translatable, and that all children acquire their respective native
languages in a similarly rapid and effortless fashion. These two
background conditions compel the conclusion that, at some level
of abstraction and function, languages are basically alike and this
commonality must match in some way the structure of the brain.
This conclusion in turn limits what a language, including its semantics, could possibly be.

Line drawings of the schemas for "over" are reproduced from George Lakoff,
Women, Fire, and Dangerous Things, Chicago, University of Chicago Press,
1987; reproduced by permission. Professor Werner Hoffmeister, Dartmouth
College, and Ms. Keitumetse Matsewane, Tufts University, generously gave me
most valuable assistance in preparing translations of English into German and
Setswana respectively for the table that accompanies this paper. Any errors in
this task are my responsibility alone, however.

Two approaches to the central missions are apparent: rationalist and empiricist. The former postulates a universal base of innate semantic "primitives" (e.g., features or concepts) that supposedly underlie the lexicon in all languages. The latter postulates a base of shared experience that is presumably caused by the effects of the real, natural world on perception, cognition, and other activity, and to which words in all languages make (rigid) designation. The rationalist school has drawn inspiration from the Cartesian tradition and is notably represented today by Noam Chomsky (1966, 1972), Jerrold Katz (1972), and Jerry Fodor (1975, 1983). The empiricist school has built on Anglo-American philosophy going back to Hume and Locke, and is represented in modern times by ordinary language philosophy of the later Wittgenstein (1953), truth-conditional semantics of Gottlob Frege (1952), Rudolf Carnap (1956), Alfred Tarski (1952), Richard Montague (1973), and by such realists as W. V. O. Quine (1960), Saul Kripke (1972), and John Searle (1975, 1983b).

The premier problem for rationalist approaches to meaning is their appeal to ordinary, commonsense notions of what the world is like to account for what people are supposed innately to know solely in virtue of the semantic component of their language. This is unsatisfactory precisely because commonsense notions are culturally acquired and culturally contingent. The empiricists' problem is explaining how humans' interaction with the causal structure of the world is directly represented in the form of language, unmediated by thought, belief, or knowledge, which themselves presuppose language and without which there would be no (human) interaction with the world to begin with.

In their recent respective works, *Semantics and Cognition* (1983) and *Women, Fire, and Dangerous Things* (1987b), Ray Jackendoff and George Lakoff have provided important statements of cognitive (or, in my terminology, phenomenologic) grammar, which represent a radical break with both rationalist and empiricist commitments and suppositions and a way around the quandaries they pose. While they do not acknowledge it, their work is situated directly in, and is derivative of, the philosophic monism of Kant, Giambattista Vico, Marx, Edmund Husserl, Kurt Koffka, and Maurice Merleau-Ponty.

Both works seek to falsify the received dogma and attendant

problems of rationalism and empiricism by rejecting the notion that meaning in language is based either upon universal, timeless, speciesless, cultureless, situationless mental forms or upon direct, rigid designation of speciesless, cultureless, objective (mass-point-space-time) entities, which are deemed in either case to exist independently of language use.

Jackendoff argues that both meaning in language and information gained from our cognitive-perceptual engagement with the world are realized at the same "level"—that of *conceptual structure*, which is mental representation. For Jackendoff, we can talk about what we experience, especially what we see, because the representation of seeing (and other sensory engagement) and the representation of meaning in language are one and the same thing. What language is about—the information it conveys—is *projected reality*, the reality that exists in virtue of the interaction of the human being with the world.

Lakoff's notion of "cognitive grammar" is derived *inter alia* from recent work in cognitive psychology, especially that of Eleanor Rosch (1973, 1975, 1977, 1978, 1981), and cognitive anthropology, especially that of Brent Berlin, Paul Kay, and their associates (Berlin 1968; Berlin et al. 1974; Berlin and Kay 1969; Kay 1979; Kay and McDaniel 1978), and Willett Kempton (1981). Like Jackendoff, Lakoff argues that the only thing language can be about is experience, not in the empiricists' sense of sensory apprehension or observation, but in the phenomenologic sense of how the world, including the individual him/herself, is posed for the embodied, enculturated mind that lives it and lives in it.

Specifically, Lakoff avers that meaning in language is part of the meaningfulness of experience, the base of which is preconceptual or pre-predicative. "We have general capacities for dealing with . . . real world objects via Gestalt perception, motor movement, and the formation of rich mental images. These impose a preconceptual structure on our experience. Our basic concepts correspond to that preconceptual structure and are understood directly in terms of it" (Lakoff 1987b: 270–71).

Perhaps the most difficult task facing an experientially grounded theory of meaning in language is to account for how its semantics represents, expresses, or succeeds in being about the *intentional* or *modal* character of all human experience, including perception and cognition. Part of this difficulty and challenge lies in the fact that the study of tropes (e.g., metaphor) becomes a central rather than a residual issue for semantics, because the tropes, especially metaphor, make explicit and conspicuous what is otherwise frequently tacit or unconscious in language use—the construction or expression of intentional or modal experience.

While the approaches of Jackendoff and Lakoff do insinuate the intentionality of experience, neither, in my opinion, squarely acknowledges or deals with the issue in their treatment of cognition (particularly cognitive schemas) or metaphor. Before offering my own proposal, I should make a brief statement of what intentionality or modality consists in.

Linguistic Modality and the
Intentional Character of Experience

While the progress of physical science and the heroic success of enterprises based on its deliverances may suggest that we command the recipe for appropriating the "really real" as objective knowledge, more and more voices from the sciences argue that this view is foolishly presumptuous. As Nick Jardine observes, "reflections on the limitations of human nature, perhaps reinforced by consideration of the extent to which the capacities of the human senses and intelligence are conditioned by our biological particularity, may convince us that there are certain vantage points to which we are forever tied by our humanity and hence cannot hope to transcend in our scientific theories." From this it surely follows that the notion of representing the world as it actually is, is incoherent, for "we could have no conception of the world that transcends all possible ways of representing it. Though the world may be prised away from our manner of conceiving it, it cannot be prised away from every possible manner of conceiving it" (1980: 24).

The only alternative to conception of an actual world is conceiving it in a certain manner. Now an object, as conceived, in the way conceived, is a "modal" or "intentional" object, as opposed to an "actual" one. For humans all objects of experience—that is, all experience—are therefore necessarily intentional. This intentionality is directly expressed in language by many modal devices such as negation, sentential adverbials, verbs of propositional attitude, indirect or reported speech, verb tenses, modes, aspects. One of the devices that cognitive grammar proposes for describing the intentional (i.e., modal) aspect of word meaning is called a cognitive model. These models (one example of which we examine in detail below) "tell" a person how percepts (or other experience) engender significance. That is, they tell us what messages experience of some object contains by virtue of that object's exemplification, instantiation, or betokening of a linguistic category or cognitive model. In more traditional wording, the "sense" that experience has arises from its linguistic categorization or representation.

Now metaphor is perhaps the most important linguistic means for expressing *novel* intentionality by its creating of novel linguistic modality. Whereas conventional collocation that appears to conform to ordinary cultural criteria for "sortal correctness" expresses already typified, conventional modality, and therefore intentionality, metaphor is the breaking of ordinary conventions of sortal correctness and the ad hoc construction of novel typification. But both "literal" and "metaphoric" uses of language are equally modal in that they express intentional reality, that is, *as it is experienced*.

These abstract points can be made clear with a few very simple, "literal" illustrations. The sentence "I saw John *wave*" expresses the fact that I saw an intentional object, waving, as opposed to the behaviorally identical but differently intended object "moving the open hand up and down." "I saw John *wink*" reports or expresses seeing an intentional object different from the behaviorally identical one "blink." "I saw the pitcher walk three men in a row" reports my seeing in terms of the intention created by knowing the rules of baseball. Ptolemy, in seeing "the sun," saw a planet. Copernicus, in seeing "the sun," saw a star. The two different intentional objects were created by the two different theories held. "I remembered my wife" makes a different intentional object of "wife" than does "I recalled my wife." For one thing "remembering" situates the agent's mental state temporally prior to its object. "Recalling" places the agent's mental state later in time than that recalled. (I can remember to call, but I can't recall to call, because the infinitive contains futurity in English). "The glass is half full" "intends" the glass's contents differently than does "the glass is half empty." "I will spare you a lecture" expresses a different intentional "lecture" than does "I will deprive you of a lecture."

With these examples in mind we can now turn to the topics of metaphor and cognitive models and see how the conception and the treatment of them within phenomenologic grammar succeed or fail to express the intentional character of experience.

Metaphor and Cognitive Models

In his account of metaphor and its relationship to (idealized) cognitive models, Lakoff states: "each metaphor has a source domain, a target domain, and a source to target mapping . . . [and] is motivated by the structure of our experience." How so is given in the answer to three questions: "(1) What determines the choice of a well-structured source domain? (2) What determines the pairing of the source domain with the target domain? (3) What determines the details of the source to target mapping?" (1987b: 276). The answers are: "(1) to function as a source domain for a metaphor, a domain must be understood independently of the metaphor; (2) and (3) are determined by correlations in our daily experience. . . . Not all correlations in experience motivate metaphors, but many do" (278). Thus, the meaning of the linguistic expression derives from an association of experiences that either have elements in common or are "analogous."

Clearly Lakoff's metaphor of the metaphoring process is based on the notion "function" or, perhaps more precisely, that of a "relation" as described in the theory of sets. Thus, to each element in a set S ("source") is assigned by some criterion a unique element of a set T ("target"). That assignment is called a function. Likewise a relation consists of a source set S and a target set T and an open sentence P(s,t), which is true for any one or more ordered pairs of elements taken two at a time, one each respectively from S and T. A function is simply a special type of relation, in which each element of the source set is mapped onto a unique element of the target set.

A weakness of this conception is that the solution set (the meaning?) of the function or relation manifests the rule of correspondence that maps elements of the domain onto the elements of the co-domain. These rules (mappings, operators, transformations) are simply a formal specification of element pairings that satisfy the function or relation. The upshot of this is that metaphor is defined as an analogy, albeit elliptically expressed. Certainly Aristotle would be content with this view, but many are persuaded that metaphor involves the breaking of strict analogy. Further, in Lakoff's formulation, the set of metaphoric predications will have to be a subset of the set of pre-predicative experiential associations, which have somehow been attained without language. This seems to limit language to principles of an associationistic psychology.

It may well be that the derivation of the meaning of one domain of experience from that of another, more "primitive," preconceptual one, by a process of a functional or relational mapping of component elements, plays a role in explaining metaphor generally. But of equal importance is the process of *restructuring* the two or more domains, thereby creating new types of categories by means of which experience is understood in qualitatively new ways. Metaphor is type-breaking, category redefining, new-schema-making linguistic creativity. In Lévi-Strauss's words, things ordinarily thought *about* become things for thinking *with*. And in metaphor the ordinarily typified things for thinking *with* themselves become new typifications.

Following Lakoff, I would argue that the words in the language that enter into metaphoric predication are understood to mean components of the experiences in reference to which the words are understood. These may involve intensions, kinesthetic body schemas, fuzzy sets, paragons, rigid designations, etc. But what does it mean to "predicate an experience of another experience"? How can a logical or syntactic relationship hold between propositions (sentences) and nonlinguistic experiences? Here Jackendoff and Lakoff have provided part of a good answer: that semantics and experience are realized at the same level, as the same thing. But one issue remains. How, linguistically, do we understand a function or relationship among experientially construed domains?

By arguing that metaphors have experiential bases, Lakoff is saying that the metaphoric mappings are motivated by the force of the source domain in preconceptual bodily (gestural) experience. Lakoff cites, for example, "verticality" as the source domain for the target domain "quantity." That is, "more is up, less is down." In another example, "source-path-goal" topography plus bodily movement along it is the source domain for the target domain "purpose." According to Lakoff, the force of these metaphors arises from early bodily experiences that are "correlated." Thus "more" is early manifest as bigger and bigger piles of something, and we look up to see rising piles. We crawl along to reach destinations, which become teleologically "purposes" (1987b: 278–79).

Lakoff says that two body-image-schematic metaphors, the "container" and the "source-path-goal," in fact are the metaphors that account for metaphor itself. This is shown above in his description of mapping functions as phenomenologically a kind of follow-the-path-from-the-elements-in-one-container-to-the-elements-in-the-other-container.

Now there may well be such kinesthetic or other lived-body metaphors that are pre-predicative in motivation. But many perfectly good metaphors seem not entirely describable as such. Some metaphors may involve mappings from very abstract (source) domains to very primitive (target) ones. "I'm *counting* on him." "Changing jobs has a significant *opportunity cost*." "He is *marginalist* in his outlook." "What's the *bottom line* here?" "An altruistic person is one who helps you *maximize your utility function* without expectation that act will increase his own." "We live in a *zero-sum* society." Or from a more engaging application of dismal science we get: He has an *ace up his sleeve*. She gave me a *fast shuffle*, or is *dealing from the bottom of the deck*. You'd better not get *lost in the shuffle*; you should have *an ace in the hole*. You *four-flusher*! Let's *lay our cards on the table*. What do we do when the *chips are down*? Stay with the *blue chips*. How do they *stack up against* the *penny-ante stuff*? Well, they *sweeten the pot* by *upping the stakes*. *Stand pat*. Just *play above board* and don't *pass the buck*. Otherwise you might wind up *in hock*. Some of Lakoff's pre-predicative orientational metaphors appear as constituents in these metaphors from poker. But the game of poker is no more reducible to them than a "wink" is reducible to a "blink."

To me the motivation and force of these metaphors and probably of most novel, compelling, apt ones found in powerful use of language are irreducibly *cultural*. From experience in significant domains of cultural meaning and/or action can emerge the same ergodicity for metaphor as is, to be sure, found with pre-predicative bodily experience. In short, metaphors do not need to be reduced to the pre-predicative to explain "force," and many metaphors, I would argue, are not so reducible at all.

Lakoff defines metaphor as "an experientially based mapping from an ICM (idealized cognitive model) in one domain to an ICM in another domain" (1987b: 417) and has sought to apply this notion to a central issue in linguistic semantics: how the various "senses" of single words are related to one another. The "classical" view of word senses is that each is a conceptually distinct and autonomous meaning unit. (See Lakoff and Johnson 1980b: 106–14 for a concise description of this classical, "abstraction" view; the fullest exposition in this vein is Katz 1972.) The fact that these meaning units are signified by the same phonologic signal (the word, or *lexical morpheme*) is considered in the classical view an irrelevant coincidence. The dictionary contains as many meaning units as it contains distinct senses of all words, and each sense (with but a few exceptions) stands for, or is defined by, either some classical (Aristotelian) category or some (rigid) semantic designator. If the senses (of a single word) are deemed to be related, it is in terms solely of some shared abstract category of meaning-*Urstoff*. If not related, they are treated as instances of homonymy.

Lakoff argues this is untrue. Rather, single words or lexical items will frequently have a basic primary or prototypical meaning, describable as an "idealized cognitive model," while other "senses" or uses of the term will involve extensions or transformations of that prototypical model. "The metaphorical mapping that relates the ICM's defines the relationship between [/among] the senses of the word, [where] the sense of the word in the source domain will be [viewed] as more basic" (Lakoff 1987b: 417). In other words, the dictionary entries that correspond to senses of the word are frequently in fact a list of past metaphoric extensions of prototypical model meanings and can be seen in part as a history of past metaphoric creativity.

One of the tasks Lakoff sets for a cognitive grammar is the discovery of the nature of cognitive models that comprise the core meaning(s) of words and the kinds of (metaphoric) transformations of those models that "generate"—that is, *motivate*—augmented and additional "senses" of the basic terms. Prominent among the forms of ICM's that describe the core or central meaning of words are "image schemas," where the various senses of a word are represented by/as transformations of a basic image schema. Although Lakoff does not make the point directly, he seems to imply that the range of a word's senses and the domain of a cognitive model and its transforms will be coincident. Thus, "lexical items are natural categories of sense" (1987b: 418). Therefore, he does not entertain the possibility that there could be a single cognitive model which several words' several senses jointly partition or that a single "sense" of some given word could arise from the melding of two or more distinct cognitive models.

The notion of "(image) schemas" used as models for understanding the meaning or information conveyed by words or sentences is not prolix. The word "image" suggests visual, or at least vision-like, experience, and the word "schema" suggests not detailed, but rather abstract or in outline. As Lakoff notes, simple sentences like "John got his hair cut," "Sue closed the door," "A bird is on the porch," or "Sally hit the ball" are all grasped in terms of images, or at least conventional, cultural typifications. Thus the first sentence would never conjure up the image of John sticking his hair up to a whirring lawn-mower blade; the second does not suggest Sue ripped the door from its hinges and placed it against the jamb; the third does not describe a penguin walking across the porch; the fourth does not suggest Sally shot the ball in midair with a bazooka.

Looking Over Over

Lakoff illustrates his account of "image schema" and its role in understanding word meaning with reference to Claudia Brugman's (1981) study of the senses of the word "over."

Consider the following from Lakoff:

–The painting is *over* the mantle.
–The plane is flying *over* the hill.
–Sam is walking *over* the hill.
–Sam lives *over* the hill.

—The wall fell *over*.
—Sam turned the page *over*.
—Sam turned *over*.
—She spread the tablecloth *over* the table.
—The guards were posted all *over* the hill.
—The play is *over*.
—Do it *over*, but don't *over*do it.
—Look *over* my corrections, and don't *over*look any of them.
—You made *over* a hundred errors. (1987b: 418–19)

Lakoff says that these distinct but clearly related senses of the word "over" are motivated by underlying features of one or more "image schemas" for that word. That is, the central sense of "over" has been extended and augmented in past usage, because the image schema invites such. Said differently, speakers of a language do not arbitrarily select words to represent new meanings; they go with words whose underlying schemas best fit the new experience to be represented.

Lakoff identifies four conventionally typified sets of senses of the word "over": (1) the "above-across" senses, described at length below, (2) the "covering" senses (as in "the board is over the hole"), (3) the "reflexive" senses (as in "the log rolled over" or "the ice spread over the pond"), (4) the "excess" senses (as in "the account is overdrawn"). He then notes several metaphoric senses based upon augmentation of these. Each of these sets comprises a core schema and its various transforms. These schemas are linked according to the transformations they undergo.

The central sense (1) combines elements of both "above" and "across" (see Lakoff 1987b: 419–25). To wit, there is a landmark (LM) and a trajector (TR) oriented according to verticality, perpendicularity, and non-contact:

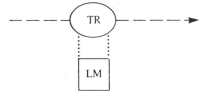

This is a schema for interpreting, for example, the sentence, "The plane flew over."

The following transformations of this basic schema are made:
(X), horizontal extension of the landmark; (V), vertical extension of the landmark; (C), contact between trajector and landmark; (E), end-point focus of trajector path. Transform (X) of (1)
yields (1.X):

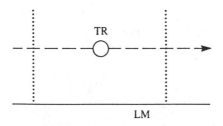

which is a schematic interpretation for, for example, "The bird
flew over the yard." Transform (V) added to (1) yields (1.V):

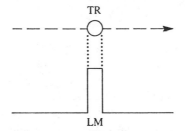

which is a schema for, for example, "The bird flew over the wall."
Adding transforms (X) and (V) to (1) yields (1.X.V):

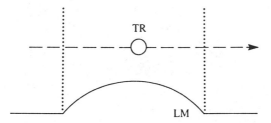

which is a schema for "The plane flew over the hill." Adding
transforms (C) and (X) to (1) yields (1.X.C):

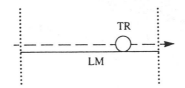

which is a schema for "Sam drove over the bridge." Transform (C) added to (1.X.V) yields (1.X.V.C):

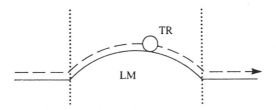

which is a schema for "Sam walked over the hill." Transform (C) added to (1.V) yields (1.V.C):

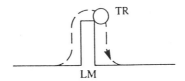

which is a schema for "Sam climbed over the wall." Transform (E) added to (1.X.V.C) yields (1.X.V.C.E):

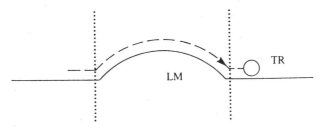

which is a schema for "Sam lives over the hill." Transform (E) added to (1.X.C) yields (1.X.C.E):

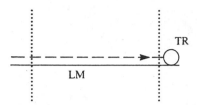

which is a schema for "Sausalito is over the bridge."

Lakoff suggests that each of the transformations is an "instance" of the basic schema. The limits on which transforms can be further transformed establishes "similarity links" among the transforms. Thus "end-point focus," (E), can only be applied to schemas with "horizontal extension," (X), and "contact," (C), between trajector and landmark.

Similar treatment is accorded the other three sets of senses of over—those for "covering," "reflexive," and "excess." The basic schemas for each of the four senses, together with their many respective transforms, are then combined in one diagram (Lakoff 1987b: 436), which shows the similarity relations (actual transformations) among the several individual schemas.

Lakoff says that we can think of these schemas in two ways.

Take, for example, a sentence like *Sam walked over the hill.* . . . We can think of *over* in this sentence as being represented by the minimally specified schema [(1)] . . . and of the additional information as being added by the object and the verb. . . . Equivalently, we can view the minimally specified *over* of [(1)] as generating all the fully specified schemas. . . . On this *full specification interpretation*, we can think of the *over* in *Sam walked over the hill* as having the full specification of the schema [(1.V.X.C)]. The verb *walk* would then match the contact (C) specification, and the direct object *hill* would match the vertical extended (V.X) specification. (1987b: 420)

Lakoff favors the generative view on the basis of the links (the restricted kinds of transformations that the schemas have undergone). We will return to this point below.

Finally, Lakoff describes (1987b: 435–40) how metaphoric extensions of the basic schemas take place to produce such sentences as:

−She has a strange power *over* me.
−Sam was passed *over* for promotion.
−You've *over*looked his accomplishments.
−Who can *over*see this operation?
−Harry still hasn't gotten *over* his divorce.
−Pete Rose is *over* the hill.

Thus, the second-to-last example is based on schema (1.V.X.C) plus two metaphors: "obstacles are vertical landmarks," and "life is a journey" (1987b: 439). And I would add a third, that "psychological coping in life is traversing a rough extended terrain." So Harry has not yet traversed the rough horizontal extent of (i.e., psychologically coped with) the vertical obstacle (the actual process of divorce) in the journey of life.

Let me try to summarize what I think are Lakoff's important claims about idealized cognitive models as exemplified by image schemas.

1. Image schemas, being ideal objects, are not reducible to a finite set of propositions. A schematic is worth an infinity of words.

2. Image schemas specify the core meaning of many lexical senses.

3. Image schemas enter compositionally into syntactic structures. The senses of other lexical items must match or be compatible with the properties of the schema. As a corollary, image schemas are not augmented with meaning supplied by the senses of terms with which the schema, via its lexical label, enters into syntactic composition.

4. Image schemas are ideal in origin and are, in part, pre-predicative.

5. Related senses of polysemous words can be described by a network of image schemas. That is, networks of image schemas are lexically sedimented as the senses of polysemous words.

6. Image schemas are subject to metaphorical, as well as conventional, extension. Conventional extension is a function of the inherent properties of the schemas; metaphorical extension involves use of a metaphor to transform some aspect of the schema in its originary domain to an analog in another domain.

Another Look Over Image Schemas

I should like to offer three propositions concerning cognitive models as exemplified by the image schema, in particular that for the word "over."

1. An image schema (and the set of its extant transforms) would only by chance be coincident, or in one-to-one correspondence, with the set of related senses of a single word.

2. Image schemas are subject to selection, augmentation, modification as a function of syntactic, semantic, pragmatic context of use.

3. Image schemas are subject to conventional-cultural and intentional principles for use or interpretation, just as are words, phrases, and sentences. Schemas are not uninterpreted primitives.

I support these propositions by means of illustration rather than by deductive argument. Consider the three sets of sentences in Table 1. The terms used in the table to refer to Lakoff's "OVER-SCHEMA" are as follows:

English: "over"
German: "vorbei," "hinweg + über" (+ accusative), "hinter" (+ da-
          tive), "über" (+ dative, + accusative), "an" (+ accusative),
          and "um"
Setswana: "kwa godimo," "godimo ga," "ka kwa ga," "mo," "mo go-
          dimo ga," "ka kwa + -eng," "mo + -eng," "ka," "kwa ga,"
          "ka kwano," and "unmarked morphologically"

As closely as I can tell from what I have elicited from native speakers of these three languages, each triad of sentences is not just a set of very close "translations," but each of a given group of three make reference in very similar ways to the same "image" or set of images of space and spatial relationships. Said differently, the set of image schema transforms represented by the sentences in English numbered 1–20 can be mapped onto a cognate or identical image in the thinking of native speakers of German and Setswana respectively. However, both in German and in Setswana, a half-dozen or more lexical items are required to denote the transforms represented in English by the various senses of "over." The question is this: why does a cross-language (cum culture) image

TABLE I

English	German	Setswana
1. The bird flew over/[past].	Der Vogel ist *vorbeigeflogen*.	Nonyane e fofile *kwa godimo*.
2. The bird flew (that way) *over* the field.	Der Vogel ist *über das Feld hinweg* geflogen.	Nonyane e fofile *godimo ga* masimo.
3. The bird flew *over* the mountain.	Der Vogel verschwand *hinter dem* Berg.	Nonyane e fofile *ka kwa ga* thaba.
4. The balloon is (floating) *over* the garden.	Der Ballon is *über dem* Garten.	Leballoon le dutse *mo* moweng, *mo godimo ga* lolwapa.
5. Sam walked *over* the hill.	Sam ging *über den* Hügel.	Sam oile *ka kwa ga* thaba.
6. Sam lives *over* the hill.	Sam wohnt *hinter dem* Berg.	Sam oagile *ka kwa ga* thaba.
7. The pot is hanging *over* the fire.	Der Topf hängt *über dem* Feuer.	Pitse e elekeletse *godimo ga* molelo.
8. Sam jumped *over* the wall.	Sam sprang *über die* Mauer.	Sam oile *otlota* leraka.
9. The plank is *over* the hole.	Das Brett ist *über dem* Loch.	Leplanka le *godimo ga* mokote.
10. Police were posted (all) *over* the hill.	Polizisten wurden *über den ganzen* Hügel verteilt.	Go ne go tletse mapodise *mo godimo ga* thaba.
11. Sam has gone *over* to the hill.	Sam ist zu dem Hügel *hinüber gegangen*.	Sam oile *ka kwa* thabeng.
12. Sam walked all *over* the hill.	Sam ist *über den ganzen* Hügel gewandert.	Sam otsamaile a tsamaya fela *mo* thabe*ng*.
13. Sam has a veil *over* his face.	Sam hat einen Schleier *über* sein*em* Gesicht.	Sam okwetse sefatlhogo *ka* lesere.
14. Sam climbed *over* the canyon walls.	Sam kletterte *an/(in) den* Kanyonwänden.	Sam opalame *kwa ga* logago.
15. Sam rolled the log *over*.	Sam rollte den Baum *um*.	Sam odikolositse morapatse.
16. Sam turned the leaf *over*.	Sam drehte das Blatt *um*.	Sam oemisitse letlhare.
17. The fence fell *over*.	Der Zaun ist *umgefallen*.	Leraka lewile.
18. Sam knocked *over* the lamp.	Sam hat die Lampe *umgestossen*.	Sam owisitse lesedi.
19. The water (in the river) *overflowed*.	Das Wasser im Fluss ist *übergeflossen*.	Noka etletse go tlala.
20. Sam asked him to come *over*.	Sam bat ihn *herüberzukommen*.	Sam omolaleditse go tla *ka kwano*.

schema mapping not correspond to a lexical translation? If we had carried out this exercise beginning with the German word *über* or Setswana *ka*, we would have had the same result: a heterogeneous list of English lexical morphemes required to refer to the set of image schema transforms, signalled by *über* or *ka* respectively.

If schemas are supposed to be experiential in origin, and in large part pre-predicative, why would different languages/cultures, even ones with such intimate cognate relationships as English and German, map image schemas onto lexical items in such different ways? What provides for the coherence and integrity of image schemas and their transforms: the extant senses of morphologically marked lexical items or "experience in the real world" or both?

I suggest that, to a large degree, the mapping of components of experience, such as image schemas are supposed to represent, onto particular senses of lexical items exhibits a certain fragmentariness and chanciness, if not arbitrariness. And yet all languages make ready reference to the same set of image schema transforms by means of a small number of lexical items. Lakoff is asserting tacitly that a collection of image-schematic senses, if glossed by a single lexical item, constitute an integral category of experiences.

But examination of the data above forces us to ask incredulously, what would have motivated the Germans to allocate spatial experience to just the morphemes cited above? What would motivate English speakers to reserve just those senses for the single morpheme "over"? Do the speakers of German and Setswana think of those experiences glossed by the English "over" as a rather fragmentary or unmotivated set, because they are not referred to by the senses of a single lexical item? Do English speakers see a natural affinity among those senses that the speakers of the other two languages miss, because of this same fact? There seems little reason to believe any of what these questions insinuate on the strength of Lakoff's analysis.

To look at this issue historically, what would have motivated speakers of English over the past 200 years to drop the "above-and-more-but-not-excess" senses of "over" listed here—and thereby also to drop the image schemas? Which words, if any, picked up the "dropped" image schema transforms? Overlip, overlord, overmore, overmost, overer, overest, overdrop, overwave, overlayer.

But note retention of overblow, overtone, overtime. While "over-take" has currently the sense of "catch up with and pass," it has lost the older sense, older image, of doing so from above, as in overnim, overget, overcatch, overhie, overhole; the "from above" sense is still resonant in words like overrun or overhaul.

Supplying imagistic schematics or icons for the extant senses of polysemous words looks suspiciously like providing a notational variant of what a list of senses plus good historical or comparative lexicography has already done. This is not, however, to question the key importance of image schemas as components of word sense. If image schemas are in part directly "experiential"—that is, pre-predicative—then there must be some way to establish their cross-linguistic, cross-cultural, transhistorical manifestation, nonrelativistically. Let me hypothecate such an approach.

A Phenomenology of Spatial-Temporal Experience

Let us approach the problem of image schemas for "lived" space-time, not morpheme by morpheme in a given language, but as Lakoff insists, from "the experience of things." Let us further suggest that fundamental lived-body experiences of spatiality are kinesthetically, visually, tactilely informed—but also that these can be linguistically/culturally elaborated or augmented.

There is an experience that would in some minimal way be shared by all languages/cultures and their speakers—that of the immediate surface of the earth and the seeming course of sun and moon. Such a "scene" would contain such potentialities for experience as these: (1) propinquity; (2) distance; (3) demarcation of spatial relationship; (4) the dial, orbit, or trajectory of sun and moon, whose light is both a point and a sweep or array; (5) cloud cover; (6) altitude; (7) courses of movement/travel through the trajectory; (8) barriers to sensory or locomotor access; and (9) behavior of entities occupying this scene.

Now any language or culture would have to cope with—and would have to talk about—certain requirements of sensorially engaging, and doing things in, such a scene. Part of this task would

be the development of symbols that represent the intentional geometry and temporality of such a scene. A cursory look at how
various languages have accomplished this (see above, for example)
suggests clearly that there are numerous ways to break up this intentional geometry and temporality and to assign resulting components to the lexicon. While the components-of-experienced-
scene to lexical-sense mapping is quite different among languages,
languages seem extraordinarily intertranslatable with regard to
their capacity to describe very subtly and precisely certain basic
experiences of this scene.

Could we with good reason hypothesize that all languages contain within either closed classes, like prepositions, or open classes,
like nouns and verbs, ready and robust codings of certain universal, materially and perspectivally grounded experiences of this one
grand scene/schema? Such an image schema would be full and
rich. The language as a whole would always lexically encode it,
but could variously schematize it in terms of how the lexicon perspectivally partitions and bestows significance on it. The senses of
any single lexical item could be rather capriciously different, so
long as the language as a whole continuously renders the primal
scene into a robust, complete field of symbols. Thus, whether or
not there is semantic "drift"—the loss or accretion of senses to
given lexical morphemes—the scene as a whole will have to remain encoded in the lexicon, for any language/culture that failed
to do this would fail in a sense to be part of humanity.

Let me push this hypothesis further, by returning to the word
"over" in English, that is, to its various senses and the imagistic
schemas Lakoff has proposed. The four basic senses of the word
"over" described by Lakoff, plus others he has omitted, plus their
various respective transforms would appear to reduce to an intentional "seeing" of this one grand scene I have described. Instead of
using some several dozen schemas, could we describe the senses
of "over" in reference to one, the partitioning of which is in part
mapped onto the various senses of "over"? We could hypothesize
that any language would encode in a small number of lexical items
all of the basic experiential properties of this one grand scene. The
collected senses of "over" in contemporary American English, for
example, express the experience of viewing a point from below

that radiates out and covers a surface and is in motion such as to describe a course, part of the trajectory of which is an arc. Other languages might, of course, use more than one lexical item to cover the same experiential domain.

The experiential counterpart of this is viewing the sun in its dial. Here we have an intentional scene in which the point can be seen as in motion or still (depending on intention). The movement of the object describes a trajectory. The object is either a point (of light) or a sweeping effect making contact with and covering the surface (rays of the sun). The gaze on this scene takes place from below the point (of light). The trajectory goes over or across terrain. At any instant, the point of light describes a point above a surface in a vertical axis. The sun makes contact with the surface via sunlight, but the sun itself is always above and not in contact with the terrain. The dial (movement) of the sun is repetitive: it creates the recurrence of identical events. At the horizon the trajectory appears to transect the surface. The view in imagination can occupy any point in the scene.

It would seem that, aspectually or perspectivally, beholding this scene can generate all the components-of-schemas that Lakoff's diagrams can generate, and many many more. Further, since this scene is a rich, full one, there may be many extensions of this scene that no typified, extant sense of "over" quite captures. For example, "overtake" used to mean pursuing with the intent of pouncing upon, coming down on from above (as one would prey). Does not the sun do this at the horizon as it "chases the night"? The sun is of course powerful; its rays can burn; its power is greatest when it is directly over one. ("She has power over me"?) What more clearly than the sun is an entity that both does and does not make contact with landmarks on the surface? What more clearly than the sun goes above, across, stands still, travels great distances, describes a trajectory, covers, reflexively moves around a central axis? (The sun goes over each day, over and over and over.) It fills the world with energy and plenty, yet too much of it (excess) can damage. Day is over when the sun sets. The sun (moon, stars) fall over the horizon. At daybreak the light floods, overflows the land. The sun conquers darkness (overthrows it).

Lakoff says experiences serve as motivations for extending the senses of words. One way I suggest this can be explained, rather than just described after the fact, is to postulate that rich, full primal experiences are subject to a potential infinity of intentional depictions, gazes, views. Some will of necessity be universal. Our existence depends on it. Others may be unique to a certain culture or language (e.g., the sex or marriage of the sun and moon).

The scene I described can potentially motivate all the experiences that are required to schematize every sense the words "over," "über", or "ka" have, had, or probably ever will have. It may also motivate experiences glossed by senses of many other positional formatives and their metaphoric extensions as well.

Now the senses of the word *über* and those of the word *ka* partition this scene differently. They represent in their respective current senses a different assemblage of gazes or perspectives. Some can be represented by some of those that *over* represents. Others not. But I would hypothesize that the set of senses of all the closed-class lexical items that represent intentionally perspectival experiences of space-time will in aggregate describe a common set of experiences, many of which are motivated by the scene I just set forth. This does not deny culturally peculiar or unique senses or gazes, which could still be motivated by unique or peculiar ways of intending it.

Bear in mind that the use of the image of the scene to understand lexical sense is always intentional, which is to say the scene is not a brute visual sensation but rather signifies in terms of categories (including image schemas) in the language. When Lakoff describes his image schemas, he tries to depict them as rather actualistic, Euclidean schematic diagrams. This ignores the key point that schemas are symbols for categories of sense; they are not simply mimetic abstractions of Euclidean space.

This misprision leads him to some difficulties too involved to explicate here, but which can be illustrated. For example, he says that the "above sense" of over precludes "contact," and "path" (1987b: 425). This is exemplified by a sentence like "The picture is over the fireplace." However, the notion of "path" is not Euclidean. Thus, we can say "the ribbon is draped over the car" (where there is contact), but not "the ribbon is over the car" (this would imply the ribbon is suspended somehow). The resolution of this seeming paradox is simple; the notions of "covering" and the notions of "path" have to be construed intentionally rather than actualistically. Thus a ribbon can be construed as describing a path provided it is laid out. And it can be construed as covering, and hence requiring contact, provided it is "draped."

In another case, Lakoff says "End-point focus . . . can only be added to those [schemas] with an extended landmark" (1987b: 423). Now this is true intentionally, but not actualistically, because extension is itself intentional. (No oxymoronic pun intended.) Thus, according to Lakoff a "wall," as in "Sam jumped over the wall," is not an (horizontally) extended landmark. So if we say "Sam lives over the wall," we imply some weird house suspended over the wall. The wall lacks "end-point focus," says Lakoff, because it is not extended. But a wall can be extended intentionally. Thus I can say, "the bird lives (just) over the wall," and clearly imply vis-à-vis a bird, just what hill or mountain or bridge does vis-à-vis Sam. Again, "where's the chipmunk's hole?" "It's just over the wall." Here the gaze of the speaker or addressee constructs the scene so as to intend a path and hence the possibility of an end point.

At another point Lakoff asserts that the "above" sense of "over" "is roughly equivalent in meaning to *above*" (1987b: 425). This statement flows from a sense of image schema that ignores intentional geometry. "Over" has an intentional horizon that "above" simpliciter does not have. "Over," in this sense, while typically precluding contact, retains the sense of intimacy of intentional connection or relation between the landmark and the object and the sense of trajectory that covers or crosses (just as the sun does not touch, but is in connection with, the earth, and its orbit covers/crosses the sky). A roof is not "above," but rather is "over" the house. A fly is not "over" the fireplace, because the intimate connection between "fly" and "fireplace" is not intended by the wall, which does create such a connection when a picture is hung over the fireplace (on the wall). "Over" signifies a relationship between reference landmark and object. We can't say "on the shelf just over" (meaning "above"). We can't say "the guest suite is one flight over" (meaning "above"), because there is no relation to the "below."

"Over" does not let go easily of its sense of arc-like trajectory. A given skyscraper may rise *above* but not *over* the city. But that very same building may be intended differently as when it towers *over*, but does not tower *above* the city. Hills may overlook the city; those hills may be above the city. A hut on those hills may overlook the city, but the hut is not *over* the city, even if it is both *above* it and *overlooks* it!

This all makes sense, perfect sense, only if we conceive of image schemas as intentional-significance bestowing devices, not as schematic diagrams of actualistically conceived geometric configurations.

Part II
The Play of Tropes

"We Are Parrots," "Twins Are Birds":

Play of Tropes as Operational Structure

Terence Turner

After a century of anthropological exegesis the well-known Bororo assertion of the title retains its frisson of irreducible alienness. Like the Nuer claim for the identity of twins and birds, and analogous statements of the Brazilian Kayapo to be considered, it seems to embody the intractable resistance of the savage mind to our own culture's standards of rationality. For this reason, such apparently irrational or "symbolic" expressions continue to be chronic

This paper has benefited from exceptionally thorough and penetrating criticism from many colleagues. My wife and colleague, Jane Fajans, has meticulously gone over three drafts of the manuscript. Her unsparing critique of both style and substance has left its mark on virtually every paragraph. Michael Silverstein, as commentator at the symposium in which the paper was initially presented, made a number of useful observations. James Fernandez, the organizer of the symposium, offered a lengthy written commentary. Paul Friedrich, Jean Comaroff, and John Comaroff also offered valuable comments, both on the subject of metaphor in general and on the paper in particular. My greatest debt is to Bill Hanks, who called in an extensive series of insightful criticisms from the delivery room in which his daughter, Madelein, was about to be born, literally (non-figuratively) pointing out contradictions between contractions. In recognition of this supreme feat of collegiality, and in gratitude to Laurie Bartman and Bill Hanks for thus bearing with me, this paper is dedicated to Madelein Hanks.

subjects of anthropological theorizing. In recent years such discussions have relied increasingly on the concept of metaphor. There have been attempts to explain both of the statements in the title as metaphorical tropes (Lévi-Strauss 1963; Crocker 1985). These attempts number among the foundational works of what has come to be known in the discipline as "metaphor theory." Like its immediate ancestor and close cognate, "symbolic anthropology," metaphor theory approaches the analysis of meaningful forms by focusing on their minimal elements (in this case, individual tropes), abstracting them from both their pragmatic contexts of social use and the more complex meaningful constructs (rituals, narratives, patterns of action) in which they are embedded. As in the case of the concept of symbol in symbolic anthropology, the result is a tendency to regard the minimal elements, for theoretical purposes, as prior in both epistemological and ontological senses to the combinatorial structures in which they are incorporated in cultural discourse and social action.

The problem for anthropological analysis is clearly to develop a theoretical understanding of the nature of metaphor consistent with the importance of its role in cultural forms that avoids the reductionist and idealist tendencies of much symbolic and metaphor theory. A possible approach lies through a critique of the metaphorical interpretations of the Bororo and Nuer assertions of the title. An effort to arrive at a more satisfactory understanding of the logical structure and meaning of these statements may provide a practical basis for reassessing the role of metaphor in their construction. This in turn might suggest new ways of conceiving of metaphor and its relation to other tropes that would allow its integration into a more broadly based approach to the interpretation of cultural forms and meanings. It should also provide an empirically grounded basis for considering the general question of the extent to which a theory of metaphor (or "symbol" or any other elementary particle of signification considered in abstraction) can be pressed into service as a general theoretical framework for the analysis of cultural structures of meaning, including metaphor itself. These, at least, are the possibilities I attempt to pursue in this article.

These issues are fraught with wider implications for cultural analysis and for the concept of culture itself. The position that individual tropes or symbols constitute the fundamental units or elementary forms of culture implies that culture is essentially to be understood in idealist terms as "a system of symbols and meanings" constituted in abstraction from concrete social activity. Conversely, if individual tropes such as metaphor can be shown to function in cultural constructions of meaning primarily as aspects of more complex, pragmatically oriented forms of discourse or activity, the implication is clear that cultural forms of consciousness and meaning, including their abstracted elements such as individual tropes or symbols, must be understood and analyzed primarily as constituents of contextually and historically situated social interaction.

Positivist and Interactionist Approaches to Metaphor: Implications for "Metaphor Theory" and Cultural Analysis

Perhaps the most fundamental issue involved in the conception of metaphor and other tropes in their generic capacity as modes of meaning is that of the nature of reference and its subjective or cultural construction. Opposing conceptions of metaphor have developed, based respectively upon positivist and interactionist or constructivist approaches to reference. Because the differences between these opposing views bear directly upon the anthropological questions about metaphor addressed in this paper, it will be useful to begin with a brief review of them before proceeding to cases.

Metaphor consists of the employment of an attribute of a given semantic domain as a predication or representation of an attribute of a different domain, on the basis of a perceived similarity between the two attributes. In the most commonly held view, based on positivist or "correspondence" notions of semantic reference, in which a sharp distinction is made between denotative and connotative meaning, it is assumed that the similarity between the features of the "source" and "target" domains is determined by the objective correspondence of each with its referent. The similarity, in other words, derives from the objective properties of referents, which are in themselves independent of (prior to) the perception or cognition of those properties by subjects. The metaphoric connection consists in a subjective recognition of this preexisting common element of denotation and its "figurative" extrapolation as the "connotative" basis of the tropic relation between the two "denotations."

This view underlies the common idea that metaphoric associations are qualitatively different (more "artificial," and therefore perhaps more creative) than the denotative semantic relations that provide their elements. The latter, which constitute the conventional stock of categories and associations of the culture or language, are regarded by contrast as "natural" or at least relatively unproblematic. The qualitative difference between metaphorical and simple semantic reference in this conventional view is variously expressed as a contrast between "figurative" and "literal," "connotative" and "denotative," or "significative" and "significational" meaning. The essential implication of all of these usages is that while metaphor creates a new relationship between domains, it does not create a new meaning as the basis of this relationship. It simply makes a new (figurative) kind of use of one that is already there. This figurative view of metaphor is implicitly or explicitly connected to the notion that metaphor, like other tropes, serves an essentially ornamental function and thus lives only so long as it remains "fresh," an unaccustomed or startling way of saying what could otherwise be said more simply and plainly in terms of conventional notions of denotative reference. Metaphors that become familiar are said to "die" because they lose their capacity to impart fresh figurative connotations to established meanings, over and beyond their basic referential denotations.

This conventional approach to metaphor is firmly rooted in the positivist tenet (itself here, as elsewhere, an expression of the dominant folk view) that "literal" meaning and the semantic domains in which it is represented are in some sense natural and thus uncreative. Creative or figurative meaning is therefore contrastively located in the "unnatural" metaphoric connection between domains. This set of assumptions implicitly or explicitly underlies much of the recent special interest in metaphor, including the tendency to set it apart from other tropes like metonymy or synecdoche, which tend to be seen as less creative because they involve only relations within the same natural domain. The championship of metaphor on the basis of such a position, although often presented as an overtly antipositivist argument for the importance of intuitive, creative, or figurative modes of transcending the limitations of positive semantic reference or "literal meaning," thus actually presupposes and reinforces the positivist conception of referential meaning it seeks to transcend.

In contrast to this conventional view stands the "interactionist" conception of metaphor associated with I. A. Richards and Max Black (although the latter retains aspects of the literal/figurative distinction) and incisively developed by Cristina Bicchieri in a recent study of the role of metaphor in scientific theorizing (Richards 1950 [1936]; Black 1962; Bicchieri 1988). In this view the common ground of the two members of the metaphoric equation necessarily entails the creation of a new meaning, not simply the recognition of a preexisting one. To say "the foot of the mountain" is to imbue both feet and the bases of mountains (and implicitly, the wholes to which feet and base belong) with a new sense not reducible to that each has in its original semantic domain.

This is clearly incompatible with the conventional view of metaphor as a "figurative" relation between two received semantic entities and their meanings, regarded as "literally" defined within the domains from which they are drawn. Instead, the metaphor becomes seen as constituting a new, integral construct, a meta-domain as it were, with a new meaning uniquely defined in relation to the context constituted by the interaction between its source and target members. Within the terms of this new meaningful construct, there can be no qualitative distinction between literal and figurative, denotative and connotative, and thus between metaphoric and conventional symbolic signification.

This interactionist view of metaphor clearly parts company with the conventional view as outlined above over the proposition that the metaphoric relation is different in some qualitative way from the relations constituting the semantic domains from which the constituents of the metaphoric relation are drawn (whether these be characterized as between symbol and referent, class and member, type and token, or prototype and example). Perhaps I misunderstand, but some such view seems to constitute an implicit premise of metaphor theory in its more common anthropological forms, at least insofar as it is based on the conception of metaphor as a sui generis mode of giving form and identity to the otherwise inchoate experience (at least, experience of self-identity) of phenomenological subjects. It is on this basis that metaphor is adduced by the preeminent architect of anthropological metaphor theory, James Fernandez (1986), as one of the fundamental elements, or perhaps the primary element or mode, of constructing relatively complex cultural forms and systems.

A similar premise, as I have argued above, is an integral part of the positivist view of metaphor as I have described it. It is also, however, assumed in some variants of the interactionist position such as Black's, which reserve for metaphor and other tropes an essentially ornamental function distinct from that of scientific models (Black 1962; cf. Bicchieri 1988: 102–3). I am not clear precisely where Fernandez's version of metaphor theory fits in this epistemological continuum, but his emphasis on a qualitatively distinct "mission" of metaphor in "expressive" culture seems to locate him somewhere within it (1986: 28–72) and thus in critical dialogue with the "interactionist" approach. A focal issue in this dialogue is the relationship between metaphoric (and more broadly tropic) constructions and nontropic forms such as anaphoric symbols and logical type or class constructs. This issue appears especially acute for Fernandez's formulation of metaphor theory because its contention that metaphor constitutes the primary cultural device for ordering inchoate life-worlds or subjective identities appears on the face of it to clash with the fact that metaphor invariably presupposes an ordered system of discrete categories (i.e., distinct semantic identities) from which it draws the elements it juxtaposes.

If the constructionist, antipositivist approach to semantics upon which the interactionist approach to metaphor is based is applied to the analysis of the nature of the symbols, semantic domains, and syntagmatic constructs that provide the source and target elements of the metaphoric relation, it becomes difficult to sustain the proposition that metaphor represents a qualitatively or structurally distinct mode of signification. In a constructionist— or what I, following Piaget, shall call an "operational"[1]—view of the nature of simple (nontropic) semantic classification, the relation between class and member, or token and type, is constructed as the product of two coordinated operations. The first is the separation or abstraction of a feature from a prototype-object that serves as the common feature of the class or type. The second is the imputing of that feature to one or more other objects, which thereby become recognized, along with the prototype, as tokens of the type or members of the class: in short, generalization.

A logical "class" or semantic "type," in this view, is essentially a coordinated bundle of these two types of cognitive operations for constructing its referent-objects, tokens, or instances. The same two operations, coordinated in the same way, are employed in the construction of metaphor. A feature abstracted from the source serves as the common basis of its relation to the target (e.g., the quality of being the base of the body as the feature by which "foot" is employed to represent the base of a mountain). The target is concomitantly treated as a second instance of this feature, which thereby becomes the general or "type" feature of a new "class"-like or "type"-like construct. This is the "new meaning" created by the metaphor in the interactionist interpretation. The relation between this meaning and the concrete elements that serve as its vehicles, which thus become instances of that meaning, is no different in principle from the relation between the general "type" or "class" aspect of the signification of a nontropic semantic domain and the referents that become designated as the tokens or instances of this generic meaning.

[1] I follow Piaget's usage of the concepts of "operation" and "operational structure" (Piaget 1968: 1–16). The essential idea is that an operation is the semiotically represented form of an action, integrated as one of a group of transformations, which is defined as a structure by virtue of self-regulation on the basis of an invariant constraint. Such an internally constrained system of transformational operations constitutes a self-regulating "totality." Although Piaget formulates these concepts in terms of mathematics and psychology, he does suggest their applicability to sociology, and I have suggested that they could be easily adapted to the analysis of cultural structures as systems of "collective operations" (T. Turner 1973).

Metaphor, in other words, consists of the employment of the general structural principles of semantic classification (the relations of type and token, the construction of referents through the semantic contextualization of signifiers) to construct a relation of semantic identity, in a new or otherwise distinct context, between elements of semantic categories not recognized in other contexts as belonging to the same semantic domain. This shift in "recognition" may be conceived as a shift in the structural vantage point or epistemological perspective of the subject. Domains that appear distinct from the subjective perspective associated with some contexts can be seen as related from the viewpoint of the context indexed by the metaphorical construction; the construction of this alternative subjective perspective and the distinct context indexed by the new association may then be seen as the point, the intentional meaning, of the metaphor (or other trope). The difference between literal and figurative meaning, or what is recognized as straightforward reference and what is perceived as metaphor, in other words, is not essential but pragmatic or contextually relative (Bicchieri 1988: 106; Hesse 1976 [cited in Bicchieri ibid.: 107]).

As Bicchieri, following the implications of this line of reasoning, argues,

If the literal and figurative are but two extremes of a continuum, the distinction one wishes to draw is a matter of degree: it has to do with the level of entrenchment of a sentence into our cognitive structure. . . . It is often the case that a statement that was previously used in a figurative sense later becomes literal: it gets "entrenched" into the language of the theory. Consider an economic expression like "the market is in equilibrium." Nowadays it is . . . taken to be literal. . . . The same expression, two hundred years ago, was taken to be figurative; it evoked an unspecified gravitational process of prices toward their "natural" values. (ibid.: 105–6)

Metaphors, in other words, begin as the expression of "a provisional connection, a link between the primary and secondary system which is new and suggestive" (ibid.: 106). This connection, however, may, if it becomes accepted, become perceived as a simple, nontropic relation within a unitary semantic domain. This is not a question of "dead metaphor," but precisely the opposite: in such cases, metaphors take on more, and deeper, "life," that is, deeper and more central meanings for the system in which they arise. This process is manifested in the reorientation and re-organization of that system around themselves. Bicchieri's com-pelling argument that metaphor may in this way play a central and lasting role in the development of scientific theories applies *muta-tis mutandis*, I would argue, to cultural metaphors of the struc-turally embedded or "generatively entrenched" sort to which this paper is addressed (on "generative entrenchment," or the effect of more deeply embedded elements of a system in conditioning those less deeply embedded, see Bicchieri 1988: 105, following W. Wimsatt 1986).

It is essential to understand the structural continuity of the step from conventional domain structure to metaphor and back again—in other words, to grasp the *nonuniqueness* of metaphor in an absolute structural sense—in order to appreciate the nature and importance of its *relative* specificity and distinctive role in the construction, and continual reconstruction, of new or distinct contexts of cultural meaning and subjective consciousness. That the difference between "figurative" and "literal" meaning is not fixed and qualitative, but pragmatic and, as it were, quantitative, does not imply that such a dimension of difference does not exist, only that it is a relative, fluid, and quantitative matter. The impor-tance of this point is precisely that metaphors and conventional domains can shade or change into one another in response to changes in context. These changes may be diachronic, as in the historical example of economic "equilibrium" just mentioned, or synchronic, as in the shift from lower to higher levels of complex-ity or between sequentially ordered phases of the same meaningful structure, as in the ethnographic examples considered below. Such shifts or transformations of metaphors into what may be cultur-ally perceived as conventional semantic domains, and vice versa, are among the more significant aspects of the "play of tropes," which, as Fernandez (1986) has suggested, constitutes the focus of the relation of a theory of tropes to one of social action and histori-cal process. The same point holds, as I shall try to show in a mo-ment, for the transformation of metaphor and other tropes into one another.

As all this implies, metaphor cannot be adequately understood in terms of a "metaphor theory" in the narrow sense of a theory concerned with the specific properties of metaphor considered in abstraction from its embeddedness in discourse and pragmatic context, or from its relations with other tropes, such as metonymy and synecdoche. Metaphor is neither a unique cognitive faculty nor a privileged, sui generis type of construction. It cannot, therefore, be considered as the fundamental element of cultural structure, much less the primary conceptual instrument for bringing meaningful order out of referential chaos. Rather, metaphor must be understood as what Marx would call a "one-sided" manifestation of general principles operative at all levels of the construction of cultural meaning. It plays a central and distinctive role in this process of construction. The nature of this role, however, can only be clearly defined if the temptation to reify metaphor as an autonomous structural principle or element is resisted. Metaphor cannot be understood, qua trope, in privileged isolation from other tropes such as metonymy and synecdoche; nor are the principles upon which it is constructed distinct in any qualitative or structural sense from those involved in conventional symbolic or linguistic constructs. On the contrary, it is metaphor's structural continuity with all of these forms, tropic and nontropic alike, that allows it to play a key role in the relations among them. This theoretical perspective on the nature of metaphor and its relations to other forms clearly emphasizes, and perhaps in certain respects amplifies, the importance Fernandez (1986) has given to the notion of the "play of tropes" in culture.

Psittacine Synecdoche Among the Bororo and Kayapo

In the remainder of this paper, I attempt to explore and develop these general propositions through the analysis of three ethnographic cases of assertions of the identity of humans and birds: two of these cases, the Bororo and Nuer, are well known, and share not only an ostensive affinity in the avian reference of their comparisons, but also a theoretical kinship that makes both directly

relevant to the discussion at hand. Both the Bororo and Nuer instances have been analyzed as cases of metaphor by anthropologists prominently associated with "metaphor theory." The third
case, drawn from my own field data on the Kayapo, a Brazilian
people of the same cultural area as the Bororo, provides useful insights of different kinds into both the other two cases. I hope
through a more concrete and thoroughly contextualized analysis
of the ethnographic particulars, to shed new light both on the specific meanings of the assertions in question and on the general
issues pertaining to metaphor and related tropes raised in the preceding section.

The Bororo Enigma

Few affirmations of la pensée sauvage have commanded the
theoretical attention accorded over the years to the Bororo assertion glossed by Karl von den Steinen as "We are parrots (araras)"[2]
(1894: 352 ff.). Von den Steinen insisted that the Bororo meant this
statement literally and in the present tense, indicative mode. His
explanation was that the Bororo, as primitives, could not distinguish between humans and animals. Von den Steinen also made
several other mutually contradictory assertions about the Bororo
concept of the relationship, some of which will occupy us below.
It is the first, and for von den Steinen, the primary interpretation
of the Bororo assertion, however, that was taken up by most subsequent commentators, such as Lucien Levy-Bruhl (1910), who adduced it as the type case of "participation," the essential principle
of his concept of primitive logic. More recently, it has received an
extended discussion from Christopher Crocker (1985), who treats
it as a case of metaphor. A critical examination of Crocker's analysis may thus serve as a convenient point of departure for a more
general discussion of the tropic construction of this and related
utterances and beliefs of the Bororo and other Central Brazilian
peoples.

Let us begin by reviewing a few pertinent facts about the use

[2] The terms "parrots" or "macaws" are often used in translating this famous
Bororo sentence. I prefer to employ the Brazilian Portuguese term "araras,"
which precisely denotes the intended species. The variety of arara in question,
unless otherwise specified, is the red, rather than the blue or black forms.

and abuse of araras among the Bororo. The Bororo consider araras
to be the preferred animal form entered and possessed by dead human souls for purposes of eating and copulation (activities souls
cannot perform in their normal disembodied spiritual state). Araras arc thus identified as the medium par excellence of the materi-
alization of human spirit-essence. The Bororo also believe that,
immediately following death, the soul passes through a series of
animal forms, one of which is that of the arara.

Some authors (Karsten 1964; J. Smith 1972; Van Baaren 1969)
have seized upon these facts as a basis for explaining the Bororo
locution as an assertion of their belief in the metamorphosis of the
human soul after death into arara form. Jonathan Smith, by far the
most scholarly and cogent of these, marshals evidence from an exhaustive survey of texts dealing with the Bororo statement, relevant ethnographic literature, and a critical reading of von den
Steinen to argue that, "The Bororo never said that they were red
parrots in the sense that von den Steinen and the majority of his
later commentators understood them. They declared . . . that
when they are dead they will become red parrots, and thus they
may speak of themselves as being red parrots in the present 'as a
caterpillar says that he is a butterfly'" (1972: 393). Crocker, published after Smith, challenges this plausible interpretation on ethnographic grounds. It is not clear from von den Steinen's text
whether the metaphor of the butterfly and the caterpillar is his or
the Bororo's own. Smith accepts it as the latter, but Crocker reports that the Bororo regard caterpillars and butterflies as distinct
species and do not recognize metaphorphosis, so that this interpretation must be rejected. He also says that his Bororo informant
confirmed von den Steinen's own reason for rejecting the postmortem metamorphosis interpretation as thc primary meaning of
the Bororo statement in question, namely that it was formulated
in the present tense (1985: 30). He also, somewhat confusingly, reports that he "found no confirmation" of von den Steinen's report
that the Bororo claim that "the soul assumes the form of a bird,
usually a red macaw, when it departs the corporeal self . . . during
dreams or at death" (1985: 15), although he later confirms that he
did find that they do believe that souls after death do just that, at
specific times and for specific purposes.

Crocker goes on to point out that the Bororo belief in the preference of dead souls for araras over living humans for periodic eating
and copulating sprees shows that they do distinguish between
araras as a species and humans, and the necessity for souls to pos-
sess araras for these purposes clearly indicates that they distinguish between araras as a species and dead souls. He correctly concludes from this that the statement "We are araras" cannot imply
metonymic identity based on shared species nature or continuity
of spiritual substance between humans and araras.

It is at this point that Crocker introduces his ill-conceived argument for the metaphorical character of the Bororo statement. That
the Bororo distinguish clearly between the respective semantic domains with which men and araras are identified (their respective
species, their humanity and animality, and the domains of spirit
and profane existence of which they are respectively recognized as
vehicles or manifestations), Crocker argues, means that the Bororo
do not understand them to be parts of the same whole or in any
sense continuous in substance. From this conclusion he argues
that, because metonymy is a relation between parts of the same
whole whereas metaphor is a relation between aspects of different wholes or orders, the relationship between them cannot be
metonymic but must therefore, by elimination, be metaphoric:
"the distinction between the domains of spirit, man, and macaw
has been established. The postulation that 'we are macaws' is thus
not founded on metonymy; it remains to be seen how it is metaphorical" (1985: 37). Casting about for a metaphorical basis of
comparison between araras and men, Crocker comes up with the
ingenious argument that both are beings in which the demands of
libidinous spirit-energy (*bope*) and essential spirit-being or soul
(*aroe*) stand in uneasy compromise.

A difficulty is posed for this theory by a surprising ethnographic
fact that Crocker adduces at this point, namely that his informants insisted that the assertion that "humans are araras" (Bororo
pronouns are non-gender-specific) applies only to males (1985: 38).
It is unclear, however, why women should be excluded from the
metaphor on the basis of Crocker's explanation, since they also
share both sorts of spiritual essence or urge. Crocker acknowledges this difficulty and attempts to account for it on ad hoc

grounds that not even he appears to find very satisfactory. This newly adduced ethnographic constraint, however, has the effect of eliminating the postmortem transformation of souls into araras for eating and copulation as the intended referent of the statement, since both activities obviously involve females as well as males.

I find Crocker's solution unconvincing on several grounds. First and most obvious, the theoretical argument by elimination is clearly a non sequitur. The opposition of metonymy and metaphor is not privative; the elimination of one does not entail the other. Second, Crocker's argument against metonymy rests on a false proposition and in this instance, as I shall argue, comes to a false conclusion. It assumes that metonymy derives from the *prior* membership of its elements in a common whole; in other words, that the character of the parts of a metonymy *as parts* must be derived from a context or contexts external and prior to the metonymy itself. Against this commonly held view, I would argue that just as metaphor creates the meaningful relation between its members, so metonymy may create the semantic and intentional whole to which its members are defined, for purposes of the trope, as belonging. Outside or prior to the metonymy itself, they may well be seen as belonging to separate wholes.

This, of course, is an interactionist view of metonymy, parallel with the interactionist conception of metaphor put forward above. In my development of that view, I argued that metaphors in effect also constitute themselves as metonymies because the emergent common meaning they create constitutes a new "whole" of which the two otherwise disparate members of the metaphor equally become parts. Though metaphors in this analytical sense must constitute themselves as metonymies, and thus a fortiori as synecdoches, however, the reverse is not true of metonymy. Metonymy does not imply metaphorical identification, and two dissimilar entities may be constituted as parts of a tropic whole without any implication that they share any specific common property. This creative, operational, or interactionist view of metonymy is, in my view, the key to understanding its role in cases of ritual and symbolic belief such as those with which we are here concerned. To see what in ordinary social existence appear as unrelated elements of different domains as parts of a single, differently constituted whole implies not only a reorganization of the object world, but equally, a reorientation or transformation of subjective perspective.

Such transformations of the subject's relation to the world, I suggest, are precisely what the ritual practices and mythical views coded by metonymic as well as metaphoric statements serve to express and effect. In the present instance, I shall argue that the Bororo conception of the man-arara relation is in at least some of its moments metonymic, in others metaphoric, and in an overall sense synecdochic. Not only are these three interpretations not mutually exclusive, but understanding their interdependence and ability to transform into one another is the essence of "the play of tropes," which I would suggest is the essential structural principle of ritual and mythical meaning. We have only to reflect on the archetypal themes of myth and ritual, such as the transfer of energy, power, disease, or fetishized forms of culture between the domains of nature and society (T. Turner 1985) or purification or pollution resulting from contact between the domains of the sacred and the profane, to realize that they are profoundly concerned with the operations of constituting disparate entities or attributes into parts of wholes, or conversely separating the parts of a discordant whole into separate domains. They are concerned, in other words, with the creation and dissolution of metonymies.

The Meaning of "Becoming an Arara" for the Bororo: Ritual Adornment and Dance as Tropic Play

A further problem with Crocker's interpretation is that it appears either to overlook or to misinterpret the significance of certain ethnographic particulars germane to his analysis. The more significant of these are, first, the mode of the verb in the Bororo statement "We are araras"; second, the fact that the assertion is made only of males; and third, the meanings and contextual uses of arara feathers.

Crocker tells us that the assertion "We are araras" is in fact commonly enough made by the Bororo to have a "customary form," and he puts all who have struggled over its interpretation greatly in his debt by finally giving us the actual Bororo linguistic form of the phrase: the three-word sentence *pa e-do nabure*. The first word, *pa*, is, according to the *Enciclopedia Bororo* (Albisetti and Venturelli 1962) a first person plural pronoun; the last word, *nabure*, is a generic noun meaning araras of the red variety; and the middle word, *e-do*, is a form of the verb "to be," in a mode which indicates, in Crocker's words, existence "in present time, as opposed to permanent states of being" (1985)—in other words, some form of focused experience or activity. The verb form is morphologically complex: again according to the *Enciclopedia Bororo*, the first morpheme, *e*, denotes "existence," that is, the state or process of existing, while the second morpheme, *do*, denotes the activity of making or doing. This latter particle occurs in combination with many stative terms in the *Enciclopedia* and appears to constitute a general productive form for transforming stative or intransitive forms into causative or transitive verbs.

It would therefore seem that the sentence in question might be more accurately glossed "We make ourselves araras" or "We become araras" rather than simply "We are araras." The gloss I have proposed is more consistent with the verbal mode of being or action "in present time" than the "permanent state of being" denoted by the usual translation (note that Crocker's metaphoric interpretation of the man-arara relationship is couched precisely in terms of a "permanent state of being," and therefore appears inconsistent with the verbal mode of the customary Bororo locution). It would also be consistent with the "metamorphic" interpretations of Smith and Van Baaren, were it not for its present-time (as opposed to future, postmortem) reference and its exclusive application to the male gender. The question therefore remains, to what *present* aspect of Bororo social existence could such a "customary form" conceivably apply?

One of the most difficult problems in interpreting the Bororo assertion is the failure of the ethnography to specify any pragmatic context for it. Crocker reports, "Informants implied that it is only Bororo *males* who are said to be macaws. This opinion emerged only during direct inquiry into the assertion. Although when the formula was mentioned, informants recognized it as a traditional expression, I never heard it uttered spontaneously" (1985: 38). In a footnote to the phrase "traditional expression" Crocker adds, "The usual phrase such explicit questioning elicited was 'pa-edo

nabure'" (ibid.: 44 fn. 20). If we are dealing with a "traditional expression," a "usual" form, for a "present condition of existence"
(or, as I have suggested, an activity in present, concrete action-
time), the implication is that there is some "traditionally" defined
context or "usual" form of activity associated with the expression.
Obviously, therefore, it is essential to an interpretation of the
tropic character of the expression to know what this context or
activity is.

Now there is one traditionally defined context, one usual form
of activity, in which Bororo men, and men only, assume a key attribute of araras, namely their feathers. This is the performance of
ceremony, for which headdresses and other regalia made of arara
feathers are essential. Ceremonial performance is a most important part of Bororo life and appears to be the most highly valued
form of social activity. Since only men perform the ceremonies,
this figures as the most culturally distinctive feature, the most
valued attribute, of maleness for the Bororo. Bororo men might
well be proud to describe themselves for this reason to an outsider
as "those who 'become araras'" by donning their feathers in com-
munal ritual, even though they would have few spontaneous occasions to use the expression to one another (a possible exception
might be the use of such a formula in the instruction of initiands;
in such a context, the phrase might be instrumental in creating
the cultural meaning of the experience of participation in ceremonial [Jane Fajans, personal communication]).

Arara feathers, particularly red arara tail plumes, are the most
distinctive material attribute of ceremonial activity. Here is what
Crocker has to say about the importance of arara feathers for the
performance of ceremonies.

Nearly all the highly diverse items in the Bororo ritual catalogue must uti-
lize macaw feathers to conform to traditional standards, which are taken
very seriously. . . . The vast majority of clan property, however divergent
in style, employs commonly macaw feathers. Hence these items are essential to Bororo ritual . . . especially those of the red macaw (nabure).
These figure in perhaps the bulk of ceremonial adornments, perhaps because . . . red is the medial color. . . . A frequent excuse for delaying a ritual is that the individuals responsible for making the ornaments have not
been able to acquire the requisite feathers. . . . [Red macaw tail plumes]

are perhaps the most important instance of a scarce non-consumable resource in the Bororo system. (1985: 34)

Ceremony is the mode of activity through which Bororo men reproduce, and thus pragmatically define, themselves and their society as "Bororo." Because the plumes of the red arara are regarded as the most essential components of the outward form of this activity, it would appear that Bororo men feel that they must make themselves araras, in a manner of speaking, in order to make themselves Bororo.

There is, as it happens, an even more cogent and specific piece of ethnographic information to support this interpretation. According to the *Enciclopedia Bororo* (Albisetti and Venturelli 1962: 100), the collective or plural form of the word for "plumes," *aroe*, *is* the word for "soul" or "spirit," as well as for "ancestor," for "Bororo" (i.e., any living member of the tribe, who is thus referred to by the term for "plumes" or "spirit"), and, as the most pertinent for present purposes among a number of further glosses, "any actor representing spirits" (as in a ritual performance, when feathers would be the most important part of his costume).

This denomination of feathers (of which arara feathers are the cultural "prototypes" in Rosch's [1978] sense) as forms of "spirit" is surprisingly omitted by Crocker from his inventory (which he apparently intends to be comprehensive) of cultural grounds for the association of araras with the notion of *aroe* (soul or spirit), but it seems to me to be the most relevant of all to understanding the cultural meaning, and thus also the tropic character, of the assertion of Bororo men that they become araras. It is certainly too consistent with the cultural meaning of feathers to the Bororo, especially in the context of ritual action, to be dismissed as a homonym. The Bororo appear to conceive of "spirit" or inner essence in Aristotelian terms, as the dynamic principle that creates the outward form of a thing. Arara plumes are the most spectacular forms of external appearance of any being in the Bororo world of experience. I suggest that the Bororo conceive of plumes (and above all red arara tail plumes, as the prototypical members of the class) as emblems or forms of spirit because they are the material medium through which the Bororo play the role of spirit toward themselves. By covering themselves with arara plumes, the Bororo create themselves *in the form* of creators of social form.

This point is fundamental, so let me, at the risk of redundancy, attempt to spell out more precisely the steps involved in the transformation of ordinary men into demiurgic araras. By detaching plumes from their original source (the living arara, reduced to its naked essence as a sort of ambulatory plucked chicken) and applying the plumes to themselves, Bororo men metonymically create a new external form for themselves as spirit beings, "actors representing spirits," who are themselves called *aroe* (plumes-spirit). By creating for themselves the external form of spirits and thus playing the role of form-creating spirit toward themselves, Bororo men empower themselves, as spirit-actors, to play the same role toward society at large through their ritual performance. The metonymic assumption by the ritual actors of feathered form as plumed "spirits" becomes the metaphoric basis of their power to reproduce the forms of society through collective ceremony (which, be it noted, is a form of action or "existence in present time"). Both steps of this tropically complex process are concretely mediated by arara plumes, as the criterial feature of self-forming spirit identity. In this culturally specific sense, then, Bororo men "become araras"; my suggestion is that they do so in order more fully to "become" themselves.

"Becoming Araras" Among the Kayapo

This interpretation may be supported from other Central Brazilian peoples of the same cultural area and type as the Bororo. The Ge-speaking Kayapo, with whom I worked, also have a traditional locution glossable as "They [meaning a collective group of Kayapo] become araras." This is the name of the climactic rite of the boys' initiation ceremony, in which the adult ritual companions (*krab-djuo*) of the small boys receiving names in the ceremony construct a circular leaf enclosure, a sort of giant arara nest, in the center of the village plaza, cover their bodies with arara feathers stuck on with their own blood, hang bunches of arara wing and tail plumes from their arms, and run around the inside of the "nest" all night, flapping their outstretched arms and crying "ra-ra-ra-ra" in imitation of araras. "They become araras," in short, to the best of their ability.

For the Kayapo as for the Bororo, red arara feathers, especially the long wing and tail plumes, are the most important item of ritual costume. Such plumes are prototypically associated with the act of flying, and the Kayapo call all ceremonial performance "flying." For purposes of my argument this more than makes up for their failure to call feathers by their term for "spirit," like the Bororo, or even to have a general term for feathers at all. Flying—and the ability of birds high in the sky to see the world as a whole—connotes for the Kayapo the ability to transcend the everyday social world and the power to encompass or subsume it as a whole within a "higher" and more powerful totality. The flight of shamans is one manifestation of this idea, but it is most vividly expressed in the lyrics of the songs with which ritual dancers accompany their steps. As the befeathered dancers (among the Kayapo, women as well as men) move in massed formations around the village plaza, they sing the songs of birds, often in the first person, thus "becoming" the bird (sometimes an arara, sometimes another species) in this sense as well:

> I fly to the trunk of the sun,
> I fly to the trunk of the sun;
> I fly to its trunk, I perch on its branches [i.e., rays],
> And stand there gazing.

> Hurl yourselves up into the sky beside me!
> Hurl yourselves up into the sky beside me!
> With your blood, stick to yourselves the feathers of birds,
> And follow me!

The ability to fly betokened by the feather headdresses, capes, and armlets of the dancers is an integral aspect of the identification with the bird, which the act of dancing and the lyrics of the songs also imply. All imbue the feathered dancer with the reflexive power to get outside his or her ordinary social identity in order to recreate it and the society that is its condition of existence.

Arara plumes and araras also figure in Kayapo death ritual and beliefs in ways relevant to this analysis. Corpses are laid in the grave with their heads pointed toward the rising sun and bunches of arara wing and tail plumes (if available) tied to their arms. The idea is that the soul "flies" out of the grave toward the rising sun. Most souls thereafter take up a terrestrial afterlife in ghost villages in the forest, but the souls of those who possessed the most honorific ritual name "Bemp-" (who in life observe a taboo against killing or eating araras) perch like araras on the rays of the setting sun, called by the Kayapo "the sleeping place of the Bemp." They, of all Kayapo, thus literally "become araras," following, in death, the lyrical exhortation of the bird in the dancing song quoted above.

If they do not explicitly share the Kayapo linguistic equation of dancing with flying, the Bororo clearly share this general set of ideas. After giving the primary meaning of *aroe* as "plumes," the *Enciclopedia Bororo* lists as the second meaning, "anything light as a feather"; the third listing is "soul." The implication is that the soul may be considered to be something "light as a feather," and that this lightness is associated with its capacity to separate from and rise above its bodily form (Albisetti and Venturelli 1962: 100). The Bororo association of the transcendental powers of souls with the "lightness" of feathers is obviously related to the role of the latter as instruments of flight. The association underlying the metaphor thus seems essentially akin to the Kayapo association of dancing with flying. The cultural notions and ritual uses of arara feathers of the two groups therefore appear to be close enough for them to be treated together for purposes of this analysis.

Of Birds and Men Among the Nuer: Further Adventures of Avian Tropes

Crocker's interpretation of the relation of araras and men as a metaphor based on their similarly ambiguous nature as manifestations of both spirit and this-worldly nature seems influenced by E. E. Evans-Pritchard's and T. O. Beidelman's writings on the Nuer. He refers approvingly to Evans-Pritchard's interpretation of totems as "manifestations of spirit" whose specific sensuous attributes are of secondary importance (Crocker 1985: 21; Evans-Pritchard 1956: 77–79). He also cites Beidelman's interpretation of the dappled

coloring of bird feathers or animal skins as bases for their association with "spirit" or the marking of sacred, mediating functions
among the Nuer and Kaguru in support of his own suggestion that
the variegated coloring of araras serves as a basis for their classification by the Bororo as "manifestations of spirit" (Crocker 1985:
30; Beidelman 1968). He does not refer specifically to the Nuer
assertion that "twins are birds," or Evans-Pritchard's and Lévi-
Strauss's treatments of this as a case of metaphor based on the
similarity of twins and birds as "manifestations of spirit," but
these interpretations, particularly Lévi-Strauss's famous reanalysis
in *Totemism*, so closely foreshadow Crocker's own argument that
a critique addressed to the latter unavoidably implies a reevalua-
tion of the former. The Nuer assertion that "twins are birds" seems
at any rate to be so much like the Bororo and Kayapo statements
analyzed above as to invite analysis within the same framework,
as a test of the wider validity of its theoretical premises.

Lévi-Strauss concurs with Evans-Pritchard's interpretation of
Nuer totems as metaphors, as well as his principle that understanding the nature of totemic concepts and their meaning can
only be reached by "following step by step the reasoning involved"
(1963: 79). At the same time, he deprecates Nuer exegeses of particular totems as manifestations of particular spirits as "not very
significant" and criticizes Evans-Pritchard's general interpretation
of totems as symbols of a tripartite relation between men, animals, and "Spirit" as "overly subordinate to Nuer theology" (ibid.:
82). I agree with Lévi-Strauss on all of these points, but it seems to
me that in his reanalysis he also fails to "follow step by step the
reasoning involved," precisely because he too remains "overly
subordinate to" the terms of Nuer theology, specifically in his uncritical acceptance of the Nuer category of "spirit" as the foundation of the "metaphorical" relationship of birds and twins.

Lévi-Strauss bases his analysis on Evans-Pritchard's report that
twins are "manifestations of spiritual power" and are therefore
considered "children of God," without considering why, or in
what specific respect, being a twin should merit this particular ac-
colade. Given this unexamined assumption, however, the rest of
his "step by step" analysis easily follows. Since sky is the abode of
spirit, twins are associated with it as "persons of the above" and

are contrasted in this respect to other humans, who are classed as
"persons of below." Since birds are also of the sky, and thus "of the
above," they are like twins; both belong to the same celestial
order. Moreover, birds may be divided into those unambiguously
of the sky (high or good fliers, birds of pure color) and those more
ambiguously associated with the ground, "birds of below" (ground-
walking and dappled species, such as the francolin or pied crow).
The latter, among birds, are thus more specifically likened to
twins, who although "of the above" are also humans and thus also
linked with "the below." The relation between "birds of below"
and twins is thus understandable as a metaphorical correspondence of their ambiguous combination of associations with sky and
earth, the above and the below, the spirit and the human worlds.
This all seems convincing as far as it goes, but when one recalls
that the Nuer themselves seem to express the relation of twins
and birds as one of substantial identity (i.e., as metonymy between
parts or species of the same order) rather than as one of metaphor,
and furthermore that the entire chain of reasoning relies on the
unanalyzed Nuer category of "spirit" as its basic logical operator,
one is likely to feel that it does not go far enough.

We should begin by asking why twins and dappled *or* ground-
dwelling birds should be considered by the Nuer to be "manifestations of spirit" in a sense that sets them apart from ordinary
creation. Let us try to answer both parts of this question by "following step by step the reasoning involved," as Lévi-Strauss recommends, or at least by suggesting a plausible simulacrum of
doing so, which is all a non–Nuer specialist like myself (or Lévi-
Strauss) can hope for.

Twins are ambiguous with respect to conventional Nuer categories of individual personhood and social identity because they
are in one sense separate individuals but in another share a common identity. In the latter respect, they may be said to be parts of
the same "individual" or totality, on both metonymic and metaphoric grounds (having shared in the same physical gestation and
birth and resembling each other in physical appearance, respectively). They thus appear, contradictorily, to be separated physical
and social individuals, yet to share their physical and social identities. That they are ambiguously both themselves and each other

implies (or at least appears to the Nuer to imply) that they are ambiguous in another sense, namely as both ordinary humans and Other, extraordinary, sacred beings. As nonindividuated individuals, they combine difference and sameness in a manner that contradicts the standards of ordinary human reality. In transcending the structure of ordinary reality, they assume the quintessentially sacred aspect of constituting a common ground of mutually exclusive yet fundamental domains of profane social existence. It is this "sacred" or transcendental aspect as union of contraries, or synthesis of contradictions, I suggest, that is indexed by the Nuer assertion that twins are "Spirit."

The structures of "Spirit," thus understood, have a dual aspect. On the one hand, they implicitly embody the power to encompass, and thus to control or order, the contradictory domains they connect. On the other, they appear themselves to constitute a separate, higher level of reality. From "below"—that is, from the perspective of one of the encompassed domains, in this case the human plane of terrestrial existence—this transcendent level appears as a source of ambiguity, even pollution, and equally of the power to remove pollution and restore the proper distinctions between categories (T. Turner 1977b).

The sky, together with its inhabitants, the birds, constitutes a separate, nonhuman plane, which not only is different from the terrestrial plane of human existence but also stands in a relation to it suggestive of the transcendental qualities and powers of "spirit." It is, to begin with, inaccessibly removed from the human plane, and thus "other" (if not necessarily "Other"). Moreover, it crosscuts its boundaries, remains unconstrained by its limits, and presents a homogeneous frame that encompasses its differences and divisions. Its relation to earth, in short, combines "otherness" and transcendence, and thus constitutes a potential objective correlative of the sacred "Otherness" of twins.

This, it may be suggested, is why the Nuer, like many other peoples, associate their concept of "spirit" prototypically with the air and sky. Birds, prototypically high-flying species of unambiguously celestial habits and light or homogeneous colors, participate in these attributes of the sky in a generic, unmarked sense. Ground-dwelling birds like the francolin or pied crow, however, with their dappled plumage combining the colors of earth and sky, present themselves as emblems of the mediation, interpenetration, or complementary juxtaposition of these contrasting domains in a special, marked sense. They are accordingly regarded by the Nuer as special mediators of the powers of Spirit to the human, terrestrial domain. As birds they are "Spirit," but in a contradictory sense they are also beings "of the below," like humans. They thus constitute an avian parallel to the case of twins among humans.

This parallelism between the relation of twins to ordinary humans and that of dappled francolins to ordinary, high-flying, monocolored birds, we may therefore agree with Evans-Pritchard and Lévi-Strauss, provides the basis of a metaphoric association between them, and this metaphoric relation is the basis for the Nuer affirmation that "twins are birds." The identification of both twins and speckled birds with "spirit," however, is not a simple ascription of quality nor, as such, the basis of a simple metaphorical comparison. It is a complex tropic construct that combines aspects of metaphor and metonymy: similarity between relationships belonging to different domains, which are simultaneously seen in a different dimension as parts of a single substantial continuum. This common substance is "Spirit," which both twins as "persons of the above" and pied crows as "birds of the below" *are* by virtue of sharing the internal structure of mediations that is the substantial being of Spirit. These parallel structures of contradiction and transcendence thus become, not merely metaphorically identical, but metonymically continuous parts of a meta-totality, the cosmic interpenetration of terrestrial and celestial domains which the Nuer conceive as "Spirit."

This combination of essential resemblance and substantial continuity as parts of the same whole defines the relation as one of synecdoche. In both cases, however, the metonymic and metaphoric aspects juxtaposed in the synecdochic relation are mutually contradictory: metonymic continuity links elements that, in the complementary metaphoric relationship, appear as members of opposed and incompatible domains. Twins are both "the same person" and different persons; ground-dwelling and dappled birds are both like other birds, the "birds of above," and different from them, as ground-associated creatures, the "birds of below." The juxtaposition of mutually contradictory tropic relations within the same synecdochic structure is resolved in each case, as we have seen, by regarding it as a manifestation of an ordering power or principle of a higher level ("Spirit") capable of encompassing and mediating the contradiction. The attribute of "Spirit" understood in these terms, however, is not merely a formal or structural property, but a substantial quality. This implies that the likeness of twins and pied crows for the Nuer cannot be merely a question of metaphor but must also be one of metonymy: both participate in, or form part of, the substantial continuum of "Spirit." This theoretical deduction seems more directly consistent than is the purely metaphorical theory with the ethnographic fact that the Nuer assert that twins are not simply *like* birds, but *are* birds, that is, share in the same substantial identity, much as twins do with each other.

The relation between twins and birds is thus not a simple metaphoric association of two entities possessed of an identical attribute ("spirit"), but an identification of two parallel cases of a special (contradictory) kind of synecdoche. This identification is itself a synecdoche, based on both formal correspondence between different entities and substantial continuity between parts of the same entity.

Theoretical Implications: Putting Metaphor in Its Place

These ethnographic cases and the interpretation of their cultural meaning that has been suggested raise a series of concrete questions with general implications for the theoretical understanding of the nature of metaphor and its relation to the other tropes. To begin with the Bororo and Kayapo, what is the tropic constitution of their statements that they "become araras"? More specifically, are they metaphoric, and if so to what extent? How much does an answer to these questions contribute to our understanding of their cultural meaning and construction? Do we learn anything about metaphor and other tropes, or their interrelations, from such an analysis? If so, what are the implications of what we learn for the project of metaphor theory?

The Tropic Structure of the Ritual Process

With respect to the first question, the statements, if I am correct, cannot be interpreted in abstraction from their actional contexts. So interpreted, they are clearly tropically complex. The act of "becoming araras" to which they refer involves metonymy, metaphor, and synecdoche, in ascending order of complexity. There is, first, the metonymic association of ritual celebrants with arara feathers: detached parts of real araras, which now become parts of the new whole constituted by the dancer in his regalia. The feathers themselves are also complex metonymic symbols, representing not only the whole arara of which they previously formed part, but also the arara powers of which they were the specific instruments or products: respectively, the power to fly and the ability to grow feathers, that is, to generate the outward form of arara-ness. These are the powers, I have suggested, that effectively compose the Bororo notion of "spirit" (the "lightness" of feathers for the Bororo metaphorically representing, as I have argued, the same capacity for transcendence that for the Kayapo is represented by their metonymic association with flight). The donning of the feathers as ritual costume, then, implies the metonymic acquisition by the dancers of the arara powers ("spirit") metonymically and metaphorically embodied by the feathers.

Here we come to the second, metaphorical level of the process; for the powers acquired through the donning of the feathers are not, of course, the concrete arara powers of flight and growing feathers, but the human powers of social and cultural creation and reproduction, metaphorically transformed through the ritual performance. To become a flying being metaphorically means acquiring the power to separate oneself from one's normal terrestrial mode of social existence, in which one acts *within* the received framework of social and cultural forms, and to assume an *external* attitude toward that framework as a whole, a bird's-eye view of it, as it were. To don feathered regalia metaphorically figures the power to generate form (in this case, social and cultural form). The generative spirit power to create form which the Bororo believe to be embodied in the feathers is thus metaphorically enacted by both Kayapo and Bororo dancers as they metonymically transform their own forms by donning the culturally elaborated feathered forms of headdresses and other ritual regalia.

The realization of these powers in the efficacy of the ritual performance itself, however, entails a third and higher level of tropic complexity. The feathered dancers, as they move in the dance within the patterns of village space, thereby recreate these patterns, and with them the key transformations of social relations that are the focus of the rites of passage they celebrate. As they produce these effects by their movements and songs, they consummate the metaphorical transformation of the metonymic powers and attributes imbued in their feathered costumes, their songs and dances. The direction of these powers into the reproduction of social form implies that that form is in itself an arara form. The form created by the arara dancers thus assumes, as a whole, the character of the "parts" (i.e., the arara dancers) who create it.

The ritual action of the dancers as they enact, and so "become," araras thus assumes the character of synecdoche, in which the metaphorically related human and arara elements become metonymically defined as the parts of a single whole of spatial and functional relations, which in turn assumes the essential character of its parts.[3] "Synecdoche" may be defined, in general terms, as a specific relationship between metaphor and metonymy, as when a part of a whole (a metonymic relation) also replicates the form of the whole (a metaphoric relation). A good example is the frontispiece of Hobbes's *Leviathan*, in which the giant body of the sovereign is made up of the bodies of his subjects. When the metaphorical associations of transcendence and form-creating power of the feathered costumes, songs, and movements of the Bororo and Kayapo dancers are ritually employed to effect the transformation and re-creation of social relations, the result is a dynamic synec-

---

[3] I have elsewhere argued that the general form of this procedure (i.e., the metaphorical projection of the control exercised over the ritual performance as the principle of the effectiveness of that performance in relation to the external situation or transformation towards which it is directed) is the essential principle of all ritual action (T. Turner 1977b: 61–62).

doche, in which the ritual acts and costumes become parts of a whole which they create in their own image.

The Dialectics of Tropic Meaning

Both the metaphoric and the metonymic dimensions of this synecdochic structure of operations depend upon one further basic feature of araras. This is that araras are not social but natural beings, that is, members of an order of being externally (again, metonymically) related to the order of society. It is precisely this metonymic externality to the social order that allows araras to serve as metaphorical vehicles of transcendence of that order. This metaphorical relation is in turn essential to the metonymic power of those members of the social order who "become araras" to transform and renew it.

The synecdochic structure of the ritual process is the essential framework for maintaining the simultaneous separation and integration of the two orders—nature (as the order of araras) and society (as the order of humans)—upon which the meaning and efficacy of the process depends. The suspension of the separation between the orders of nature and society within the encompassing totality created by the ritual depends in turn on the suspension or mutual relativization of the metaphoric and metonymic relations between them. The essence of this mutual relativization is that the same relation that functions as metonym at one level or context functions as metaphor at the next. The juxtaposition of feathers and men that creates the metonymic totality of the feathered dancer becomes the basis, in the dance, of the metaphoric identification of the feathered dancing movements of the men and the feathered flying movement of the birds. As a corollary, orders or systems of relations (e.g., "nature" and "society") that appear as separate totalities in everyday life become suspended at the higher level created through ritual action as interdependent parts of a single totality.

The relativity of tropes thus depends upon the relativity of totalities (or "domain boundaries," in an alternative jargon). These two dimensions of relativity, moreover, are not just supplementary features of tropes or domains/orders/totalities considered as things-in-themselves, but integral features of their construction.

They are, in other words, fundamental principles of the operational structure of tropic meaning. Tropic meaning is thus essentially dialectical (the essential principle of all dialectic being the mutual relativization and interdetermination of parts and wholes). Tropes and their meanings are dialectical constructs. As such, they must always be understood in terms of their internal relations to their total contexts of use, rather than theorized in abstraction from those contexts (on "internal relations," see Ollman 1976: 26–40, 256–62).

The cultural meaning of the Bororo and Kayapo assertions that they become araras becomes clear only in the context of this synecdochic orchestration of metaphoric and metonymic relations in ritual action. For the Bororo and Kayapo, to "become araras" is to become fully human, in the sense of a social being capable of transcending and recreating the structure and meaning of social life. To attempt to characterize the cultural meaning of a complex process such as this in terms of a single trope (e.g., "it's metaphoric") is to fail to recognize that both tropes and cultural structures are constructed through a "play of tropes," a dialectical process in which meaningful wholes are simultaneously integrated as parts of larger wholes and differentiated into new patterns of relations among their own parts. Not only is meaning constructed in such a process through the interplay of distinct tropes, but the same symbolic elements (e.g., feathers) figure in different tropic capacities at different levels of the structure of the same ritual, myth, or other type of meaningful construct.

Tropes figure as essential aspects of this process, but they need to be put in their place as aspects of more encompassing structures of operations, which constitute their actional contexts and govern their mutual relations and transformations. To conceive of such structures simply as agglomerations of tropes would ignore the dialectical relations of interdependence and transformation among their tropic and nontropic aspects, above all their syntagmatic structures and intentional meanings, which cannot be reduced to tropic categories. These latter aspects play a decisive role in determining how each trope is constituted as an aspect of the whole. A theory of tropes, in short, can supplement, but cannot substitute for, a theory of cultural structures, and both converge in a dialectical conception of the construction of meaning. In any specific case, the analysis of the tropic aspects of expression must be supplemented by an analysis of the specific structures of operations that constitute their context.

Operational Structures

It is crucial that the structures in question be recognized as *operational* structures, that is, as functional procedures for constructing the objects or qualities predicated in the tropic relation. "Structure" in this operational sense bears little resemblance to the "structuralist" concept of static patterns of contrastive relations formulated from a vantage point external to the context and process of construction, such as Saussurian *langue*. From this structuralist perspective, as from that of positivism, the members of the tropic relationship appear as inert, preconstituted objects, "debris of experience" whose significations are already determined by their participation in other, prior structures. The transformation of meaning in the "play of tropes" as envisaged in the foregoing analyses of the Bororo, Kayapo, and Nuer examples presents such a theory with the paradoxical question of where the "literal" meaning or denotative reference of the tropic elements goes when they become engaged in tropic interplay. From the standpoint of a critical, "interactionist" approach, this question closely resembles that often posed to children, of where mommy's lap goes when she stands up. The meaning is in the doing, in the operations, in the construction of the form, in the standing up and sitting down, in the flying and the dancing, rather than the flight, the dance, the araras, or the lap, as positive entities or synchronic relations.

An operational analysis of the role of metaphor in the Bororo and Kayapo statements that they "become araras" thus converges with the interactionist view of tropic meaning outlined earlier. In both, metaphor and metonymy, rather than functioning as primary and mutually autonomous tropic principles, emerge as relatively secondary, contextually specific, and internally related refractions of the more complex master trope, synecdoche. In both cases, a total operational structure is seen to constitute the essential context for both the cultural construction and the analytical interpretation of individual tropes.

The general implications of these conclusions can be stated as follows. Tropes such as metaphor or metonymy must be defined relative to the specific operational structures within which they are embedded rather than as context-free "elementary structures" in their own right. Any theory of metaphor powerful enough to deal with the contextual relativity and transformations of metaphor and metonymy in cultural structures and processes of meaning-construction must therefore become something more than and different from a "metaphor theory."

Tropes as Poetic Constructs

The minimal "complex structure" that has emerged from this analysis is constituted by the interdependence of metaphoric and metonymic relations within the encompassing structure of synec-doche. Our analysis of tropic structure thus converges with the concept of structure developed in the Prague School tradition, as a relationship between the axes of "selection" and "combination" (of which metaphor and metonymy are, respectively, instances). To repeat our earlier conclusion, then, there can be no adequate metaphor theory apart from a more encompassing theory of structure, for the simple reason that metaphor is always defined as an aspect of a *structure* of relations in the Pragueian sense of the word. This conclusion is not only important in itself, but is the essential foundation for formulating the relationship between tropic analysis and a structural poetics.

There is little space here to develop this point, but a reconsideration of Roman Jakobson's formulation of the "poetic function" of language may suffice to indicate the general point. Jakobson defines the poetic function as the projection of the principle of equivalence from the selective to the combinatorial axis of language structure (1960: 358; see also my discussion of this formulation in T. Turner 1977b: 142–45). Although his discussion is primarily concerned with aspects of the sound structure and metrics of poetic language, Jakobson emphasizes that the same principle potentially applies at other levels, such as semantics. Meter, however, provides perhaps the clearest example. Meter consists of taking a certain combination of stressed and unstressed syllables as a "repetitive figure of sound," or metrical foot. This unit, identically repeated, becomes a modular paradigmatic form and, as such, serves as an integral constituent of such higher-level combinatorial forms as lines, stanzas, or whole poems. Rephrased in terms of tropic relations, then, we have a certain metonymic juxtaposition of relations as the basis of a metaphoric equation of distinct segments of verbal content and the further metonymic regimentation of the metaphorically equivalent units thus created into more encompassing units (the line, stanza, or whole poem), which in turn stand in part/whole relations toward even higher levels of structure. This formulation of Jakobson's "poetic function" could stand equally well as a formulation of the tropic structure of ritual in the foregoing Bororo and Kayapo examples.

Metaphor is often discussed as if it consisted only of the figurative identification of the features of source and target overtly involved in the metaphoric comparison, but this of course ignores the process of abstracting those patterns and features in the first place, which is equally part of the metaphor considered as a total operational construct. The essence of this process is the figurative equation of two parallel "systems of differences," *treated for purposes of the metaphoric equation* as metonymic patterns of "combination" of parts into wholes. In this equation, each system as a whole is metonymically represented by the specific feature foregrounded in the metaphoric equivalence. In certain cases, the *whole* system of differences of the source domain may be explicitly applied to the target, as in Lévi-Strauss's (1963) conception of totemism: this does not affect the metonymic character of the internal relations among the different components of each system since here the whole system still metonymically stands for itself. In a metaphor, then, two parallel patterns of metonymic "combination" are made the basis of a paradigmatic "equivalence"; the "principle of equivalence" is thus "projected" from its usual context, the axis of paradigmatic selection, onto that of syntagmatic (metonymic) combination. The resulting structure of relations, a specific relationship between the metaphoric and metonymic dimensions of association, is an instance of synecdoche as defined above.

The poetic function, again to follow Jakobson's formula, thus has a profound affinity with synecdoche. To paraphrase Jakobson's notion of poetic construction in tropic terms, it consists in a "play of tropes" similar to that identified in the ethnographic examples analyzed above: the basic move consists in the transformation of a metonymic combination into a metaphoric equivalence, followed (in more complex poetic or ritual forms such as those discussed) by a further transformation of the metaphoric relation thus established into a metonymic constituent of a higher-level totality. This use of the same pattern of relations in alternating tropic modes to construct higher levels of coherence or integration is the essence of poetic construction, as well as of the Bororo and Kayapo ritual patterns discussed earlier. The same procedure is the essence of synecdoche, in which a part appears as a microcosm (i.e., a metaphorical replication of the same pattern) of the whole to which it (metonymically) belongs.

Poetic meter again exemplifies this synecdochic relation. Metrical feet are *both* segments of differing verbal content metaphorically equated in terms of their identical stress pattern *and* metonymically connected parts of the same whole (the line, stanza, or poem). At the level of the individual metrical foot, the metrical stress pattern *is* the structure of the whole, that is, of the foot as a totality; at the level of the larger whole (the line, stanza, or poem) of which it forms part, it becomes the structure of a part of a whole, although of a special kind of whole, all of whose parts have the same structure. The structure of the *part* in this special poetic sense thus becomes identified with the structure of the whole, much as—to reapply the example of *Leviathan*—individual bodies define Leviathan himself/itself in their own image. The essence of the "poetic function" in Jakobson's sense might thus be formulated, in tropic terms, as an extrapolation of the principle of synecdoche, in which the relativity of relations between different levels of structure is exploited to produce an ambiguous identity between whole and part. In this play of transformations, what is whole at one level becomes part at the next higher level, on the condition that this higher level is itself created by the uniform replication of the same holistic form by the lower-level units. The higher-level whole thus becomes defined as the invariant form of its constituent parts and implicitly charged, as such, with the demiurgic power of self-creation.

My point is not to try to reduce poetics to synecdoche, but on the contrary to emphasize that tropes are neither the unique instances nor the primary sources of the structural relations or principles they exemplify. Rather, they represent only one manifestation of those principles (perhaps the simplest, but not necessarily for that reason the most fundamental). The same principles are manifested at higher structural levels, in more complex and specific forms such as poetic discourse (as we have just seen, following Jakobson), in ritual (as argued earlier in this paper and by numerous others, including myself: T. Turner 1977b), in mythical narrative (T. Turner 1977a; 1985), in forms of social organization such as moiety structure (T. Turner 1985), and in many other domains of language, culture, and social organization.

The Role of Tropes in a Pragmatic Interactive Approach to Cultural Meaning

The Nuer identification of twins and birds involves a complex interaction of metaphor, metonymy, and synecdoche in a play of tropes very similar to the Bororo and Kayapo cases. The feathered bird-men and "flying" dancers of the Central Brazilian peoples partake of ambiguous properties formally similar to those of Nuer twins and pied crows, combining attributes of the opposing domains of sky and earth, birds and men, in emblems of sacred transcendence or "spirit." It is not the figurative freshness of the metaphoric elements in this play that gives meaning to the resulting constructs; rather, meaning is revealed by the way these constructs provide a basis for linking domains that are separate at the level of ordinary existence, but become recognized, through the shift in perspective accomplished by the metaphoric identification, as metonymically contiguous parts of a more powerfully integrated totality brought into being by ritual action and "spiritual" power. Paradoxically, these cultural metaphors of magical transubstantiation have more in common, from both a functional and a structural standpoint, with the metaphorical components of structures of scientific theory analyzed by Bicchieri than with the rhetorical figures of speech and stylistic ornaments which normally serve as type cases in literary and anthropological discussions of tropes. In both the scientific and the cultural cases with which we have dealt here, metaphor and its corollary tropic constructs in the play of tropes serve, not as ornaments for precoded denotative meanings expressed elsewhere by transparent referential constructions, but as the central building blocks in the construction of a meaningful world.

What is accomplished through the play of tropes in both the Central Brazilian and the Nuer instances is that what would be irresolvable ambiguities, antinomies, or contradictions at their own basic level of definition are resolved through their embedding in more encompassing, higher-level structures. This process of hierarchical embedding becomes itself the icon and essential referent of the qualities of transcendence and power that it defines. The construction of the "supersynecdoche" that constitutes at once the framework and the instrument of this embedding process thus generates a final tropic dimension, albeit one accessible only to the critical analyst or actor: irony. For the critical consciousness, the normal actor's unawareness of the reflexive relation between the superhuman powers of "spirit" or ritual action, which are thought to be indexed by the synecdochic construct, and the human creation or ritual re-creation of that construct is the fundamental irony on which the whole system depends. At this point, structural analysis of the play of tropes merges with critical analysis of the alienation of social consciousness, and trope becomes fetish.

The issue of fetishism inevitably arises in a critical discussion of metaphor theory because its tendency to focus on individual tropes as isolated instances leads it to fetishize the trope (and specifically metaphor) as the *fons et origo* of conceptual (and a fortiori cultural) structure and meaning. This tendency is readily discernible among some "single-issue" metaphor theorists like Lakoff and Johnson (1980b), but it is present in more or less implicit and subtle forms among other, more literarily or culturally oriented metaphor theorists with less totalizing (or at least less explicit) theoretical claims. Against this, I have attempted to demonstrate in my analysis of the Bororo, Kayapo, and Nuer data that metaphors and other tropes (including some that have played central

roles in the development of anthropological metaphor theory) occur in their natural ethnographic settings not as pure types but as
relatively undifferentiated aspects of more complex, polytropic
constructs. Theoretically, I have argued that precisely because individual tropes manifest the same principles as the higher-level
(poetic, mytho-poetic, ritual, social, or other) semiotic and pragmatic structures of which they form part, they cannot be assumed
to be the primary sources or a priori forms of these more complex
combinatorial structures. Taking synecdoche (often in variously
multiple, "negative," and hierarchically ramified forms) as the
prototype of such naturally occurring constructs, I have argued
that theoretical analysis and empirical evidence converge to suggest that such syntactically complex constructs of intentional,
pragmatically oriented meaning, rather than individual tropic elements, should be taken as the ontologically and epistemologically
primary forms of cultural meaning and consciousness.

The analyses of the avian tropes of the Nuer and Central Brazilian peoples I have presented have been designed not only to
demonstrate the cogency of this approach but to point out the
ways in which attempting to understand them as cases of individual tropic mechanisms or principles leads to serious distortions of
their pragmatic, intentional, and conceptual meaning. Reducing
these naturally occurring forms to instances of individual tropes,
whether metonymy or metaphor, leads to interpreting them as exclusively ideal phenomena and suppressing their pragmatic and
interactional aspects. Against this, I have tried to show how ap-
proaching the same forms from the top down, so to speak, emphasizing the irreducibility of their character as complex constructs,
leads directly to an awareness of the nature of such constructs
as interactive, pragmatically oriented processes of constructing
meaningful social relations.

Such complex constructs and the pragmatic processes in which
they participate may be subsumed under the general tag of the
play of tropes. The use of this term, however, should not be taken
to suggest that the construction of intertropic relations and syntagmatic forms is somehow secondary or epiphenomenal to the
radical tropic elements involved, or that it lacks significant properties of its own apart from particular tropic principles defined in

abstraction from the "playful" process of construction. On the contrary, the analysis presented leads rather to the conclusion that relatively complex, interactive tropic constructs are the more fundamental basis of cultural discourse and social performance. To privilege individual tropes such as metaphor as the atomic elements or primary sources of the cultural structures in which they are embedded is, in sum, to reify them, in a way ironically analogous to the reified positivist or correspondence theories of objective and referential meaning that metaphor theorists typically see themselves as combatting. A deeper irony is that the attempt to account for metaphor itself by means of a metaphor theory conceived along such lines must lead almost unavoidably to the fetishization of metaphor as the player in the play of tropes.

Embedding and Transforming Polytrope:

The Monkey as Self in Japanese Culture

Emiko Ohnuki-Tierney

When we talk about "tropes," we seldom confront their multiplicity of function—how a symbol functions as a different trope depending upon the context—although it has long been recognized that "meaning" in discourse or "significance" in language (Todorov 1982) is never singular. And this failure to confront persists despite the abundance of literature on tropes. In part, this may be due to a less than satisfactory rapprochement between literary

James W. Fernandez's invitation to participate in the metaphor theory session at the 1987 American Anthropological Association meeting provided me with an opportunity to rework my material on the monkey. I thank him for the invitation and for his detailed comments on an earlier draft. I have profited from recent exchanges with Paul Friedrich, whose comments on an earlier version were much appreciated. Judith Shapiro's perceptive comments and suggestions on this paper were invaluable, as were those by Robert Fogelin, whose own work on figurative speech has been most provocative (Fogelin 1988). The ethnographic and historical work had been done for my own book (Ohnuki-Tierney 1987), first while I was on leave with a Guggenheim fellowship, and then at the Institute for Research in the Humanities, the University of Wisconsin, and at the Institute for Advanced Study at Princeton. The final revision of the paper was completed at the Center for Advanced Study in the Behavioral Sciences at Stanford, California. I am most grateful to all these institutions for their generous support of my research.

fields and the fields of linguistics and anthropology. The former—the homeland of scholarship on tropes—have, until recently, focused on literary works primarily of the elite of various Western societies. Even Bakhtin (1981, 1984b), who highlighted the multiple voices of the carnivalesque dialogism, is not an exception. This emphasis on high culture is in part responsible for a dominant position in the literary fields according to which tropes are individual creations of literary geniuses and not a matter of cultural collectivity. The fields of anthropology and linguistics, in contrast, are the homeland of "hierarchy of meaning" (Ohnuki-Tierney 1981; Todorov 1982; T. Turner 1977b) and multivocal symbols (V. Turner 1967)—all emphasizing the multiplicity of meaning. Yet until recently anthropologists and linguists often regarded tropes as lying outside their fields of inquiry, failing to recognize that they are used in the day-to-day discourse by ordinary people in any culture.

Like meanings, tropes are not frozen onto particular objects or beings, or in their linguistic expressions in the language. In addition to historical changes in its tropic functions, a symbol becomes a different trope depending upon the actor's use. The use of tropes as a *symbolic action* in Kenneth Burke's (1966) sense has been expounded by several anthropologists, including Christopher Crocker (1977) and David Sapir (1977) in their concerns with the social function of tropes, and by James Fernandez (1986) with his emphasis on "performance." Thus, a monkey or a lion is not ipso facto a metaphor, a metonymy, or a synecdoche, but becomes a particular type of trope when used and/or interpreted by particular actors—including interpreters like anthropologists—in a particular context, both social and historical. There are various ways in which multiple tropic functions of a symbol operate.

This paper examines the complex nature of *polytropic* symbols,[1] which I define as polysemic symbols whose multiple meanings in various contexts function as different types of trope. At times these multiple tropes of a symbol are constructed simultaneously by different actors involved in the discourse, and at other times different tropic types are sequentially used/constructed—one type at a time—depending upon the context, historical and so-

---

[1] An early draft of this paper was entitled "Polytropic Symbols and Synecdoche as an Interstitial Trope." Paul Friedrich also uses the term "polytrope."

cial. In most cases, however, multiple tropes are completely embedded or interpenetrated. It is the layering of multiple tropes of
a symbol and the tension between them that has received little
attention.

My choice of focus in this paper is a type of polytrope that
*simultaneously embodies the metonymic and metaphoric prin-
ciples.* I call this *synecdoche,* although traditionally synecdoche
has been regarded as a subtype of metonymy, which is itself a subtype of "contiguity," as we will see later. The focus on this polytrope is chosen because it illustrates best the complexity of the
tropic behavior. On the one hand, it involves the embedding of
more than one trope, thus illustrating the tension between tropic
"layers." On the other hand, it also highlights the tropic function
as a process whereby one trope *becomes* another.

In this paper, I use the term *metaphor* to refer to a trope charac
terized by similarity or shared feature(s) between the tenor from
one semantic domain and the vehicle from another,[2] whereas
the tenor-vehicle relationship for *metonymy* is contiguity or
part-whole within the same semantic domain. I also attempt to
elucidate the distinction between the synecdoche whose metonymy is characterized by part-whole and the one characterized
by contiguity.

Although every trope is defined in many ways, synecdoche is
notoriously pedantic as well as ambiguous—often serving as a label for what does not fit in the better delineated tropes of metaphor, metonymy, and irony. While there is, therefore, considerable
danger in using this term, I do so in order to point to the polytropes that simultaneously involve metaphor and metonymy in a
way that makes them distinct from both metaphor and metonymy
as such.

As a broader issue, this formulation of synecdoche is proposed
in order to demonstrate how the two dimensions of meaning—
contiguity and similarity—are inseparable in poetic processes involving polytropes of this kind. Although the structuralists' notion of two intersecting axes—paradigm and syntagm or analogy
and contiguity—has been a powerful analytical tool, the biaxial

[2] The terms "tenor" and "vehicle" were originally proposed by Richards
(1950). See also Basso 1976.

notion has prevented us from recognizing an almost complete interpenetration between the two axes in our thought. Through a discussion of synecdoche, I hope to show the simultaneous presence in the poetic meaning of these two axes.

All the tropes—metonymy, metaphor, synecdoche, and irony—are symbols in a broad sense. I use the term *tropes*, then, in order to differentiate for analytical purposes poetic meanings of symbols from semantico-referential meanings. For instance, a monkey is a symbol, representing a category of animals. In this case we are dealing only with the semantico-referential meaning of the monkey. But it becomes a trope if someone uses it as a metaphor of the Japanese self, for example. However, I later elaborate how the distinction is artificial and not tenable in the actual perceptual process.

To illustrate my arguments about trope theories in general, I have chosen as an example the monkey in Japanese culture, which has served throughout history as the dominant verbal and visual metaphor of the self for the Japanese. Most, though not all, ethnographic and historical data were first presented in my book *The Monkey as Mirror* (1987), which did not, however, include a discussion on tropes. My paper starts with the Japanese monkey.

The Monkey in Japanese Culture: Human-Animal Distinction

Although the difference between beasts and humans is delineated in every culture, each culture defines the demarcation line in its own complex manner (Ingold 1988). In the normative picture of the Japanese universe, humans live in a harmonious relationship with beings of nature, including animals, who constitute their Shinto deities. The official Buddhist doctrines also offer a fluid demarcation line, since humans and animals alike undergo transmigrations, and thus the essential distinction between them is denied. The demarcation line can be crossed by metamorphosis of a human into an animal, and the act represents a form of transcendence. The Japanese notion of the distinction between humans and animals is in stark contrast to beliefs of the Judeo-Christian tradition, in which the distinction is a divine creation and the transgression of its boundary constitutes an act of blasphemy (cf. Douglas 1966).[3]

Yet there is another side to the Japanese notion of animals. Especially in later history and in the plebeian culture, animals are lowly beasts without supernatural power. Indeed, perhaps the most important curse word in Japanese (which, as we will see, is quite poor in its repertoire of curse words) is "Beast" (chikushō). In the plebeian culture the transcendental and the beastly nature of animals are but the two sides of animal deities—and of humans. The human/animal distinction, therefore, is a highly significant and sensitive issue for the Japanese, as it is for other peoples.

In this regard, the macaque, native to the Japanese archipelago, has served for the Japanese as "the Beast in Every Body" (cf. Fernandez 1986), embodying both the positive and negative sides of animals and humans. Macaques are uncannily similar to humans— at least the Japanese think so—both in their bodies and in their behavior. No other animal has figured more prominently in deliberations of who the Japanese are as humans vis-à-vis animals and as a people vis-à-vis other peoples. The meanings and tropic functions assigned to the monkey therefore enable us to tap the essential dimensions of the Japanese conception of self. The monkey provides us with a strategic window into the Japanese worldview and ethos.

Before urbanization and industrialization chased them off to the mountains or to "reservations," macaques were familiar figures; the Japanese had frequent opportunities to observe them and their behavior. The monkeys often shared the human habitat, coming down from the mountains into the fields. In the spatial schema of the Japanese at the time, the mountains were the abode of deities, whereas the fields belonged to the humans. The macaques ate people's crops, thus sharing their food. In this cosmos, the monkey was a sacred messenger to humans sent by the Mountain Deity.

Perhaps the most important basis for the affinity that the Japa-

---

[3] This line of interpretation, proposed by Douglas, may actually represent only one of many ways of understanding the human/animal relationship in various Western cultures. Some argue that the distinction in the West is only a matter of degree, rather than kind, as seen in the evolutionary theory that is also a product of Western thought.

nese have recognized between themselves and the monkey is the fact that the monkey is a social animal, like humans. The self in Japanese culture is defined in interaction with the other, defined either collectively in relations to other peoples or dialogically in relation to another individual in a given social context.

Let me first briefly discuss the Japanese self in social context, which is clearly expressed in daily discourse and in which the self is always defined dialogically, in Bakhtin's (1981) sense. In Japanese speech, a context-free utterance rarely exists. There are about thirty linguistic forms that may be syntactically classified as pronouns, each chosen on the basis of the gender of the actor, his/her relationship to the addressee, and the nature of the social context, including the degree of formality. Despite this availability of a great number of pronouns and their equivalents, the Japanese usually avoid them. In their stead, speech levels are used extensively. The choice of an appropriate speech level is determined by a set of similar criteria to those used for choosing pronouns. Thus both a pronoun and a speech level are chosen on the basis of the self as dialogically defined in relation to the specific other in a given context of discourse. The position of the self is neither fixed nor permanent. In addition, the first rule for the use of the speech level is to address "the other" (the addressee) as someone of a higher position than the speaker, especially when the two meet for the first time. The other by definition occupies a higher status than the self, be it the dialogically defined other in social context or the transcendental self in cosmology, which is perceived as the other, as we will see shortly.[4] In a discourse that presupposes sensitivity and good understanding of finely tuned rules, powerful insults can be delivered by a strategic choice of speech level.

The dialogically determined self in social context is intimately related to the basic notion of humans in Japanese culture, most succinctly expressed in the two characters that stand for humans, combined to form the term *ningen*: the character for *nin* means "humans," and that for *gen* means "among." Thus humans are by

---

[4]This contrasts with the egalitarian emphasis in American discourse, in which equal status between the two speakers is held as ideal and the hierarchy is expressed only through nonverbal means.

definition *among* humans; an individual human cannot be conceived of without reference to others (cf. Watsuji 1959: esp. 1–67).

In a culture that defines humans only in the company of other humans and in which the self is rarely defined in the abstract, the monkey, the social animal par excellence, is an apt symbol of humanness.[5] At the same time, an animal so similar to humans is threatening. It is dangerously close to being human, pressing hard on the demarcation line in Japanese cosmology between humans and nonhumans. It thereby threatens the throne on which the Japanese have sat, unique as humans and as a people. Seeing the macaques as too close to humans, the Japanese have deliberately established their distance from them. It is no accident, then, that the monkey is seldom involved in the metamorphosis between humans and animals—a theme quite popular in Japanese folktale, since human metamorphosis into animals, most of which are deified, is a form of transcendence. Thus, although metamorphosis of humans into snakes, foxes, badgers, or other animals is welcome and commonly alluded to in folklore, throughout history metamorphosis between humans and monkeys is far less frequent (Nakamura 1984).

Distance is also created by emphasizing the dissimilarities between macaques' bodily and behavioral features and the corresponding features of humans. Thus, when the Japanese wish to accentuate the animality of the monkey, they laugh at its "ugly" eyes, nose, buttocks, and so on, whose equivalents in humans are thus defined as "superior," as I elaborate in a later section of this paper.

Realizing the similarities between monkeys and themselves, the Japanese have long deliberated upon their identity as humans vis-à-vis animals, and as Japanese vis-à-vis other peoples, by using the monkey, as it were, as a sounding board. In part this is done by

---

[5] I do not wish to imply here that the dialogical and dialectical definition of being human in Japanese culture translates into "groupism"—a portrayal of Japanese as always interacting harmoniously with each other and sacrificing themselves for the goals of the social group. This view of "group-oriented" Japanese is sometimes presented in the genre of writing known as *nihonjinron* (theories about the Japanese).

treating monkeys as various tropes in verbal and nonverbal discourse, including visual arts. For example, a newspaper editorial might admonish the Japanese by stating, "We Japanese should not engage in the monkey-imitations (*sarumane*) of the West," just as keeping up with the Tanakas (Joneses) is frowned upon as a "monkey-imitation."

These two sides of the structure of meaning assigned to the monkey in Japanese culture are expressed in historical changes of the meaning of the monkey—from a sacred mediator to a secular scapegoat—as defined in the context of Japanese cosmology. Let me, therefore, briefly discuss the dualistic universe of the Japanese, which constantly ebbs and flows between two opposite principles: purity and impurity, good and evil, order and its destruction. With opposing forces simultaneously present, it is a universe in which negative elements are as integral as positive elements. I posit here that the dualism of Japanese cosmology corresponds to the cosmology represented by *yin* and *yang*.[6]

⁶I further speculate that although historically the yin-yang principle was introduced from China to Japan, a similar dualism had already characterized Japanese cosmology before the introduction of the yin-yang, which then provided a formal expression for the native dualism.

To characterize the cosmology of the Japanese throughout history in terms of the yin-yang principle alone may seem to be a sweeping generalization. Indeed, there has been discernible shift in the basic attitude toward life between Ancient, Medieval, Early Modern, and Modern periods. William LaFleur, for example, documents how the Medieval cosmology (which he refers to as "epistome") was characterized by the notions of karma and *rokudō* transmigration—Buddhistic principles that were unfamiliar to the folk during the ancient period and have lost their strong hold on people in contemporary Japan (1983: 30–31, 59). These Buddhistic principles, however, are basically in accord with the dualism of yin-yang described above. Thus, the *rokudō*, or "six courses," is characterized by "the belief that karmic reward or retribution for anterior acts pushed every kind of being up and down the ladder of the universe" (ibid.: 27). This system of belief espoused relative rather than absolute hierarchy, and each person was individually responsible for his or her own future. The *rokudō* belief, therefore, is in accord with the yin-yang principle, which negates absolute hierarchy.

A development in Buddhism during the Kamakura period (1185–1392) also demonstrates that these Buddhistic doctrines are basically compatible with the yin-yang principle. A movement called *jikkai*, considered of critical importance by scholars of Buddhism, formalized the belief that "good and evil are

Two significant features characterize this type of dualistic universe: first, the complementarity of the two principles and, second, the universe as a process or movement. Referring to the Chinese system of yin and yang, Maurice Freedman remarked that "*yin-yang* is a system of complementary opposition, not (as was sometimes thought in the past) a dualism of mutually antagonistic forces" (1969: 7). As graphically expressed in the iconographic representation of yin-yang, the two small eyes are of paramount significance in indicating that yin always has a yang element and vice versa. Yin and yang, therefore, represent relative proportions or degrees of significance, rather than a separate and antagonistic quality. The two principles are complementary to each other, for neither is meaningful without the other.

The second important characteristic of this type of dualism is that the universe represents a process or movement in which one principle grows in time into the other, and vice versa. When the small eye of yang in yin grows large enough, it becomes yang with a small eye of yin in it. The curved dividing line between the two halves of the iconographic image consequently is not a permanent line. Rather, it represents a movement.

The resulting universe consists of complementarity, a state in which neither asserts absolute hegemony over the other, since the two forces are constantly in slow motion, gradually changing sides.[7] The dualistic principle is thus as much a principle of syn-

---

not seen as absolutely opposite but, on the contrary, mutually dependent" (ibid.: 53).

These examples of formal Buddhistic doctrines illustrate that in terms of basic principles, the yin-yang principle discussed in this section underlies the formal Buddhistic beliefs, just as it underlies the concept of the stranger deities originated in native Shinto religion. In a deceivingly "modernized" and industrialized contemporary Japan, there is a profusion of what I call "urban magic," much of which operates on the yin-yang and Taoistic principles (Ohnuki-Tierney 1984).

For the Chinese yin-yang, see Porkert 1974. For the yin-yang in Japan, see LaFleur 1983; Ohnuki-Tierney 1987 (esp. 130–33); Putzar 1963; Yokoi 1980; and Yoshino 1984.

[7] Seen in this light, noteworthy are the original Chinese characters *liang-i*, which denote dual, but not separate, meanings. As Porkert reminds us, *liang-i* "is used metonymically for *t'ien-ti*, heaven and earth, i.e., the cosmos. There-

thesis and an expression of totality as it is a principle for ordering and classifying the universe, which is conceived as an ever-moving process. In this universe, both the deities and humans are characterized by the dual qualities and powers. The role of ritual is to harness the positive power of divine purity in order to rejuvenate the lives of humans, who also consist of both the negative, degenerative quality and the positive, energizing quality.

In ancient Japan, the role of rejuvenating human lives was assigned to mediators, such as shamans, who were simultaneously musicians, dancers, and religious specialists. At that time, monkeys as messengers of the powerful Mountain Deity were trained to dance human dances, and their dancing was imbued with the supernatural power to heal the illnesses of horses and bless new rice crops and human lives in general. In mythology Japanese deities descend to earth on horseback. Horses, indispensable in agriculture, represent the agrarian establishment (Ohnuki-Tierney 1990a). Likewise, rice is the most sacred food for the Japanese; it is *the* food for commensality between deities and humans, on the one hand, and among humans, on the other (Ohnuki-Tierney n.d. b). Thus the monkey regularly performed its dances at stables of warriors and farmers to protect their horses, and at the time of rice harvest, the monkey danced to bless the new crop of rice. In short, monkeys were sacred counterparts of human shamans, and, like shamans, they possessed mediating powers. Thus the significance of the monkey was determined within the cosmological context in which the principle of purity and impurity has served throughout history as the most important principle of classification in the Japanese universe, as well as the most psychologically powerful set of moral values (for details, see Ohnuki-Tierney 1984: 34–35; 1987: 137–40).

But in this cosmology there is another means of maintaining the purity of human self, besides its restoration by a mediator. It is to transfer its impurity onto a scapegoat. The monkey turns into a secularized beast, shouldering the impurity of humans. From the

fore, *yang* signifies the beginning, while *yin* denotes the completion, and a number of paired complementary concepts are expressed by *yin-yang"* (1974: 13, and generally 9–43; see also Granet 1977: 48).

perspective of the reflexive structure of the Japanese, the monkey as scapegoat carries out the same function as the mediator, but in reverse. As scapegoat, the monkey is laughed at because it is *short* of being human—it looks like a human but is too ugly to be one, and it tries in vain to behave like a human. This conception of the monkey as scapegoat arose later in history than that of the monkey as mediator, although the monkey has been a polysemic and polytropic symbol throughout history, with one or two meanings being dominant during a given historical period.

Thus in the dualistic cosmology whose elements ebb and flow, the monkey has performed a crucial role in the Japanese effort to remain pure—by fetching purity from outside or by removing impurity from within.

Tropic Predication and the Process of Objectification: Poetic Meanings and Significances

The process involved in the predication of the Japanese self upon the monkey as a polytrope encompasses several analytically distinct levels of abstraction. Historical and ethnographic details of the cultural representations of the monkey suggest that the conceptualization of the basic resemblance between monkeys and humans is concretized at another level, where the basic analogy is expressed in the equivalence of a set of selected physiological parts—the eyes, the nose, the buttocks, and the hair—that both monkeys and humans have. Note, however, that these body parts are simply equivalent and do not specify the content of equivalence: monkey eyes are similar to human eyes but not quite the same, and so on. Note also that each body part, such as the monkey's nose, is a metonym for the monkey, just as a human body part is a metonym for humans, by being a part of a whole—a point I return to at the end of this section.

Yet at another higher level of abstraction, worldview and ethos enter the picture in assigning significances—poetic significances, in this case—to the monkey. The poetic significance becomes a particular meaning in a social context, which always has two dimensions: the historical context, which provides the structure(s) of significance, and the context of a particular discourse, which constrains or engenders a meaning(s) of a symbol. Historical contexts are often neglected in our anthropological and linguistic discussions despite an almost commonsensical understanding that the significance of a word or a lexeme often changes with time. In the case of our monkey, its dominant meaning changed over time from mediator to scapegoat, and the change is due to the historical contexts. In the immediate context of verbal and nonverbal discourse, such factors as "framing" (the "definition" of the context as ritual, secular performance, ordinary discourse, etc.) and readings by different actors, whose "voices" are often multiple, are all responsible for the emergence of a particular meaning of a monkey.

A few specific representations of the monkey, chosen from different historical periods, illustrate how the equivalence between humans and monkeys in specific contexts is given various meanings, as actors—through the use of monkey as a trope—move the monkey and consequently the humans (Japanese) around, up and down in the scale,[8] while deliberating upon their own identity.

The oldest record of a monkey figure is the "Monkey Deity" (*Saruta Biko*), which appears in the *Kojiki*, compiled in A.D. 712, and the *Nihonshoki*, compiled in A.D. 720—the two oldest writings that contain accounts of mythical-historical events of early periods. The Monkey Deity appears in an episode in which the Sun Goddess (Amaterasu Ōmikami), considered to be the ancestress of the Japanese,[9] decides to send her grandson to earth to govern there. As the grandson, accompanied by several other deities, is ready to descend, a scout, who has been sent earlier to clear their path, returns to report his encounter with the Monkey Deity at "the eight cross-roads of Heaven."[10] The scout describes the Monkey

[8] Compare the notion of the "quality space" (Fernandez 1986).

[9] Although Amaterasu Ōmikami is popularly believed to be the ancestress of the imperial family, she achieved this status only after the Yamoto state and the imperial system had become well established. Before her, Takami Musubi was the ancestral deity to the imperial family. For details, See Ohnuki-Tierney n.d. a.

[10] The number eight is the most favored in early Japanese numerology, which favored even numbers; eight is the only number under ten that can be

Deity: his nose is seven hands long, his back is more than seven fathoms long, his eyeballs glow like an eight-handled (-handed) mirror, and a light shines from his mouth and from his anus (Sakamoto et al. 1967: 147–48). Saruta Biko explains to the scout that he has come to greet the heavenly grandson.[11]

In Japanese culture, light and mirrors are symbols of deities, and the deities in turn represent the transcendental self of humans. The Sun Goddess, providing light to the Japanese universe, once hid herself in a building,[12] thereby depriving the world of light. Myriad deities assembled in front of the cave and, while making merry music and laughing, told her that there was a superior deity in front of the cave. Her curiosity aroused, she opened the door to the cave and saw herself in a mirror hung from a branch in front of the cave. Upon mistaking her image in the mirror for a goddess superior to her, she reentered the Japanese universe, which in turn regained light. Even today shrines ensconce a mirror as the soul of the guardian deity. In other words, a mirror represented the other that is in fact the transcendental self.

These anonymous "chronicles" describe the Monkey Deity, symbolically situated at a crossroads, as a mediator between de-

---

divided three times and give even numbers. Japanese preference of odd numbers in later history is due to Chinese influence.

[11] For descriptions of Saruta Biko, see also Kurano and Takeda 1958: 127; Philippi 1969: 138, 140, 142; Shimonaka 1941: 118. Various factors identify Saruta Biko as the Monkey Deity. First, the term *saru*, which forms a part of his name, means monkey. Also, the deity's physical characteristics include red buttocks, a prominent characteristic of Japanese macaques (Shimonaka 1941: 118). Furthermore, in the *Kojiki* Saruta Biko is said to have had his hand caught in a shell while fishing (Kurano and Takeda 1958: 131; Philippi 1969: 142)—a behavioral characteristic of macaques, who gather shellfish at low tide. A monkey with a hand caught in a shell is a frequent theme in Japanese folktales (Inada and Ōshima 1977: 392). The description of Saruta Biko's shellfish-gathering behavior and his physical characteristics are cited by Minakata (1972: 401) as evidence for the unquestionable identity of Saruta Biko as an old male macaque. Others have suggested that, since Saruta Biko welcomes the Sun Goddess just as Japanese macaques "welcome" the rising sun with their loud morning calls, he must be a macaque.

[12] In the popular rendition of this episode, the goddess is said to have "hidden" in a "cave." However, Saigō (1967) argues that she "isolated" herself in a "building." See Ohnuki-Tierney n.d. a for details.

ities and humans and between heaven and earth. The transcendental quality is *objectified* as the glowing eyes and anus. Here the monkey is moved up the scale, above humans into the category of deities.

Note, however, that transcendental qualities are assigned to the same body parts that were also selected later in history when the Japanese chose to assign a beastly quality to the monkey. The "monkey face" (*sarumen kanja*)—a common insult in Japanese— is an ugly human face. The face as representative of the entire body and hence the person him/herself is a common metonym found in many cultures besides Japan. It is often expressed in the use of masks, which in Japan occurs extensively in folk festivals as well as the Noh drama. By donning a mask, a person becomes another person represented by the mask.[13] Thus, the metaphor of "monkey face" (*sarumen*) on the surface only laughs at an ugly human face but in fact it declares that the person is not a human but a monkey.

The "monkey eyes" (*sarume*) are human eyes that are sunken and ugly, like those of a monkey. Although the term *okume* (rear eyes; sunken eyes) may also be used to describe this type of eyes, to insult someone one uses the phrase "monkey eyes," not *okume*. The eyes in Japanese culture, as elsewhere, are not simply physiological parts or vision per se. When the three monkey theme—no see, no hear, no say—was originally introduced from China, it represented three *tai* (close identification) based on the philosophy that espoused the use of the three senses in making close observations of the world (Iida 1973: 158).

In addition to being one of the faculties for the perception of reality, the eyes in Japanese culture represent another crucial difference between humans and animals—the capacity for emotion, especially sadness. Emotions have always been highly valued in Japanese culture, and *emotion*, instead of rationality, has been

[13] The ritual and dramatic uses of masks have fascinated many anthropologists. Noteworthy here is the original contribution by Mauss (1985), who pointed out that the Latin *persona* means a mask, although his scheme of universal evolution from *personnage* to *persona* to *personne* is untenable and his emphasis on "legal rights" characterizing the *persona* must be reevaluated (Carrithers, Collins, and Lukes 1985). On the mask, see Hollis (1985).

considered unique to humans. Of all emotions, *sorrow* has been particularly important throughout history, and shedding of tears has been considered a unique human behavior. For example, we find debates over this matter in Medieval literature (LaFleur 1983: esp. 34–35), and an important element in the Kabuki theatre is a number of stylized ways of crying. Importantly, the traditional repertoire of monkey performance includes the replication of these various types of crying in the Kabuki theatre by a monkey. In contemporary Japan, the *enka*, a genre of folk songs characterized by pathos and sadness, is extremely popular, and movies are classified into three categories by the number of handkerchiefs necessary to soak up the tears, with "the three-handkerchief movie" being the best.

The eyes therefore represent the unique human capacity for sadness; through the eyes humans *perceive with senses* and *feel with emotions* the outside world.

In one performance from the traditional monkey repertoire, a trainer, representing his monkey, sings a song in which the monkey laments: "Because of the karma of my parents, my face is red, my eyes are round, and, in addition, my nose is flat and ugly" (Yamaguchiken Kyōiku Iinkai Bunkaka 1980: 41). The monkey imitates weeping, covering its eyes with a handkerchief. This seemingly simple performance embodies complex workings of the face and eyes as polytropic symbols that allow us to tap the core of the Japanese cosmological scheme involving the relationship between humans and animals.

Similarly, "the monkey hip" (*sarugoshi*) is a human hip that looks like the hip of a quadruped. It should be noted here that the vital step in the training of monkeys for performance is teaching them bipedal posture, which symbolizes the uniqueness and superiority of humans over animals. The choice of the hip (*sarugoshi*), points not simply to the anatomical difference or difference in physical appearance, but to the difference between quadrupedal animals (*yotsuashi*) and bipedal humans, which is crucial in the Japanese conception of who they are as humans.

Because a major difference between humans and animals is that humans alone are able to control sexuality, the *red* buttocks of the monkey symbolize for the Japanese the uncontrolled sexuality of monkeys or of animals in general. Note that not only the control of sexuality but also the control of the bodily functions in general is involved here. Often during a performance, a monkey, unlike "trained" humans, may urinate and defecate when threatened or excited. When a monkey does this out of nervousness and excitement, children in the audience almost always become excited; they have just mastered toilet training, and thus the monkey's inability to control the bodily functions allows them to feel quite superior to the monkey. The red buttocks, therefore, express something quite opposite of the dancing that was once the primary aspect of the monkey performance, for dancing represents the utmost control and willful and skillful manipulations of the body. While the dancing monkey is endowed with superhuman power to heal illnesses of horses, the monkey with the red buttocks is a beastly animal, which cannot control its basic bodily functions, let alone its sexuality.

Note also the Japanese "definition" of the monkey as "a human minus three pieces of hair." Head hair is a unique physiological characteristic of humans. As in many cultures, head hair in Japanese culture is a powerful metonymic symbol, representing the essence of a person (Yanagita 1951: 121–22). There are numerous practices in which a person's hair is used to represent the person him/herself. Even today a Japanese who prays to a deity—for instance, for the recovery from an illness—will cut a tuft of head hair and offer it at a shrine, in lieu of him/herself. In this "definition," the monkey is characterized as lacking the quintessential quality of being human.

In sum, the physiological parts of the monkey that are simple equivalents to human parts may be objectified positively or negatively, depending upon which poetic meaning is given to the monkey in a particular historical context and by a particular actor. The metonymic parts representing the monkey are defined and redefined through positive and negative analogies to the equivalent human body parts and thus objectify certain crucial characteristics that distinguish the two in Japanese culture. Actors can use not only body parts but also behavioral as well as moral and aesthetic characteristics, such as sensory and emotive "feelings," to strategically move the monkey and, conversely, human beings or a particular human up and down a scale. By so doing, the Japanese can "adorn" or "disparage" (Aristotle 1960: 187) themselves by moving the monkey. Instead of using one symbol to adorn and another to disparage, the monkey as a polytropic and polysemic symbol can be both a (spineless) jellyfish, a metaphor for disparaging a man, and a (brave) lion, a metaphor to adorn a man.

Thus, in addition to establishing analogy between the monkey and the humans, the selection of certain body parts elucidates how the Japanese have defined and redefined their own notion of being human. Put another way, we learn what characteristics in particular are seen to be important in defining humans by the choice of these body parts and the meanings assigned to them.

Metaphor, Metonymy, and Synecdoche

In the remainder of this paper, I offer a formulation of synecdoche and delineate the interrelationships between synecdoche and metonymy, on the one hand, and between synecdoche and metaphor, on the other. Each tropic type is seen to emerge during a *continuous* conceptual process in which one tropic type transforms into another as actors "play" with the tropes. I begin with a discussion of metaphor and the semantic tension involved in it, since it is this tension that offers us an insight into synecdoche as defined here.

Semantic Tension in Metaphorical Predication

That both similarities and dissimilarities are at work is often pointed out in discussions of metaphors. Most frequently the arguments point to the presence of similarities in the dissimilar. Aristotle emphasized this when he stated, "a good metaphor implies an intuitive perception of the similarity in dissimilars" (1960: 212–15 [3: 1412a 1412b]). Kenneth Burke's well-known statement reads: "It [metaphor] brings out the thisness of a that, or the thatness of a this" (1955: 503). In discussing the power of metaphor, Clifford Geertz, while stressing semantic tension, explains, "When it works, a metaphor transforms a false identification . . . into an apt analogy; when it misfires, it is a mere extravagance" (1973: 211). S. J. Tambiah emphasizes that metaphor "highlights a resemblance" (1968: 189).

Although metaphor does foreground a particular feature of similarity in the dissimilars, I would argue that for certain metaphors the tension between dissimilarities and a similarity (or similarities) of the tenor and the vehicle is the source of their metaphorical power, as I. A. Richards (1950) long ago emphasized. Rather than simply offering a delightful discovery of an unexpected similarity in the dissimilars, a metaphor may present an uneasy tension pointing to an unwelcome similarity between the tenor and the vehicle.

A brief comparison of the monkey as self in Japanese culture with such well-known metaphors as "George the Lion" and "The Attorney General is a jellyfish" (Fernandez 1986) will illustrate my point about the tension. A lion or a jellyfish has such a remote resemblance to a human that its use as a metaphor places in prominence only one particular feature of unexpected similarity. In these cases, the "poetic genius" is emphasized; the actor is credited with powerful creativity, evident in his/her ability to unveil the unexpected similarity. The distance between the semantic domain of the tenor and that of the vehicle is so great that the two domains remain separate except for that feature—the lion's courage or the jellyfish's absence of backbone. Consequently, the metaphoric predication does not bring the two semantic domains closer together. Despite the particular feature of similarity, basic dissimilarities remain intact.

In contrast, there is another type of metaphor whose affective power rests on the tension between semantic categories. In the case of a monkey in Japanese culture, the proximity between the animal and humans is recognized even without a metaphorical predication. The role of metaphor then is to bring to the fore an inherent metonymic relationship (sometimes uncomfortable to acknowledge) between the two semantic categories by emphasizing similarities. Suddenly, then, humans and monkeys are placed side by side in *a metonymic relationship through the metaphorical emphasis of the likeness.* In a given context, a particular feature of similarity stands for the general analogy shared by the two domains, which at the referential level are kept separate. The semantic tension underlying the monkey as a metaphor derives from the specific nature of proximity between the two domains that Japanese culture assigns.

The case of the Japanese monkey is an example of a general phenomenon in which an animal considered close to humans in a given culture is used as a metaphor. Edmund Leach (1964) illustrates varying degrees of proximity or distance seen to exist between humans and certain animals in various cultures. "Dog" becomes a powerful insult in British culture precisely because dogs are seen as so close to humans that a clear demarcation line must be drawn; the tension inherent in the tenuous classificatory boundary is the basis for the metaphor to turn into an insult.

Thus macaques and dogs have served for the Japanese and the British, respectively, as "the Beast in Every Body" throughout history precisely because these animals are uncannily and often unwelcomely similar to humans when they are or should be dissimilar. The "mission" of some metaphors is not to offer an insight into certain similarities between two dissimilar forms. Rather, their mission is powerful precisely because they simultaneously juxtapose similarities and dissimilarities, thereby creating the tension that is the source of affectivity of metaphor, which in turn is the source of the metaphor's illocutionary power.

Put the other way, "the Lion" leaves George and the rest of humans alone, except for a particular feature of similarity, while "the monkey" or "the dog" is ready to lump humans and these animals in a single category. We should be aware of the difference between these two types of metaphor, since, as a consequence, the nature of the performative power of metaphors in each type is different.

Synecdoche as an Interstitial Trope

The metonymic relationship established by metaphoric predication must be examined further in order to elucidate the interrelationships among tropes. I do so by examining the conceptual principles involved in the figures we call the "mediator" and the "scapegoat"—the two roles assigned to the monkey in Japanese culture. Although "mediators" and "scapegoats" are not tropes, the principles that define these figures are of contiguity and analogy/similarity—the conceptual principles defining metonymy and metaphor, respectively.

Both mediator and scapegoat stand in metonymic relationship to the self of humans. The monkey as a marginal deity is situated at the edge of the semantic category of deities or Other and thereby next to the semantic category of humans. It is metonymically related to the self through the contiguity principle. Conversely, the monkey as scapegoat is positioned within but at the margin of the domain of humans or Self, as expressed succinctly in the aforementioned Japanese "definition" of the monkey as "a human minus three pieces of hair." In relation to the self, then, a scapegoat is closer than a mediator. A scapegoat is one's own kind but is lacking some qualifications; it is metonymically related to the self through the part-whole principle.

The monkey's proximity to humans is in turn the basis on which the monkey becomes a messenger/mediator, bringing, during a ritual, the purifying energy of deities to humans whose life, without the replenishment of purity, would degenerate into a state of impurity. Humans, who consist of both purity and impurity, are placed in an analogous relation to the monkey as mediator through sharing purity. A scapegoat, on the other hand, at the classificatory margin, becomes the repository of impurity—it shoulders the impurity of the self, which in turn becomes purified. It is analogically related to the self through sharing of impurity. These three structures—self, mediator, and scapegoat—are analogous structures, consisting of both purity and impurity; purity is foregrounded in the case of deities and mediator, but impurity overshadows purity in the case of scapegoat.

Thus, the monkey as a mediator belongs to a semantic category distinct from, but next to, the category of humans, and is linked to the latter through *contiguity* in the syntagmatic chain, while it is also related to the latter through *analogy* in the paradigmatic chain. The monkey as scapegoat transforms itself from a metonym of humans through contiguity, to a metonym of humans through a part-whole relationship by occupying, albeit at the margin, the same semantic domain, and finally to a metaphor of humans by sharing impurity. The monkey as scapegoat, therefore, is related to humans through being in a *part-to-whole* relationship, as well as through the *analogy* of sharing impurity.

The monkey as mediator and the monkey as scapegoat represent two types of synecdoche characterized *simultaneously* by analogy and either contiguity (A) or a part-whole principle (B). These two types of synecdoche are two phases of the *conceptual process* of symbolic representation. In the case of the monkey symbolism, its historical transformation in fact was from synecdoche A to synecdoche B, but the model is not meant to represent a historical process. As a general model, synecdoche B may transform into synecdoche A as well.

Synecdoche B is the type of trope most broadly applicable to studies of ideology and political economy. Defining synecdoche as being characterized by whole-for-part or part-for-whole relations, Friedrich points to its "terrible power," which "surfaces from its workings in the political economy when allegorical individuals . . . or an entire population ('The Americans,' 'The Germans,' 'The Russians') . . . are accused of atrocities and mass crimes in which only a tiny fraction of the population was engaged" (1989: 306).

We can also turn his argument around to find the beguiling power of synecdoche. "We, the Japanese," for example, often negates the presence of minority groups, who are represented by the dominant group, to which "we" in fact alone refers. Thus the label, "the Japanese," has always meant the dominant Japanese— the elites in the agrarian sector—and yet it has been seen as "naturally" representing *all* Japanese (see Lincoln [1987: 152] for a reference to a similar use of pronouns of the first person plural).

This is clearly illustrated by "the special status people"—a minority group in contemporary Japan.[14] In my original work on the monkey (Ohnuki-Tierney 1987), I examined the historical transformations of the meaning of the monkey in relation to the historical transformations of the meaning assigned to the special status group, often referred to as the former "outcastes," because

[14] I borrow from Susan Tax Freeman the designation in English of "the special status group," since it has neither positive nor negative connotations and so enables me to refer to people whose meaning in Japanese society has changed through time. In Japanese they are referred to as *burakumin* or *hisabetsu burakumin*.

monkey-training is one of the traditional occupations of this group. The meanings assigned to the special status people, or at least to some of them, have gone through the same transformations as the meanings attached to the monkey—from mediator to scapegoat.

Historical evidence suggests no unilinear descent line linking the special status people in different historical periods as a cloistered social group. Although some have argued that they are of Korean descent, there is very little evidence that these people actually had a different ethnic origin from the majority of the population. Throughout history they have held primarily non-agrarian occupations. Some were traders, artisans, religious specialists, and performing artists. Others held occupations that dealt with culturally defined impurity, including specialists in purification rituals and a number of occupations related to animal and human deaths. The formation of the special status people as a minority in Japanese society was a gradual process, resulting from interplay among a number of factors. They include, for example, the development of a hegemonic role played by the agrarian value system that devalued nonagrarian occupations. Another factor was the establishment of impurity as radical negativity sometime during the latter half of the Medieval period, resulting in an extremely negative valuation of occupations dealing with death and other culturally defined impurity. In 1572 people in such occupations became legally codified as "outcastes" in Japanese society. Since then, the special status people have been a minority in Japanese society. Above all, they have been seen as "impure."

In relation to Japanese society at large they constitute synecdoche B, being subsumed by "we, the Japanese." Like the monkey as a scapegoat, the special status group is related to the dominant Japanese through the sharing of impurity, which the dominant Japanese have imposed on these people, and through being part to the whole of Japanese society. In addition, "the Korean descent theory" exemplifies how a minority–dominant group relationship may be inferred to be a historical development from synecdoche A to B so that the dominant group can deny its identity with the minority.

This conceptual model is then a general model explaining the relationship between dominant and minority groups. Synecdoche

B explains the negation of the presence of minorities in the discourse in which the generic "we." or "the Americans," for example, is used to refer to an entire population. The model also serves to explain how an establishment of synecdoche A (the entire social group) from two separate semantic categories (two distinct social groups) is implicitly suggested and understood as an *actual* historical process. An equation of the conceptual and the historical processes thus creates a tension, threatening to separate into two distinct categories.

The conceptual model draws attention to the fact that synecdoche A inherently involves the uneasy tension between the two original semantic categories; the tension inherent in synecdoche B is the threat of fission into two distinct categories. A and B are, therefore, *interstitial* tropes in the sense that they involve the process of *becoming*. Our poetic construction thus represents a movement of thought; it involves temporality. Just as metaphoric predication involves a process, both types of synecdoche are not simply the end results of conceptual process. Rather, they embody two processes: the analogic synthesis of classificatory categories and the discursive process of classificatory fission. The two modes of thought are thus enacted as conceptual processes in our poetic construction of synecdoche.

In sum, synecdoche is not only characterized by the embeddedness or interpenetration of more than one tropic function but is also interstitial, or even more accurately, processual. Each tropic type is seen to emerge during a *continuous* conceptual process in which one tropic type transforms into another as actors "play" with the tropic principles, while in fact retaining a previous trope as it transforms into another.

Polytrope

The fluid and complex nature of polytropes, especially synecdoche as defined and illustrated above, challenges trope theories, especially the biaxial model. The two dominant approaches to tropes are (1) one that makes a fourfold distinction of metaphor, metonymy, synecdoche, and irony; and (2) one that recognizes only two types, metaphor and metonymy. Without going into the details of the two schools and their arguments, my discussion focuses upon the interrelationships between metaphor, metonymy, and synecdoche.[15]

For Jakobson (1956), Lévi-Strauss (1966: 150), and Leach (1976), metaphor is characterized by similarity, and metonymy is characterized by contiguity, cause and effect, end and means, and container and content;[16] in this schema, synecdoche is subsumed in metonymy. Recognizing these two types of tropes, these scholars have wrestled with the interrelationship between them. Lévi-Strauss called attention to the "transformation and counter-transformation" between metonymy and metaphor, as noted earlier. Similarly, those who hold metaphor as the most central of all tropic figures emphasize that a metonymic principle is often involved in metaphor. For example, Paul de Man (1979: 65–66) insists that striking metaphor depends upon metonymic connections, and Gerard Gennette (1972: 42–43) emphasizes coexistence and mutual support, or the interpenetrating relation of metaphor and metonymy.

Metaphor as Temporal Movement

Even when these interpenetrations and copresence are recognized, the biaxial model,[17] especially that of Lévi-Strauss, has denied the essential fluidity of tropic movements by equating metaphor with paradigm and offering primacy to metaphor.

First, in this model, metaphor is equated with simultaneity, and metonymy, characterized by contiguity, is seen to have temporality, or "diachrony," as Lévi-Strauss expressed it. In the original use by

---

[15] Needless to say, the available literature is too vast even to present an adequate overview of this field of trope theory. Some representative overviews are included in: Black 1962; Culler 1981; Ortony 1979; Ricoeur 1987; Sacks 1979; Sapir and Crocker 1977; Todorov 1987; White 1983.

[16] Leach separates out the "cause and effect" principle to set up a third figure, signals.

[17] This dualism is persistent in trope theories and inherent even in Susanne Langer's (1980) discursive vs. presentational symbols, although her emphasis on the presentational symbols is otherwise an important perspective that has not received enough attention.

the Prague School, the term *diachrony* refers to irreversible historical changes. Yet Lévi-Strauss (1967: 208) *mis*uses the term—as Tim Ingold (1986) and Terence Turner (1977a) point out—by equating it with the temporal sequence involved in *la parole* in his scheme of /synchronic : diachronic :: *la langue* : *la parole* :: paradigm : syntagm/. Lévi-Strauss's diachrony then refers to speech—*la parole*, actual utterances that are, in his scheme, permutations of the linguistic codes (*la langue*). Although speech does have temporality, by emphasizing it, Lévi-Strauss ultimately denies the temporality in the other pole, involving paradigm and metaphor.[18]

Second, when the biaxial framework is combined with an emphasis on paradigm and metaphor, it not only denies the importance of the syntagmatic chain, which is the temporal dimension in this scheme, but it also negates the temporality or the processual nature of metaphor itself. As seen in the formation of both types of synecdoche we have discussed, a metaphor *in practice* entails movement—a process whereby the semantico-referential categories of the tenor and the vehicle are moved closer together

---

[18] Because I have stressed temporality (and processuality) in the poetic process, let me clarify my use of this term. Temporality in the poetic meaning should be distinguished from various other terms—diachrony, history, "process" as in "ritual process," etc. It should be distinguished from diachrony in the sense of irreversible historical changes, as defined by the Prague School, or diachrony as *la parole* in the Lévi-Straussian scheme. Diachrony, history, and historical processes all involve actual time flow, which is not involved in the temporality or processuality of poetic construction. Poetic temporality is akin to historicity or historical consciousness—the way people experience and understand history. People often relate the past and the present either metaphorically through analogy or metonymically through contiguity. Thus historical consciousness is characterized by temporality as a mode of thought, but does not involve temporal process itself. Likewise, concepts of time do not include actual flow of time, but rather patterns of thought (Ohnuki-Tierney 1973). "Process," as in ritual process or the process of social interaction, on the other hand, does involve time flow, and yet it should be distinguished from historical process. I should like to reserve the term "history" or "historical process" for temporal processes that are of far greater magnitude than the process involved in ritual or a social process, including discourse. What I am stressing here is a tripartite distinction: temporality in poetic meaning and modes of thought; short duration of time flow as in ritual process and social interaction; and historical processes.

as a result of the actor's enactment. Perhaps we must reexamine not only the biaxial model in figures of speech but also the distinction seen between two modes of thought—the analogic and the discursive or prepositional; although figures of speech and modes of thought should be distinguished, they are nonetheless related, requiring further inquiry into interdependence, in addition to distinction, between the two modes of thought.[19]

Why Master Trope?

Another major controversy in trope theory is the choice of a master trope. The orthodox argument—held since Aristotle (1960: 187 [3: 1405a], 206 [3: 1410b]) and by many, including Vico (1961: 87 [I 404]), Jonathan Culler (1981), de Man (1979), Fernandez (1986), and Stephen Ullmann (1964)—has been that metaphor is the figure of figurality or the master trope, that is, the most creative and powerful of all tropes. Recently, David Sapir (1977), Tzvetan Todorov (1970), and others have argued that synecdoche is the figure of figurality. Sapir's synecdoche is characterized either by anatomical mode (whole-for-part or part-for-whole) or taxonomic mode (genus-for-species or species-for-genus). Terence Turner also chooses synecdoche as a master trope, while assigning it a special kind of part-to-whole relationship: "a specific relationship between metaphor and metonymy, as when a part of a whole (a metonymic relation) also replicates the form of the whole (a metaphoric relation)" (see his contribution to this volume, p. 148). Friedrich, on the other hand, would choose irony if he were forced to choose only one trope (personal communication).

The question of the choice of a particular trope as *the* figure of figurality seems spurious when we consider that a particular meaning or a tropic type emerges in a social context as it is used or interpreted by an actor (see Ohnuki-Tierney 1990a). In this paper, I chose to focus on synecdoche, not because I consider it to be the master trope or figure of figurality at all times but because such a formulation seems to offer insight into the dynamics and complexity of polytropes.

[19] A further discussion of this topic is beyond the scope of this paper, however, and would involve a more systematic examination of the terms and concepts such as the analogic and the discursive.

Summary and Conclusion

Using the Japanese monkey as an example, I have presented a formulation of *polytropic* symbols—symbols that transform into different tropic types in a given context. The foregoing discussion offers several important points that have broader implications for our understanding of the process and structure of poetic construction and tropic behaviors in general.

We recall that the first stage in the poetic construction of the meaning of the Japanese monkey is the selection of physiological parts. Each constitutes a metonym for the monkey, but these metonymic forms are chosen to represent the monkey because of their metaphoric capacity for linking monkeys with humans. These forms are, therefore, simultaneously metonymic in relation to the whole monkey and metaphoric in relation to human body parts. The monkey as a metaphor, therefore, is based upon "fragments of syntagmatic chains" (Lévi-Strauss 1966: 151), but these syntagmatic fragments constitute the distinctive features defining the monkey precisely because of their capacity for metaphorically linking monkeys with humans. As a general model, I suggest that the syntagmatic or metonymic chain remains embedded in a complex trope like the monkey, and, conversely, the paradigmatic power is engendered because of its syntagmatic capacity.[20]

The process of metaphor-metonymy transformations involves several "stages" of poetic construction. The physiological parts of the monkey are chosen as metaphors because they represent certain crucial behavioral characteristics that are seen by the Japanese to constitute essential distinctions between humans and animals. But these behavioral characteristics in turn represent moral/aesthetic characteristics that mark "humanity" as opposed to animality. Thus, the "monkey eyes" represent (1) a physiological part; (2) the behavioral function of vision; (3) the perceptual/in-

---

[20] The original insight into the transformation and countertransformation between metaphor and metonymy was offered by Lévi-Strauss (1966: 150), whose understanding, however, is constrained by his flawed biaxial model, as noted above. See also Fernandez (1982: 557–62; 1986: 43–51) for detailed discussion of this subject. The arguments by these scholars are summarized in Ohnuki-Tierney 1987: 218–21.

tellectual capacity of humans to perceive reality; and (4) the aesthetic/moral capacity to feel emotions, especially sadness. Importantly, these stages remain embedded as multiple layers that constitute the source of complexity of a polytrope in general.

As exemplified by the Japanese monkey, a trope with a complex structure of meaning is often embedded in the cosmology of the people who use it. A broader implication is that symbolic forms anchored in cosmology have the capability to engender illocutionary power. They are likely to remain powerful for a long time, as exemplified by the Japanese monkey, since these forms often stay important in cosmology even when their meanings undergo significant changes through time.

The preceding discussion makes it sufficiently clear that the monkey is never an "objective" entity in nature offering its morphology and meaning as given. Poetic meaning is involved even in the perception of the monkey—its eyes are glowing or sunken and ugly or even both. A broader implication of this finding is that an artificial separation of a referential meaning and a poetic meaning is untenable. There is never "pure reference," and "poetry also refers," as Friedrich emphasizes (1986: 126).[21]

Another broader implication of the poetic construction of the Japanese monkey is how *objectification*[22] constitutes a continuous interactive process whereby a subject interacts with the external world through a simultaneous externalization of itself and reappropriation, in turn, of this externalization. Thus, the Japanese themselves are construed and redefined as they assign meanings to the monkey because the latter forces the Japanese to contemplate themselves. Neither the subject (the Japanese) nor the object (the monkey) claims priority; both are becoming through the process of objectification.

While polysemes of a polytrope do often constitute "layers," it is also important to understand the construction of these tropes as

[21] See also Friedrich 1979; Ohnuki-Tierney 1981, 1988. See also "Speech acts" of Searle (1983b), and Silverstein's (1976) critique of the Austin-Searle approach in which a clear-cut distinction is made between "performative" acts of speech and the "semantic" content.

[22] See Hegel (1977) and Benjamin (1986). For most recent work, see Miller (1987) and Humphrey (1988).

movements. In particular, I argue that not only metonymy but also metaphor represents a movement, thus involving temporality. In order to elucidate this point, I propose a definition of synecdoche: *a polytrope that involves analogy between two semantic domains metonymically linked as a result of metaphorical predication.* As an interstitial trope, a synecdoche thus must meet two conditions: (1) two *distinct* semantic categories *become* metonymically related—either through part-whole relationship or through contiguity; and (2) there is an interpenetration or embeddedness of metaphor and metonymy. On the one hand, synecdoche is distinguished from metonymy, which is also characterized by part-whole or contiguity principles, by the involvement of two semantic categories. On the other hand, synecdoche is distinguished from metaphor by the formation of the metonymic relation between the two domains.

As for the conceptual principles involved in relating a vehicle to a tenor, synecdoche involves the metaphoric and the metonymic principles, rather than an altogether distinctive principle. As a trope representing the *interpenetration* of metaphor and metonymy, however, synecdoche is a more complex form of trope and thus differentiates itself from an ordinary metonymy or metaphor.[23]

[23] Since synecdoche is a more complex form of trope than metaphor or metonymy, one might suggest that it involves a higher degree of articulation or motivation than metonymy, in which a part and the whole are connected "intuitively" or "naturally," as in the case of a leaf representing a tree. Yet it is questionable whether the part-whole relationship of synecdoche is always articulated in the mind of the actor who uses it. Fernandez's (1986: xi–xii, 50) concepts of "revelatory incident" and "primary process" focus on times when an actor suddenly becomes cognizant of the meaning of a symbol or a figure that he/she has not been aware of previously. Actors are not always fully cognizant of either the meaning of a symbol or its tropic capacity. The analytical importance of an actor's role or the performative power of a trope must also be distinguished from consciousness or articulation of the meaning of a symbol. Even political leaders using the synecdochic "we," thereby negating the presence of minorities, for example, may not have articulated this synecdochic exclusion. Furthermore, if we take the life course, as it were, of a trope—from the time a poet, for example, "invents" a tropic figure to the time when it becomes a dead or frozen metaphor—we see various degrees of motivation on the part of actors in a given context. Elsewhere (Ohnuki-Tierney 1990b) I have discussed the *routinization* of the meaning of a symbol in historical perspective.

Synecdoche, like metaphor, presupposes both a classificatory scheme—underlying two distinct categories—and a synthesis of categories through analogy. Furthermore, its metonymic dimension reveals a *movement* whereby a new category is created. Seen in this light, synecdoche, governed simultaneously by metaphoric and metonymic principles, represents a trope that is truly processual.

The notion of synecdoche in particular and that of polytropes in general therefore seriously challenges both the biaxial framework of the structuralist approach to tropes and to discourse in general, and the choice of a particular tropic type as the master trope. Even when scholars emphasize the interdependence between metaphor and metonymy, their representation through a Saussurian image on counterposed axes falsely denies their interpenetration. It fails to portray the essential characteristic of polytropic symbols, which transform from one trope to another in a fluid process. Synecdoche as defined above illustrates how the two axes interpenetrate, thereby showing how the equation of /paradigm : syntagm/ with /synchrony : temporality (diachrony)/ is false. Our monkey as a polytropic symbol illustrates the interdependence of the two axes as they conjoin in a continuous process in which a symbol is transformed from one tropic type to another. Both axes involve temporality and the two join hands in the movements of a polytropic symbol. Likewise, the choice of a particular trope as the master trope—often metaphor, but recently synecdoche or irony—also negates the contextual construction of a tropic type. More generally, as with meanings, tropes are not out there waiting for us. They are *not* things unto themselves. A particular symbol is construed to be a particular trope by an actor in a given social context.

The intellectual appeal of tropes may very well be that they remind us of multiple realities and multiple representations and, ultimately, of the centrality of indeterminacy in our conceptual world. Yin always grows into yang and vice versa, in a fluid process of interdependence and interpenetration. Tropes remind us that the world out there is not as statically classified and delineated as we might (at least at times) assume. Indeterminacy indeed is the very mechanism that enables creative energy to engender polytropic and polysemic symbols. Flights of imagination may lead us to transcendence, and yet that transcendence may remind us of our animality. The tension in metaphors and the creation of synecdoche then arise from the irony and paradoxes of the kaleidoscopic realities whose dynamic processes and movements let us reach the height of moral imagination, but not nihilistic chaos. Ultimately, the new creations are enacted by individual actors who are constrained but not determined by the received categories at a given historical period and by the context of their social interaction.

Tropical Dominions:

The Figurative Struggle over Domains of Belonging and Apartness in Africa

Deborah Durham
James W. Fernandez

Before the climactic battle in D. T. Niane's retelling of the classic Mandingo epic of the founding of the Mali Empire, the hero Sundiata engages in a war of words with his rival Soumaoro, the king of Sosso, who has conquered the Mali region.

Speaking through an owl, the enemy king claims: "I am the wild yam of the rocks; nothing will make me leave Mali."

Sundiata, through his own owl, replies: "I have in my camp seven master smiths who will shatter the rocks. Then, yam, I will eat you."

The argument of images continues: "I am the poisonous mushroom that makes the fearless vomit."

"As for me, I am the ravenous cock, the poison does not matter to me."

"Behave yourself, little boy, or you will burn your foot, for I am the red-hot cinder."

"But me, I am the rain that extinguishes the cinder; I am the boisterous torrent that will carry you off."

"I am the mighty silk-cotton tree that looks from on high on the tops of other trees."

"And I, I am the strangling creeper that climbs to the top of the forest giant" (Niane 1965: 60).

Soumaoro is thwarted: he is unable to create a metaphor that dominates or a resultant universe that he can dominate. He presents himself and the contested region to Sundiata in the form of metaphors, which not only locate him in a separate domain but also insert him into a hierarchy imputed to that domain. Soumaoro is not simply likened to a mighty tree, he is the tallest tree in the forest that is Mali; he is not just a stubborn plant, but the yam on an impervious rock face. Sundiata does not counter these challenges with stronger but distinct metaphors from other domains; instead he enters each of Soumaoro's figurative domains and undermines or trumps his rival's position by focusing on the more complex relationships between elements within the domain. That is, he makes associated elements of the domain of figurative struggle chosen by his opponent work against him. He suggests that rocks exist in worlds where men and their tools can smash them and that yams do not just cling but are gathered or eaten.

Sundiata asserts for himself his own superiority vis-à-vis his enemy both within the analogical discourse and outside of it. This is only fitting in the context of the epic, for the unsubtle Soumaoro (who in Niane's version of events is a smith and not of the caste from which rulers come) has attempted to hammer out an empire by force and force alone. His reign is predicated, as are his metaphors, upon one-dimensional relationships. Sundiata, on the other hand, succeeds in overthrowing his enemy and creating the Mali state through the multiple relationships he has forged in the course of the narrative with neighboring princes, with the castes of Mandingo society, and with the spiritual forces that pervade his culture. He is also able to subvert his rival's hegemony of words and people by bringing to the fore, reexamining, and subverting Soumaoro's implied metonymic status—his dominance in the domains he has figuratively created.

There has been, as our symposium of papers in this volume signifies, a bringing back of metaphor into the center of focus in the social sciences, with the result that, in spite of the variety of approaches, there is a basic consensus on what it is and how it works. Metaphor juxtaposes two apparently distinct domains, sometimes called the tenor and vehicle or target and source, to effect a transfer of meaning from the former to the latter, enrich-

ing, transforming, or constituting and creating our understanding
of the target domain. But meanings, as we have learned from this
century's linguistics, are not necessarily unitary, free-floating ideas
to be picked up or put together randomly. They become significant
within conventionalized systems of contrast and association. And
so a source domain is not, as Soumaoro learns, simply an undifferentiated lump of meaning with which he can hammer Sundiata. It has a structure and hierarchy, which may be played upon
to question and reorder relations within the target domain—in
this case, the domain of political relations in the early Mali Empire. Metonymy and synecdoche are the tropes that substitute
terms for one another inside a conceptual domain. The metonymic associations that link terms within a domain, whether
hierarchical, causal, or contiguous in some other way, are multiple—and subject, as we see, to playful manipulation. And, indeed, as has been recognized by many and is surely recognized by
Soumaoro, it is the interplay of the metaphoric and metonymic associations that makes tropes truly effective in ways interesting to
anthropologists: that is to say, ways that make subtle rhetorical
impact on social relations.

Paying Attention to Metonymy

Metonymy, however, has received far less attention in the recent renewed focus on tropological matters than has its inter-
domain counterpart. As a result, the interplay of the two tropes
comes to be variously understood, or even underestimated. At
the start, there is some confusion as to what we should call a
metonymy, or metonymic relationship, and how to define it. This
problem extends itself and can make more complex, if not bring
into question, the nature of "domains" themselves.

David Sapir, in his important paper dissecting the "anatomy of
metaphor," illustrates the two most common approaches. As does
Quintilian, Sapir lists the specific relations that might exist between metonymic substitutes and their referents. Thus, cause can
substitute for effect, or vice versa, container for contained, agent
or instrument for act, and so forth (1977: 19). Such an oft-repeated

list emphasizes the figurative use of metonymy in discourse, the actual substitution of one distinct term for another, calling soldiers "khakis" or "guns" or reading "Homer" instead of his works. In a broader vein, however, Sapir also suggests that "metonymy replaces or juxtaposes contiguous terms that occupy a distinct and separate place within what is considered a single semantic or perceptual domain" (ibid.: 4). And it is this replacement or juxtaposition that is central to the rivalrous exchange between Soumaoro and Sundiata. Since the terms in metonymic manipulation are associated by many possible contiguities and do not necessarily share features or properties, the associations are less constrained than suggested by the usual list of "cause/effect" relations that is given in discussing metonymy. Thus the nature of the associations that might spring up when domains are brought into relation is not easily defined or bounded by any obvious natural (cause/effect) criteria, but is instead susceptible to diverse contiguities that can always be reconceptualized under the spur of ongoing social relations.

Sapir suggests that the metaphoric juxtaposition of tiger (as source) and fuel (as target) in the slogan "put a tiger in your tank" extends metonymically to associate the tiger with the car and also with the driver. In this metonymically sensitive understanding of a metaphor, the tiger in the fuel tank acts to create a new perception of the entire domain of car and driver. Those features not overtly shared by the tiger and the fuel (say, the jungle conventionally associated with the tiger and the highways of the car), although remaining semantically distinct within the new conception, still add what Sapir calls "coloration" to one another through an implicit though unexpected metonymic association. Practically every metaphor that works effectively to associate domains, therefore, carries metonymic implications; often enough inadvertent, perhaps, but not for that reason of less concern to a discipline interested in the vicissitudes and volatile transformations of human relationships—interested in the way, that is, that metonymies can transform metaphors and unrealized contiguities can create new similarities.

An earlier pertinent and related approach to metaphor and metonymy may be found in Roman Jakobson's (1956) language-anchored paper on aphasia. Metaphor, as a substitutive process, becomes a counterpart in discourse of the selection function of speech. Metonymy (here subsuming synecdoche) becomes by contrast a figurative part of the combinatory, or syntagmatic, function. Any complete discursive act relies on both a selection of terms and a predication upon them: it must be both metaphoric and metonymic, although cultural or personal predilections (or, in the case of aphasics, pathologies) may favor discourse oriented around one or the other figurative pole. Realism as a genre, for example, is metonymic in preference, exploring in careful detail the specifics of given domains, while romanticism favors the frequent shifting of domains by means of metaphor.

Jakobson notes that metonymy has received little attention in the critical literature—and, as noted, this continues to be the case—possibly because the essentially metaphoric construction of metalinguistic discourse itself predisposes it to be more sensitive to that trope. Perhaps because of the multiplex and not easily predicted possibilities of association by contiguity, as we have said, metonymy is less readily understood. Though his work was influential on such later students as Roland Barthes and Claude Lévi-Strauss, neither they nor Jakobson himself make extensive analysis of metonymy. Essentially, the apparent assumption is that it operates in the field of associations in a volatile way where many different forms of locational contiguity can lead to some predicative or narrative relationship, or, as in the case of Soumaoro and Sundiata, some social advantage.

The linguistic analogy (or metaphor) of the two axes provided by Jakobson (found earlier in Saussure, to be sure, and picked up later by many others) graphically presents the interdependence of metaphoric and metonymic relations as the interaction of two planes of experience, although the model tends to obscure the dynamic of metonymy as regards the conventional constraints of culture on the one hand and particular pragmatic circumstance on the other. The model is certainly a persistent one in Western thought. W. J. T. Mitchell, indeed, reads Jakobson's metaphor/metonym dichotomy as paralleling a resemblance/juxtaposition, icon/symbol, and finally natural sign / conventional sign set of oppositions that permeate Western thought from Hume to Gombrich (1986: 59).

But, as we say, the dichotomy can also serve to obscure the essential conventionality which underlies associations within domains (whether these rest upon perceived cause/effect relations or on some conceived contiguity) and which is a conventionality that, in fact, delineates the domains themselves. For example, in spite of the fact that Saussure attempted to deny it (1966: 124–25), the received view of his ideas on syntagmatic relations situates those relations within the idiosyncratic and temporal realm of speech. Here the elements selected from a language are associated for some pragmatic purpose, assembled for the moment—*in praesenti*—but in no constant group. By this same received view associative, or selective/substitutive/paradigmatic, relations exist within the atemporal realm outside discourse, in memory or "the inner storehouse that makes up the language of each speaker" (ibid.: 123). Therefore, associative relations, which Jakobson and others have likened to metaphor, are widely recognized and should be shared by all speakers; syntagmatic ones on the other hand, likened to metonymy, are more highly individualized and are freely assembled and disassembled according to particular experience and circumstance. This view of the volatility of the metonym and the persistence of metaphor may partially explain why the former is so little studied and the latter so celebrated.

Cultural Conventions in Metonymy

In fact, however, the metonymic relations latently invoked in a metaphor can be highly conventionalized, part of the "inner storehouse" of a culture and its sets of cultural assumptions or models. In one society a house might be metonymic of male homeowners, in another of the female homemakers, although both occupy it. To return to African examples, Basotho women may refer to men by the blankets that enclose them as part of their everyday dress, but in a second metonymic association blankets belong to a domain of nocturnal play. This problem has not gone unremarked in the literature: Mark Turner notes that "one of the most common forms of metonymy depends on conventional cultural associations, such as the association of evil with darkness" (1987: 21). Even George Lakoff and Mark Johnson, in an empiricist train that tends to "naturalize" metaphor—in the sense conveyed by Mitchell— by rooting the metaphoric constructions of the cognitive world in primary "experiential gestalts," note that these gestalts, or basic domains, vary from culture to culture (1980a: 478, 462). Sapir, in the quote above, says that metonymic terms occur within *what is considered* a semantic or perceptual domain; and Jakobson, too, writes that "such metonymies [as used by aphasics with a 'selection deficiency'] may be characterized as projections from the line of a *habitual* context into the line of substitution" (1956: 84; emphasis added).

So where does this bring us? Metaphors often rest upon linkage to highly conventionalized domains, and the metonymic "entailments" that a source domain carries over to the target domain provide for the target an internal structure paralleling that of the source. Two important points emerge; we discuss one here and return to the second below. Understanding a metaphoric assertion implies an understanding of the structure of the domains involved in a predication, and this, in turn, requires a previous understanding dependent upon an immersion in culture. Hence Theodore Cohen (1979) suggests that metaphors cultivate intimacy, or even a sense of complicity in language, between the speaker and the audience. One person's making of a metaphor, readily grasped by another, can become an instrument of consensus and thus community between them. This assertion can be related to Victor Turner's thesis linking the liminal experience of communitas with creative insight into similarity relations and thus with the emergence of basic metaphors (1974: 50–51). Liminality and communitas, the conditions of a consensual antistructure, act, for Turner, to provide a "world of prophetic, half-glimpsed images." These images are metaphors whose internal structure is only later worked out, under conditions of societal and corresponding conceptual structure, by the "thought technicians" of the world of structure (1974: 28). Turner's communitas, like Lakoff and Johnson's primary experiential gestalts perhaps, generates these metaphors, which are the opposite of the "imageless thought" of modern reason; they seem instead to be more "thoughtless images," which are culturally acceptable and whose associated metonymies can later be thoughtfully elaborated.

But metaphors do not juxtapose two incoherent domains. They do not work—that is, make any sense—unless one recognizes and accepts the structure of the source domain and is also willing to accept an understanding of the target in terms of that structure. The creation of the metaphor and subsequent metonymic manipulation is not arbitrary, but may indeed be said to be "motivated," in Saussure's sense (1966: 132–33). It is a joint recognition of these shared understandings—that is, culture in a fundamental sense—that constitutes Cohen's intimacy or community.

Metonymic Manipulation

But, of course, the argument of images going on between Soumaoro and Sundiata produces the very opposite of "intimacy" in its normal sense. Here we must look further. While acceptance of a metaphor as apt may mean the acceptance of the authority of its producer and of the culturally established vision of the world that he provides, such acceptance is susceptible to manipulation. In their epic "argument of images," Soumaoro, in the interest of his own hegemony, attempts to coerce his challenger Sundiata into accepting a particular vision of the world, in this instance a particular set of relationships between trees and between men. Should Sundiata acknowledge the organization of Soumaoro's domains as presented, he would also acknowledge Soumaoro's authority, as did the conquered peoples of Mali. Instead, by focusing through metonymic manipulation on the basic associative relationships in the source domain, Sundiata questions Soumaoro's understanding of the world and his ability to continue to define his position. He refuses to participate in Soumaoro's community or to truckle to the dubious "intimacy" of domination which Soumaoro proffers. He "turns the tables" on him!

A second point, which we promised above to examine, is as important for understanding the Mandingo war of words as the inherent authority putatively presented via metaphor. Metaphor does not simply juxtapose two domains, but ultimately joins them, uniting them metonymically in their parallel structures. It creates a more concordant model of the world, a single, more encompassing organization. Not only do they draw the author and the audience into intimacy, metaphors also see "intimacy" in the world and draw the world together into a larger community. Sundiata, adding elements to Soumaoro's metaphors (the smiths, the torrent of water, the vine that smothers the tree), not only challenges Soumaoro's ability to impose and sustain a particular convention but also contests the unity or appropriateness of worldview implicit in that convention. He denies not only the convention, or commonplace understanding, of the source domain, but also the external relationships posited for it in relation to the target domain. He denies Soumaoro's ability to create a world by the linkage of domains. It is in the realm of metonymic associations, indeed, that conventions may be challenged, and hence metonymy is a trope most suitable for either asserting or challenging established hierarchies and conventions—for asserting and/or challenging worldviews indeed![1]

Disenfranchisement, Language Hegemony, and the Protest of Tropes

These points—and matters having to do with the creation or separation of worlds—may be illustrated by looking in some detail, and with the play of metaphor and metonym in mind, at another, although contemporary, African example: the Soweto uprisings of 1976 and the black poetry of protest that has emerged in the 1970's and 1980's in South Africa. On June 16, 1976, in Soweto, schoolchildren were shot down by police while protesting Afrikaans as the language of instruction—in fact, they were met-

[1] It is important to emphasize the dynamic potential of figurative speech in both its metaphoric and its metonymic aspects. Praise poetry of southern Africa, for example, is highly metaphoric, layering one image upon another in describing its subject. Metaphor upon metaphor is made of the subject, both increasing his personal extension and also situating him firmly (and metonymically) in a larger world.

onymically challenging the cultural and political domain of action being hegemonically imposed by the South African state. The language of schooling and the schools themselves are assertions and implementations of the role of cultural definition and control assumed by the state.

In the 1940's, it will be recalled, discontented with inadequate mission schooling, Africans had called for "state responsibility for education"; in 1953 the Bantu Education Act located that responsibility in the Department of Native Affairs (Hirson 1979: 40, 45). Schooling became a means by which the creation of separate cultural categories was doubly undertaken: the races were segregated and provided with different curricula, and, by a circularity of hegemonic reasoning, the curricula themselves provided the cultural distinctions upon which the segregations were based. Dr. Verwoerd, architect of apartheid and head of the Department of Native Affairs, outlined the task to the Senate quite baldly:

When I have control of Native Education I will reform it so that the Natives will be taught from childhood to realise that equality with Europeans is not for them. . . . What is the use of teaching the Bantu child mathematics when it cannot use it in practice? That is quite absurd. . . . The school must equip him to meet the demands which the economic life will impose on him. . . . There is no place for him above the level of certain forms of labour. . . . For that reason it is of no avail for him to receive a training which has as its aim absorption in the European community. (Quoted in Hirson 1979: 45)

Although later labor requirements required more skills from the Bantu Education system, the principle by which it created and defined the "native" and "native" cultural possibility persisted. The immediate event that precipitated the Soweto protests was only a reaffirmation of that principle. It was decided that, beginning in 1976, half of all instruction was to be in Afrikaans and that, specifically, Afrikaans would be the medium for instruction in mathematics and social studies, the latter encompassing history and geography, those fields, indeed, in which social and political relations are taught and understood.

In 1948 the Afrikaners had been voted into political power in South Africa, and with them came the formal institutions of apartheid, themselves anchored in Afrikaans. Afrikaans was the language of the framers of Bantu Education that was associated with the systematic disenfranchising of the non-white population of the country. The relationship of state-to-education-to-populace was a relationship that delimited and defined the constituents of this triad and the hierarchy prevailing between them. It was also a hegemonic model of possible cultural understanding provided by one segment of that domain, the Afrikaans state itself. In denying and counteracting that hierarchy, the children carried school exercise books on the covers of which were written the slogans of protest: "Down with Afrikaans," "Abolish Afrikaans," "Blacks are not dustbins—Afrikaans stinks" (Hirson 1979: 180). The schoolbooks contained both the slogans and, in their display, the act of appropriating to the children the power inherent in those books. The rebellion was challenging the essential relationship between state and education, challenging the hegemonic relationship of the one to the other, and challenging the ability of the state to impose an inhibiting cultural definition, a separation of worlds, on the black populace in the form of language or text.

This metonymic reconfiguration is illuminating because the immediate terms of the protest—the language of instruction and the state system that it represents—are brought into question as part and parcel of the protest. The systematic relationship between them, the hierarchy by which one dominates through the other, is the contested object of dispute. What is more, the contiguous part-whole relationship between the schoolchildren and the texts and between the schoolchildren and the state is one of an inhibiting contiguity and encompassment that is being here challenged and transformed.

Afrikaans, it should be said, is not the only language of cultural hegemony protested in black South Africa. English, too, and specifically the literary use of English, has recently come into contention. In 1986 Njabulo Ndebele charged English with being itself the instrument of cultural hegemony—of representing and imposing the values of a still-imperialist West, in effect metonymically constituting part of a domain of self-serving subordinances with regard to the African, who was given an inhibited Western culture by means of the agency of language itself. Ndebele also charged

English with being the medium of control insofar as "native" English speakers attempted to determine grammars and terms for proper use of the language (Ndebele 1987).[2] This issue surrounds the construction of protest poetry in the 1970's and 1980's and contributes to both its form and, indivisibly, its content (see especially McClintock 1987).

The hegemonic place of English in the whole picture of apartheid has not always been so challenged. Throughout Africa in the colonial era, education and literacy were viewed as means to attain European material and political advantages. In South Africa, as over much of the continent, that education, whatever subsequent protests over cultural hegemony, was predominantly in English, and there the language came to serve a number of functions. Es'kia Mphahlele wrote (from exile) in 1962: "Now . . . the Government is using institutions of a fragmented and almost unrecognizable Bantu culture as an instrument of oppression. . . . We have got to wrench the tools of power from the white man's hand: one of these is literacy and the sophistication that goes with it. We have got to speak the language that all can understand—English" (quoted in Alvarez-Pereyre 1984: 4). English, then, was to be the language of power, the means of communicating the oppression and the struggle to overcome it, and it was also to be the common tongue of the many linguistic communities united under apartheid. And written English, literature, became one of the powerful vehicles of expression and protest.[3]

Nonetheless it was ultimately perceived that even that usage was subjected to complacent hegemonic judgment. For example, "classically" trained black writers in the 1950's produced work that Nadine Gordimer rated as "some of the best on the continent" (1973: 51). Their works were, however, a celebration of the values of the liberal white European society. Aesthetically, the pri-

[2] We do not intend here to break into the theories of the relationship between language and culture that inform Ndebele's critique. The matter at hand is the relationship as it is conceived and as this conception gives form to action.

[3] Of course, the "literature of commitment" in South Africa is not confined to English. There is a rich body of poetry and prose in Afrikaans and in Zulu as well. English, however, has been the most commonly used medium and, for reasons developed above, takes a very complex role in the struggle.

mary worth of poetry was identified with "individual creativity, imm[a]nent and 'universal' literary values" (McClintock 1987: 612). More disconcerting uses of the language were questioned. Gordimer, for example, in evaluating the black corpus of fiction, doubts that writings by "the testifiers of social change . . . will last," and she seems to be looking for the timeless aesthetic qualities that perdure outside of any historical, and political, context—outside, that is, matters of hierarchy. Moreover, while praising the theme of political struggle, she faults the bulk of African writers for not dealing with "human motivation" and the psychological underpinnings of their characters (1973: 7, 19)—for example, the representation of the universal individual, shaped by the conditions of society but retaining the universal humanistic traits that allow him to transcend those conditions, as valued in a liberal framework. Indeed, African writers with such interests—that is, those writers who were trained in the mission schools and whose writings, albeit political, still stressed the transcendent validity of private and individual experience—left the country following the Sharpeville massacre in 1960 and the state bannings of their writings.

A new generation of writers emerged in the 1970's and 1980's who were not trained on Shakespeare and the classics of British literature (indeed, not even on the writings of their banned and largely expatriate compatriots), but instead were brought up in the Bantu Education schema with its hegemonies and also on the tenets of Black Consciousness, which emerged in the later 1960's. The literature that they developed—much of it poetry—had to deal with the increasingly violent conditions of black life in an increasingly oppressive South Africa. At the same time, the Black Consciousness movement was urging, and confirming, the possibilities of a strong and valuable broad-based black cultural community (although the movement itself was confined to an educated and urban population).

The poetry of this period, therefore, turns against the conventions of European culture and has most recently rejected the traditional aesthetic of the English poetic art.[4] Jacques Alvarez-Pereyre

[4] The appeal to a common cultural identity based upon the conditions of apartheid has drawn the criticism of some Marxist critics, who argue that this

notes that rejection in the fact that this poetry, by contrast to normal English usage, makes use of slang, phonetic spellings, tran-
scriptions of the spoken language of the townships, and com-
posite, portmanteau words ("brainwhitewashed") (1984: 261–64).
Anne McClintock suggests that the incorporation of many elements from traditional oral forms, the appropriation of elements
of jazz, jive, and black Americanisms as well as township speech
lead to "signs of an imminent abandonment and destruction of the
text," as the written form becomes more closely intertwined with
oral presentation in public readings, in performances incorporating other media, and at rallies and protest meetings (1987: 615,
623). The rejection of a "classical" canonical English is practically
visceral. Wrote Mothobi Mutloatse, "We are going to pee, spit, and
shit on literary convention. . . . We'll write our poems in a narrative form; we'll dramatize our poetic experiences; we'll poeti-
cize our historical dramas" (quoted in Vaughan 1985: 197).

The keepers of aesthetic value, the Praetorian Guard of classic
English, were naturally hostile—hostile and defensive, decrying
the way in which the conventions of artistic usage and respect for
the traditions of the expressive English language were disregarded
in favor of political messages (McClintock 1987: 619). But the
township poets appropriate to themselves the power of asserting
their own values through both the imagery of popular experience
and the linguistic forms of that experience; "syntax, a means of
enslavement, can, when it is rejected or denied, express revolt"
(Alvarez-Pereyre 1984: 263).

Still there is a subtlety to this expression of revolt, this symbolic rejection of the crucial metonymic part that controls the
whole of the entire dominant culture. The Soweto poets may reject the particular Afrikaans or English that holds hegemony over

---

set of terms obscures the capitalist conditions of oppression and inhibits the
development of a working-class-based consciousness (see Vaughan 1985: 201).
A second critique of literary protest notes that the form itself, insofar as it is
drawn from European traditions of creativity, "focuses upon the way in which
individuals experience conditions of oppression: the way in which individuals
encounter imaginatively these conditions" (ibid.: 196). It is possible, however,
that the movement toward performative and public creativity (necessitated in
part by persistent bannings of published material) may itself respond to this
critique (see McClintock 1987).

them. But they accept the understanding of language that makes it both the symbol and the agent of expressive identity, of the power of self-definition and assertion. They accept it as the crucial part of the whole. Thus, their poetry serves mainly to redefine the relationships between conservative (if politically liberal) "native" English speakers and their language and culture and the nascent black community that wishes to take control of its own worldview.

Studies of this protest poetry of South Africa tend to take two approaches. First, they evaluate the use of language in the construction of aesthetic form, as discussed above. Second, they discuss the extent to which the expressions of the oppressed, the revelations of the indignities of black life in the apartheid state, the predictions and exhortations of doomful action can effect any real change in the political order. We have discussed above the practical challenge constituted in the writing of this "poetry of commitment" to hegemonic control over the English (or Afrikaans) language and the culture it is metonymically tied into. But the images of social disorder and order contained in the poetry, the reordering of the domain, as part of the power of the pen can hardly be underestimated. Soon after the Soweto revolt, in 1978, *Staffrider* magazine was introduced as a vehicle for protest literature in South Africa. It was banned almost immediately for undermining "the authority and image of the police" (Publications Directorate, quoted in McClintock 1987: 599). The police, too, as the metonymic minions of the cultural and political domination of the state—the agents and synecdochic embodiments of it—are an image implicitly understood by all participants in the arguments (see Vaughan 1985: 215) and ripe for recasting. We read here a poem by Hein Willemse.[5]

> the stormtroopers are in the streets
> the poets have buried their metaphors
> the preachers are exiled prophets
> the young boys are walled in
> the young girls are violated

[5] Hein Willemse, "Poem," in David Bunn and Jane Taylor, eds., *From South Africa: New Writing, Photographs, and Art* (*TriQuarterly* 69 [1987]: 180–81; rptd. Chicago: University of Chicago Press, 1988); reprinted here by permission of *TriQuarterly* magazine, a publication of Northwestern University, and of the author.

the stormtroopers are in the streets
the women wash dishes with their tears
the old women's knitting needles are broken spears
the men smash jugs of wine against panzers
the old men forget their front-stoop newspapers

the stormtroopers reign in the streets
they lob schoolboys from armored car to armored car
the streets are not empty
the stormtroopers reign in the streets

the writers die in exile
the preachers call to their gods in vain
the raped prime their barrels with thunder

the stormtroopers are in the streets
the youths carry spears

the stormtroopers are walled in
the children are in the streets

The stormtroopers of this poem are both metaphoric and metonymic of the state. As metonyms, they are the agents of the state,
the arms of its power and agents of armed infiltration into people's
lives. As metaphors stormtroopers figuratively represent the state
in a context in which, in effect, the stormtroopers and the state itself can be metonymically reconfigured by the transforming power
of the elements with which they associate. These associated elements, too, cannot but be transformed themselves by the intru-
sion of the police, in a complex and dynamic figurative process.
The state penetrates the community in the embodiments of its
enforcers; and the presence of these actors in the community
transforms the objects of people's lives—their dishes and knitting
needles, their wine, their bodies. The community is being pene-
trated, surrounded, walled in by casspirs[6] and police.

A formal analysis might note that the verbs in the first stanza
are predominantly in the passive voice, rendering the boys, girls,
and preachers acted upon and powerless. The only action by the
community—the burying of metaphors, which are, as noted above,
a medium of creativity—is an end to action, moreover one that

[6] Casspirs are armored vehicles used by the South African police.

was completed in the past. Only the stormtroopers are in control
of themselves and their environment, situating themselves "in
the streets." But slowly the power of the community to act develops, from action directed at the immediate environment (dishes,
needles, jugs), to futile acts directed outwards, counterpointed by
the forcefulness of the police, to a final mobilization of the instruments of the community to create a condition in which the
stormtroopers themselves are trapped, ineffectual in the streets.
Through the transformations effected upon the forms of its life,
the community in turn redefines the place of the troopers. The
troopers end up themselves surrounded, walled in, under seige.
And so the state as a whole is increasingly rejected as a constituent—and dominating—part of the lives of the black community.
The value of the state is contained in the oppressive image of the
police: challenging the validity of the latter, poets of protest in
South Africa challenge the validity of the European state in their
society. But beyond that, by questioning the validity of the lan-
guage(s) of the state, their accustomed associations, their structures and hierarchies, they question the organization of the entire
social order. If it is not a new world the poets present, it is surely a
drastically reorganized one.

Buried Metaphors, Lively Metonymies

We have noted that metaphors predicate an internal structure
to uncertainly understood domains, and that this structure is
mainly conventional; it rests upon a joint recognition of the correspondence between those domains. Metonymies operate within
those domains and can operate upon such conventions. Unlike
metaphors, while they are not creative of new understandings and
new worldviews, they can be creatively manipulative of old ones—
as in our examples from old Sudanic Africa and modern South Africa, where the configurations of power and the parties in the conflict both form and contest the structures within which arguments
take place. The argument of images can thus serve to confirm the
organization of conceptual domains, but such arguments can also
serve, as in our examples, as the foci of challenges to a received or

an asserted view of the world without attempting to replace it entirely.

At this juncture, it is relevant to note Jakobson's observation that aphasics with what he called a "similarity disorder"—that is, those who had difficulty with the substitution or selection or paradigmatic process of speech and relied heavily on context and the process of combination—had great difficulties in starting a dialogue. They could carry one through, however, once one was started for them—they were "reactive" (1956: 77). Similarly, we saw that Victor Turner proposed that "thought technicians"—the specialists of metonym—followed up on other metaphoric flashes of insight, spinning out their associations and ramifications.

Hayden White's (1978) reading of Vico accepts a similar distinction, in which human history, ideologically conceived and ideologically transformed, passes from an initial stage characterized by the predication of a metaphoric understanding of the world to one predicated upon the manipulation of metonymies. These ideological conceptions are intimately linked, moreover, with the actual organization of human society, which in the latter metonymic condition becomes far more diverse and, we might say, "organic," capable of challenging an established, would-be classical, sense of order. And so we might see Sundiata in ancient Mali, weaving new metonymies into and so subverting Soumaoro's metaphoric domains of self-assertion, reorganizing a society of more complex associations (predicated on differentiations of castes) out of the basic unified empire created by Soumaoro. The same may be said of these impious visceral poets of Soweto whose metaphoric powers of creation may be buried but whose metonymic powers to reorganize given domains are alive and well.

This analysis of the relations between metaphor and metonymy has focused primarily upon the use of these devices in discourse—upon the relationship between how they serve as organizing or reorganizing images for the construction of the world and how, more particularly, their use may serve to construct or reconstruct the world of social relations. The work of V. N. Voloshinov (1986) on the reporting of speech in Russian demonstrates the ways in which speech is not simply a series of vehicles (symbols, icons, indices) representing concepts or cognitive formulae. More than that, it is the very embodiment of social interaction, its grammar and form both organizing that interaction and being organized through it.

We have suggested various ways in which tropes may construct, or reconstruct, social hierarchies: through the affirmation or denial of the authority of the trope-maker to define the world, through the definitions or redefinitions of relations within existent metaphoric domains that also configure relations between participants in a discourse, and also through the models that metaphors and metonymies present of more unified or less unified and structured worlds.

With this "evolutionary epistemology" of the play of tropes in mind, let us, finally, consider the views of Michael Shapiro and Marianne Shapiro (1976: chap. 3) on the tropes and semantic change. They are concerned with the "inherent dynamic of tropes," the way that metonymies, which are claims on parts of wholes, can become metaphors, which are claims on wholes calling our attention to another domain of interest.

Every metonymy thus contains the potential for sliding into metaphor. Of course, both tropes can still coexist in the same linguistic vehicle, thus facilitating the slide of an original metonymy into metaphor. The word *head* used to denote the person in charge is metonymic in that one part of the human body is taken to stand for the entire body (person). It is simultaneously metaphoric, as an analogy (semantic similarity) is drawn, on the one hand, between the dominance of the head physically and physiologically over the rest of the human body and the dominance of a leader over the group on the other. These two coexistent figural components of *head* are themselves, naturally, not unranked: the metaphoric component markedly dominates the metonymic. This rank order is consistent with the principle that metonymy tends strongly to be superseded by metaphor. This means that metonymy is the more basic, less complex of the two tropes. (1976: 15–16)

The basic dynamic that the Shapiros point up is the dynamic of hierarchization, dehierarchization, and rehierarchization. Metonymy is, par excellence, the hierarchical trope; to extrapolate a bit, it is obliged to feature and thus exalt some part for a whole or vice versa: the container for the contained or vice versa, the cause for the effect or vice versa, the inner for the outer or vice versa, the farther for the nearer or vice versa, the upper for the lower or vice versa. Any metonymic or synecdochic (as the main metonymic strategy) predication, then, implicates a hierarchy, for "in metonymy there is a differentiation of some totality with the necessary concomitant" of "the relative ranking or hierarchization of the constituents" (ibid.: 11), whereas in metaphor, where two terms are juxtaposed as similar, relations are dehierarchized, reversed, and neutralized (ibid.: 7).

The Shapiros give primacy to metonymy, making it the more primal and natural trope than metaphor on the basis, apparently, that we must begin with some ordered structural state, a contiguous integument as it were, before we can transpose it metaphorically. They begin with the world created and inevitably hierarchical insofar as men and women have any choice to make about where they find themselves in the integument. Vico and White do not accept such unbegun beginnings and wish instead to begin with the world made anew by metaphor. In our own analysis here, we have tried to take into account both the creation of a world contained in a metaphor and the liberating manipulation within the hegemonies of that world made possible by metonymy. But there can be no doubt that matters of hierarchy, either accepted or rejected, deconstructed or reconstructed, lie at the heart of these predications and these manipulations.

Conclusions

In conclusion we return to our main point, a point brought out in the imaginative struggle between Soumaoro and Sundiata. We have seen that metaphoric assertions contain within themselves metonymic structures of associations wherein can be discovered the seeds of world manipulation, transformation, or even destruction. Indeed, only in the presence of these latent metonymies would metaphoric structurings make any sense. One powerful way of challenging the structure of the world, as sustained by an authoritative and legitimating metaphor, is the challenge to the internal metonymic structure of the metaphoric domains. The imagery of protest or rebellion may lie in a new metaphoric assertion, but it

may also lie, as we have seen, in metonymic reworkings of metaphoric assertions, reworkings that challenge conventional, culturally specific structurings of the social order implied in conventional
metaphor. Metaphor has, as Jakobson pointed out, dominated the
attention of most students of the tropes. But for anthropologists at
least, whose main interest must be social order, metonymic reorderings of that order, which is to say struggles over hierarchy,
must be of equal or greater interest.

Part III

Metaphor and the Coherence of Culture

Reasonable and Unreasonable Worlds:

Some Expectations of Coherence in Culture Implied by the Prohibition of Mixed Metaphor

Dale Pesmen

> *Sir, you may fight these battles as long as you will, but when you come to balance the account you will find that you have been fishing in troubled waters, and that an ignis fatuus has bewildered you, and that indeed you have built upon a sandy foundation, and brought your hogs to a fair market. . . . I am, sir, yours, &c.*
>
> *Joseph Addison*

There is an etiquette of metaphor—and mixing metaphor is not allowed. From Aristotle through the Enlightenment to the present time, textbooks on rhetoric and style forbid it. Why?

This essay suggests that certain expectations of reality are implied by the interdiction of mixed metaphor—expectations that also inform current discussions of consistency and eclecticism in anthropology, philosophy, and aesthetics. I will argue that the prohibition against "taking up cross-scents" stems from a wider ideology of coherence inseparable from our intuitions of the "rightness" or "goodness" of theories, thoughts, and ways of operating in the world. This notion of coherence governs our judgments of the "truth," "validity," and "realism" of pictures of that world and distinguishes things we *can* think about from things we find objectionable and/or impossible to think.

I am indebted to James Fernandez for his patient readings of drafts of this article and for his helpful suggestions at every stage of the writing. For comments that sparked my imagination as well as watered it, I am grateful also to Steve Coleman, Paul Friedrich, Alaina Lemon, and Bob Peters.

A typical example of the prohibition of mixed metaphor is that of Thomas Gibbons, in his 1767 treatise on rhetorical tropes. Gibbons calls mixed metaphors disgustful, spoiled, repugnant, absurd, and miserable incongruities, and writes that "though the Metaphor is so excellent and lovely a Trope, there is nothing so disgustful as a Metaphor ill-chosen and ill-conducted, according to the old maxim, *corruptio optimi est pessima,*" and "after we have begun a Metaphor, we are to beware lest we spoil it, by introducing something repugnant and dissimilar to the first image" (1969: 28). Gibbons agrees with Quintilian's comment that to "set out with a tempest [and end with] a conflagration" has an effect of "most shameful inconsistency" (1891: 136). These writers are not alone in finding mixed metaphor "offensive and repulsive"; it is generally considered "one of the most intolerable faults of composition" (Gibbons 1969: 34). Having been shown a mixed metaphor in *Paradise Lost*, Coleridge told Wordsworth that he could not sleep all the next night for thinking of it (Bett 1932: 242).

This is the sort of language that writers on rhetoric, style, and poetics have used to describe their responses to the "vicious combination of metaphors" (Constable 1731: 104). The other response (besides this one, formulated often in terms of nausea) seems to be that mixed metaphor is intolerably absurd, literally laughable, as in the example of the *New Yorker* section "Block that Metaphor." But is ridicule "the test of propriety"? ("T.D." 1825: 723). I would like to argue that this laughter in response to mixed metaphor is nervous laughter, laughter in response to a threat to "the familiar landmarks of . . . *our* thought, the thought that bears the stamp of our age and our geography—breaking up all the ordered surfaces and all the planes with which we are accustomed to tame the wild profusion of existing things." Thus Michel Foucault describes his experience of reading Jorge Luis Borges's "Chinese encyclopedia" taxonomy. Foucault describes a wonderment in which "the thing we apprehend . . . that by means of the fable, is demonstrated as the exotic charm of another system of thought, is the limitation of our own, the stark impossibility of thinking *that*. But what is it impossible to think, and what kind of impossibility are we faced with here?" (1970: xv). Whatever kind of impossibility it is, the mixing of metaphors produces the same sort.

Because mixed metaphors suggest impossible worlds, I will examine the various attempts made over the years to explain why metaphors ought not to be mixed. I believe that these attempts describe implicitly what worlds we consider "possible." However, although *all* style texts forbid and/or ridicule mixed metaphor, there are in effect very few explanations, and those that do exist can be seen as the same explanation invoked in various ways. It is not for the purpose of discussing metaphor or style that I am using this material; I would like rather to look at whatever implicit assumptions are made explicit in the course of prohibiting mixed metaphor. I shall then move from these assumptions and from the various arguments against, to use Foucault's word, the *Heterotopias* (as opposed to Utopias) (ibid.: xviii) implied or generated by mixed metaphors to examine the notions of order that these "impure unions"—as mixed metaphors are so often called in the style texts—imply.

The Problem

> It is forbidden diet. In prose writers, unclean; in poets, abominable.
> "The reason why" is another matter; for [the laws of critics and
> grammarians], like those of the comets, are inscrutable to common
> intellect. . . . What anathema of Nature's is there against changing
> a metaphor as often as a man pleases?
>
> "T.D.," "On the Use of Metaphors"

The anonymous author of the above quotation is one of the few staunch defenders of mixed metaphor. Writers as a rule do not deny that things can be successively compared to any number of things "if considered in several distinct lights"; the problem is one of when and how this may be done. For example, Joseph Addison writes that "an unskillful author shall run these metaphors so absurdly into one another, that there shall be no simile, no agreeable picture, no apt resemblance, but confusion, obscurity, and noise."

My question about these objections begins much like that of "T.D.," who speaks of critics and grammarians as

members of a class of persons, who, like certain secondary animals, live and are fed upon those of greater importance than themselves . . . [and] have put ["mixed" or "broken" metaphor], as an Otaheitan would say, "under Taboo."

Why is it of necessity to fill up a sentence or a period, or a paragraph, or any assignable space—neither more nor less, like Shylock's pound of flesh, on peril of cancelling the bond? What jurisdiction has Matthews or Hoyle to compel us to play out the suit thus before we try another? Are we bound to run down the first similitude we start, like beagles, or be lashed by some whipper-in of a pedagogue for taking up a cross-scent? What law is there to compel us to let our first metaphor, like our first wife, die a natural death before we take a second?—or what canon is there thus coupling a metaphor and matrimony, and insisting that our comparisons, like our wives, if we will have them, shall be pure, and only by one at a time? Has any critic shown the existence of such laws, either in reason or out of it? (1825: 721–22)

Where I do not agree with "T.D.," however, is in the finality of his conclusion: "The forbiddance of mixed metaphor is founded then upon assertion." The prohibition is not without foundation but rests on certain notions of commitment and fidelity. As we are told, "What God therefore hath joined together, let not man put asunder" (Matthew 19: 6).

The marriage metaphor for metaphor use is actually quite popular—"T.D." jokes about "sinful flirtations with first one metaphor and then another," "being happily converted . . . to the blessed communion of 'one at a time, for better for worse,'" and "the great licentiousness of [Shakespeare] in joining heterogeneous metaphors" (ibid.: 723), but mixed metaphor *is* often called "monstrous union" and similar names by most of its critics. This is an indictment with sensual over- (or under-) tones which I shall come back to throughout this essay. There is a sense in which mixed metaphor is an infidelity: a metaphoric predication implies an association not only of two terms, but also of two worlds, in what is felt as a sort of promise of union. Perhaps the initial observation of an analogy is not yet perceived to be "satisfying" or "substantial," and so immediate movement to an entirely different domain is felt as leaving a set of potentialities behind. However, I would like to follow the rhetoric and style texts through some descriptions of the experience of this phenomenon.

There are several descriptions of mistakes that lead to the generation of mixed metaphors. Broken metaphors are perceived as being impure unions, "the mythical mermaid—what begins as a human being ends up otherwise" (Kellogg 1895: 132). That is, "incompatible" images are set too close together for comfort. The territory of a faithful metaphor is variously described as a sentence, a period, an idea, or "the same connection or clause"; we also find vaguer warnings against "sowing them too thickly" (e.g., Addison 1859: v. 1, 411). In general, mixed metaphor is when we "shall find Metaphors . . . whose meanings can no more accord with one another, than the iron and clay in the feet of the image in NEBU-CHADNEZZAR's dream" (Gibbons 1969: 28).

The same error can be made when mixing metaphorical with literal language, such as (from Hunt 1891: 104):

> He was cured of his pride and his leprosy.
> The orator drew forth their sympathy and their purses.

The distinction between literal and figurative language leads to the issue of dead metaphor. In the words of "T.D.," "To be sure, like hares, they are so like the ground they sit on, that it requires a sharp eye now and then to make them out" (1825: 720).

If, as it has been argued, language itself is "a dictionary of faded metaphors" (Tompkins 1897: 310) that have lost their identity as such, then metaphors inevitably mix in any sentence. This is not experientially disturbing, however, because conventional metaphor does not call itself to our attention as figurative language. A metaphor, used as such, refers to something outside the discourse—an image. Dead metaphors have lost most or all of the richness of their imagery. Thus we can elaborate on T.D.'s "taboo": "you may mix old metaphors as you will, but of young ones beware" (1825: 722). Thus it is in our *creative or spontaneous use* of metaphor that we run the risk of offensively mixing metaphor. Gertrude Buck, in her book on the psychology of rhetoric, has a chapter on "Pathological Forms of Metaphor." She claims that metaphor is only mixed "because it has ceased to be a metaphor. Though maintaining the figurative form, it has become, in the mind of the speaker, a literal statement." When, for example, honor demands that one be "firm as a rock in blotting something from one's soul," Buck contends, one does not really *experience* the image of a rock *blotting* something—"The image of the rock obtrudes itself for no appreciable time into the consciousness" (1899: 65). As there is no incongruity to the writer, there is none for a reader who, persuaded, reduces the original figure to a literal statement (or accepts it) with the same rapidity as the author. Mixed metaphor has to do with *being conscious* of the shifting of images. For the author, "the second figure does not jar with the first, for the first has ceased to be figurative" (ibid.: 64). The implication is, of course, that no one could *want* to mix images and that the experience of mixed metaphor can cause us to become "disenchanted"—that is, conscious that figurative language is at work on us.

Deception and Claims on Reality: Visualization and Validity

It is hoped that some of the seed will not fall on deaf ears.

Nelson Goodman (1976: 34–35) considers the extent to which deception is the measure of realism, reducing the notion to absurdity. Since I am looking at the *experience* of mixed metaphors as unrealistic, the issue of deception persists as relevant. If the consciousness that a rhetorical device is being used can effectively shatter our belief in the "reality" of what we are experiencing, then this element of everyday belief and persuasion is important.

Wallace Stevens makes an argument related to Buck's when he says, "There is no such thing as a metaphor of a metaphor. One does not progress through metaphors. *Thus reality is the indispensable element of each metaphor.* When I say that man is a god it is very easy to see that I also say that a god is something else, god has become reality" (1969: 179; emphasis mine). This sense of "reality" apparently refers to a constant relationship that should ideally be maintained between the metaphorical domain and that of which it is predicated. The "man" we describe as a god is a "real" man, even if he is a fictional character. Not only is it assumed that the domain the "man" "lives" in is a "coherent," "real world," but the same very particular assumptions are brought to bear upon the "world" the "god" inhabits. These are assumptions that take the form of *expectations* about what relations are "natural" within the metaphorical world. In mixed metaphor, these expectations are violated.

In the course of this essay I hope to show that this traditionally demanded internal "order" is not just an order expected of metaphoric domains in relation to specific domains "in the service of which" they are created; for the remedies offered by the writers of style texts to correct the tendency to mix metaphors show that their criteria or organizing principles are related to those used to judge "realism" in visual art and pictures in general. In addition, these same criteria are much in evidence in the "coherence" and "unity" and "autonomy" we expect of formal structures, systems, and scientific paradigms.

Metaphoric-literal shifting and mixed metaphor are often said to occur, if not exactly because of forgetfulness, as Buck proposes, then because of "loose and careless speech": John Constable explains that authors, too easily following the heat of imagination, cannot fix it sufficiently *"for the finishing out of the true sequel of notions"* (1731: 104; emphasis mine). Speaking in an impassioned way can have the same effect, and I shall speak of passionate speech later. In these cases, one is assumed to have become, to borrow an example from a style text, swamped in the meshes of one's argument. This is considered a fault, which there is only *one* developed way to avoid, a technique suggested by most of our writers, who quote it in each other back to the Greeks. This technique is to "surrender one's thoughts *to the picture suggested* until it is wrought out as far as needed" (Tompkins 1897: 311; emphasis mine). This technique is seen as bringing metaphor "to the test of nature" by *visualizing* the image suggested to us! Thus Buck recommends "picturing" as a way to assure that consciousness of earlier stages of the metaphor is retained as the continuation of the idea is being written.

Gibbons offers a critique of lines written by "Dr. Young,"

> One eye on Death, and one full fix'd on Heav'n,
> Becomes a mortal, and immortal man.

and

> Together some unhappy rivals seize,
> And rend abundance into poverty;
> Loud croaks the Raven of the Law, and smiles

He protests, "who, but he who has a disorder in his sight, can at the same time have one eye full fixed on one object, and the other eye upon another? . . . Who ever heard of a raven's smiling? And how unfortunate is it that *what cannot agree with a raven in its original, should be made to agree with it in a metaphorical state?"* (1969: 37–38; emphasis mine). This kind of argumentation (by ridicule) is the verbal counterpart to the "picturing method." It implies that between certain conceptions and characteristics of sense-perception, thought-experiments based on it (visual imagery in particular), and the correct use of metaphor there is a logical relation that allows one to speak of *truth*. Addison makes this an explicit principle: he, like Gibbons, writes that it is improper to make any being in nature or art do things in its metaphorical state which it could not do in its original. Now, given that metaphor does indeed "serve to convey the thoughts of the mind under resemblances and images which affect the senses" (Addison 1859: v. 2, 387–88) and that mixed metaphor is perceived as being unclear, confusing, disgusting, and funny to some degree by virtually all writers, we still have not seen reason to consider mixed metaphor *invalid*, "a mighty deformity by the inconsequent combination of objects" (Constable 1731: 103; translating Quintilian); yet this is exactly the argument against the mixing of metaphors, an argument that implies that mixed metaphor is an *untrue* thing to do, proof being that the image created in the mind is not, in some particular sense, "realistic." As Arnold Tompkins has it, "If the parts, when pictured out by a painter, be incongruous, put your Metaphor in the fire, lest there should stand before you a goddess, horse, and ship, all in one" (1897: 312).

Herbert Spencer, A. R. Radcliffe-Brown, and other social scientists could *logically* justify the use of metaphor in the development of their theories only as useful "illustrations" and "scaffolding" without which inductions would nevertheless stand by themselves. Yet in the same breath as they thus defend the use of metaphor, they call their analogies (for example, between society and an organism) "real and significant," "essential," and "true." "In the absence of physiological science . . . it was impossible to discern the real parallelisms" (Spencer 1981: 388). These "essential parallelisms" are "disclosed by modern science" (ibid.: 391–92) and are still appearing; Spencer anticipated that further scientific and technological developments would allow for further "revelations" of parallels between society and the functioning of an or-

ganism (ibid.: 433) and subsequently had to energetically refute the
charge that he "based Sociology upon Biology" (1967: xl–xli), by
allowing the metaphor he claimed to use only as scaffolding to inform the directions of his inquiry. Radcliffe-Brown (1952) also repeatedly uses the word "real" to refer to the organic analogy and to
social structures, thereby validating social science as an empirical
branch of the natural sciences. This same application of the idea of
"reality" or "realism" to the use of figures appears in discussions
of literary style.

Theodore Hunt writes that "just as from a good outline of an
historical painting we would be able to fill out the scene, so from
the metaphorical terms used we should be able clearly and vividly
to see the truth," and quotes James Russell Lowell's remark that
"A Metaphor, if the correspondence be perfect in all its parts, is
one of the safest guides through the labyrinth of truth" (1891:
103). And J. H. Gilmore gives, alongside the "picturing" method,
the logical "test for analogical comparison" from Aristotle, advis-
ing us to "strip it of its verbiage and reduce it to an equation of
ratios. E.g., $X : Y : : A : B$. Thus, 'the ship ploughs the sea' becomes: the ship is to the sea, as the plough is to the land. The application of this test frequently shows that the resemblance is fan-
ciful or remote; or that it involves more than four terms—that is,
it is a mixed metaphor" (1891: 157).

Yet the fact that the requisite consistent relationship of the
metaphorical domain to the domain of the matter at hand can be
put in logical form *changes nothing* of its mystery. It still remains
to be discussed what criteria are invoked in a judgment of "resemblances" as inconsistent or invalid.

When Addison writes "I bridle in my struggling Muse with
pain," he controls his muse as he would bridle a horse. Once he has
begun using an equestrian image to speak of the difficult subject
of creative process, by continuing to say that this Muse-horse—
itself "no very delicate idea," as Dr. Johnson (Bett 1932: 243) observes—"longs to launch into a bolder strain," Addison is charged
by Henry Bett with committing the following "fault" or "inac-
curacy": "She is in the first line a *horse*, in the second a *boat*; and
the care of the poet is to keep his *horse* or his *boat* from *singing*"
(ibid.). This still seems to equate a certain surrealism in imagery

with low truth value or logical incoherence. Foucault might say that "what is impossible is not the propinquity of the things listed, but the very site on which their propinquity would be possible . . . where could they ever meet, except in the immaterial sound of the voice pronouncing their enumeration, or on the page transcribing it?" (1970: xvi). If by "site" we understand something so wide as to include assumptions about categories, expectations of coherence, etc., I agree; yet what the second part of this quotation from Foucault implies is what our style texts respond to: if the only possible locus for the described phenomenon is a text or discourse, the phenomenon is not "real," is not an acceptable use of figures. But how many styles in art have been labeled "realistic" that could only exist in the medium in which they were created![1]

And again, it is not "just style," but explicitly the "truth-value" of the metaphor that is at issue. The "clearness and safety" of a given metaphor as a way to negotiate intellectual and expressive labyrinths "truly" is what is imperiled by mixing images. None of the explanations I found in the literature escape or go beyond that assumption, based on a prescribed identification between domains.

What *kind* of coherence and autonomy must "worlds" exhibit to merit the authority we grant them?[2] The complexity of this problem is summarized by Goodman:

> A version is taken to be true when it offends no unyielding beliefs and none of its own precepts. Among beliefs unyielding at a given time may be long-lived reflections of laws of logic, short-lived reflections of recent observations, and other convictions and prejudices ingrained with varying degrees of firmness. Among precepts, for example, may be choices among alternative frames of reference, weightings, and derivational bases. But the line between beliefs and precepts is neither sharp nor stable. (1978: 17)

I would like to cite two sources as to what constitutes "realism"; one is George Marcus and Dick Cushman on ethnographic real-

[1] Goodman (1976: 10–19) illustrates how eminently conventional and distanced from everyday physical experience is the "realism" of Renaissance perspective. Below, I discuss Ouspensky's work with the point-of-view metaphor, and Harries' discussion of point of view and perspective in art.

[2] In Needham's (1985) article on Psalmanaazaar, the authority of a wholly fabricated account of an invented culture is attributed to the articulation of details into systems (as opposed to the mere accumulation of a mass of ethnographic data).

ism, and the other is Karsten Harries on realism in artistic representation. I choose these two from many such descriptions relating
to diverse media, all of which have a striking "family resemblance." "Realist ethnographies," observe Marcus and Cushman,
"are written to *allude to a whole* by means of parts or foci of analytical attention which constantly evoke *a social and cultural totality*" (1982: 29). (From this, with a few alterations, we can also
derive some descriptions of successful "realist" projects in fiction
writing.)

It is, of course, an expectation (as described by James Clifford
[1983] and others) that ethnographers find systematicity in cultures and represent these cultures as systematic in the ethnographies they write. An examination of how we expect coherence in
worlds of many sorts can help us build up a context in which to
examine the particular case of systematicity in both the object of
anthropology and anthropological endeavors. As Harries writes,
"the presentation of interpretation and analysis is inseparably
bound up with the systematic and vivid representation of a world
that seems total and real to the reader" (1968: 29).

Harries traces this "wholeness" to the Platonic notion of a state
of timeless "being" from which man perceives himself to have
fallen and toward which he strives. This realm of forms or ideas,
says Harries, has represented for man "completeness," satisfac-
tion, "true being"; he contrasts it to Edmund Burke's notion of the
"sublime." Burke, relying on the Platonic definition of beauty, associates the latter with pleasure and the experience of being integrated in a community, and distinguishes this from the experience
of the sublime, a new image of "reality" and "nature," associated
with pain and danger, which "confronts man as an alien power"
(Harries 1968: 39). The resulting paradox of "how to reconcile the
immensity of the sublime with the beginning, middle, and end
which Aristotle demands of a work of art" (ibid.: 41) is one of
many related paradoxes in descriptions of the relation of engaged
people (and participant observers) to what they consider or call
"real," "true," etc.

What does the concept "realism" imply when applied in the
case of metaphor? In *what* does picturing the metaphor ground it?
If "realism" is the criterion from which truth emerges, it would be
good to know what its authority is like. Goodman (1976) examines

some possible parameters of "realism," including resemblance, deception, the amount of information presented, ease of access to this information, and faithfulness. These all relate to realism in different ways, but ultimately, he says,

> reality in a world, like realism in a picture, is largely a matter of habit. . . . For the man-in-the-street, most versions from science, art, and perception depart in some ways from the familiar serviceable world he has jerry-built from fragments of scientific and artistic tradition and from his own struggle for survival. The world, indeed, is the one most often taken as real. . . . Ironically, then, our passion for *one* world is satisfied, at different times and for different purposes, in *many* different ways.   (1978: 20)

Yet this constant psychological shiftiness, this eclecticism, this bricolage of realities, is not often acknowledged in the idealized, commonsense notion of reality.

Changing Points of View: Spatial Perspectives

> *It will be for you to say whether this defendant shall be allowed to come into court with unblushing footsteps, with the cloak of hypocrisy in his mouth, and to withdraw three bullocks out of my client's pocket with impunity.*
>
> *W. Crafts and H. Fisk,* Rhetoric Made Racy or Laugh and Learn

Satisfying that passion for *one* world in *many* different ways, "at different times and for different purposes," is something we do not usually notice ourselves doing. However, there are *unaccustomed* kinds of juxtapositions and "shifts" in "point of view" that *do* alert us. We notice shifting in Foucault's example of Borges's encyclopedia. Foucault describes the experience of reading that animals are divided into (a) belonging to the Emperor, (b) embalmed, (c) tame, (d) suckling pigs . . . (n) those that from a long way off look like flies, as taking place, by virtue of language, in "an unthinkable space," as "fragments of a large number of possible orders glittering separately . . . in sites so very different from one another that it is impossible . . . to define a *common locus* beneath them all," a "mythical homeland Borges assigns . . . to that picture that lacks all spatial coherence" (1970: xvii–xviii [empha-

sis mine], xix). "Lack" and "impossibility" are the judgments we
have seen in response to mixed metaphor; but the *rhythm* of the
classification a, b, c, d, . . . also suggests to me a process of *shifting*, a radical shifting in the case of the Chinese encyclopedia, as in
mixed metaphor.

What kind of shifting? How can we describe what happens
when animals are one moment instantiated as innumerable, the
next as drawn with a very fine camelhair brush, the next as "et
cetera," and the next as "having just broken the water pitcher"? If
each of these implies a different "possible order," and a locus
within it, the tendency is to read this classification as asking us to
move very quickly, impossibly quickly, from picturing one kind
of action or position in a particular context (or "domain") to another action or position, perhaps in a different setting. What's
more, we are asked to do this not only in space, yet somehow spatially nevertheless, or at least that is how we describe it. If this is
the kind of "shifting" mixed metaphor asks us to do, the language
traditionally used to describe mixed metaphor, "repulsive," "nauseous," "disgustful," "spoiled," "repugnant," etc. seems less gra-
tuitous; what is being described is a kind of metaphorical motion
sickness.

Shifting of "points of view" and the associated idea of "space"
are fundamental heuristic devices in the examination of literature
in the critical writing of Boris Ouspensky in *A Poetics of Composition* (1973) and of Wayne Booth in *The Rhetoric of Fiction* (1983).
The changes in point of view in the narratives that Ouspensky and
Booth discuss are sometimes abrupt or shocking; the shock, I suggest, is akin to that of a mixed metaphor, for reasons I have discussed above. Along what lines, then, can "point of view" shift?

Ouspensky specifies four "planes" or "basic semantic spheres
in which viewpoint may generally be manifested . . . planes of investigation in terms of which point of view may be fixed" (1973:
6), only one of which is the "spatial and temporal plane." Foucault
writes that the Chinese encyclopedia order is "spatially incoherent," but a comparison with Ouspensky shows in what a complex way Foucault means "spatial." Ouspensky cites (using Yuri
Lotman's description of) the character of the Nose in Gogol's story
of the same name. The Nose has a face; it walks, stooping; it runs

up stairs, wears a full dress coat, and prays with an expression of devout piety. All of these attributes of the Nose "completely destroy the possibility of imagining it in three-dimensional space" (ibid.: 78). Gogol's description of the Nose is indeed primarily *spatially* distressing, whereas Borges's list of definitions of "animal" moves us in a much more complicated way in terms of our implied involvement with the "animal" in question and the whole domain or context of the encyclopedia entry. In this way, the exotic and foreign "Chinese" encyclopedia demands a flexibility we do not consciously have in *much* more complex and conceptual ways than does the Nose, which merely defies visualization. Yet Foucault calls Borges's incoherence "spatial."

Benjamin Lee Whorf and many other writers have situated this spatializing tendency deeply within the European "relation of habitual thought and behavior to language." What Whorf calls "metaphors of spatial extension" for the expression of the experiences of duration, intensity, and tendencies are just one "part of our whole scheme of OBJECTIFYING" (1956: 145). This conceptualization of various aspects of life in spatial terms and the resulting treatment of them as such entails the bleeding over of certain ways of knowing space to these other realms. Because of this conflation of many dimensions of existence into the notion of space, Ouspensky's and Booth's works (although this is far from their intended purpose) can help us examine the range of experiences and conceptions we automatically treat in spatial terms.

Ouspensky's work shows that the "point-of-view" metaphor condenses "ideological," "phraseological," "psychological," and "spatial and temporal" planes. Because of the richness and complexity of this condensation, we can afford to lose sight of the fact that "point of view" is a metaphor. We forget about the sense of formalism that the adamantly spatial idea of "composition" brings; "point of view" implies that *position* is divorced from *what is being observed from that position*, a form-content dichotomy in which we recognize the split between "spatial form and spatial formless continuum," which Whorf (1956: 147) observed was inseparable from our tendency to deal with various aspects of life as images, as spatial.

Harries discusses the manifestations of point of view in art, showing its movement from a "pre-Cartesian" form, where there *is* point of view, but no orderly Academic perspective—"every part of the painting stands in a relationship of tension to other parts: its different parts cannot be synthesized from one point of view. We cannot take its measure" (1968: 42)—to the development of the Renaissance unity we have come to identify and expect from art—a unity that "has its foundation in the demand that the work of art be designed with respect to *a particular point of view.* This results in a new homogeneity; all objects are located in one space and are enveloped by the same light and atmosphere . . . *the world . . . in the image of reason*" (ibid.: 16–17; emphasis mine).

But can worlds really be constructed in the image of reason? They might be reduced to it, yet seem to be constructed more poetically or opportunistically than reasonably. James Fernandez (1982), in his studies of revitalization movements in which new worlds are attempted, finds in them a shiftiness in this regard. Indeed, he goes on to argue (1986 and unpublished lecture, 1987) that this "shape-shifting" is characteristically human and that in everyday life we *constantly* shift from metaphor to metaphor in our quest for understanding of situations. (Yet, as we have noted, *if* we were truly committed to the self-consciousness that strives to make assumptions explicit and to be theoretically consistent and truthful to what we start, we ought *not* to shift.) The implications of any particular predication we make on the world when we think it and act in it never get completely worked out. Shifts occur in our understanding, in the "image" we have of the situation, and suggest different ways of performing. This way of operating, which is very practical, differs from *our idea* of systematic scientific examination. Yet we see that the methods of art and of science are, in practice, not so absolute: throughout the unfolding of his organic metaphor for society, Spencer shifts, using any number of discrete versions of organic models, supported by a constant sliding from literal to figurative senses.[3] It is a creative mode of thought, and it

[3]For example, a potentially troubling difference that Spencer notices between the organic and social organizations is that "while the ultimate living elements of an individual organism are mostly fixed in their relative positions,

behaves like one. What I would like to call attention to, however, is that the definition of reality or truth taken from science and philosophy is permeated by ideological notions or norms of consistency and parsimony which are related to the desire for "objectivity." These norms and expectations are brought to bear upon the social sciences and the arts, resulting in a formalism or separation of form and content.

Certainly figurative language has a dizzying reservoir of possibility. Since in such language "all nature opens her stores, and allows us to collect without restraint," style texts give us rules to guide our choices, invoking the golden mean, some ideal of a safe, prudent way between extremes. Metaphors "must be suited to the nature of the subject; neither too numerous, nor too gay, nor too elevated for it," adds Richard Parker (1852: 117; he paraphrases Hugh Blair). Metaphors of a "discreet Author" are not too long: one writer, with a tendency to "run it on into the tiresome lengths of childishness and affectation," is recalled by Addison as "having said by chance that his mistress had a world of charms, thereupon took occasion to consider her as one possessed of frigid and torrid zones, and pursued her from one pole to the other" (1859: 388). "The reader is wearied, and discourse becomes obscured" (Parker 1852: 118). This moderation points again to a valuation of the invisible rhetorical artifice, and to how mixing metaphor, by *calling our attention to the device*, results in failure to produce persuasion. Our notion of reality, that by which we are persuaded, is of a state of mind from within *one* model. It was traditionally a tenet of art that the means of creating the illusion must never be noticeable, lest the illusion fail. We have seen this ideal in both art and science.

---

those of the social organism are capable of moving from place to place." He makes good of this, though, realizing that "while citizens are locomotive in their private capacities, they are fixed in their public capacities" (1981: 396); a shift from a literal to a metaphorical sense of "place." In another such case, where the "reality" of the metaphor is challenged, Spencer juggles several senses of the word "feeling": physical sensibility, emotional and intellectual sensibility, and consciousness (ibid.: 397). On one page, a person is a liver cell, passing away and being replaced; the next moment, however, blood cells are coins, and humans the active agents who propel the currents of commodities (ibid.: 418–19).

Arguments and Scientific Models as Spatially Grounded: The Notion of Structure

Mr. Speaker, I smell a rat; I see him floating in the air; I hear him rustling in the breeze; but I shall nip him in the bud.

W. *Crafts and H. Fisk,* Rhetoric Made Racy or Laugh and Learn

The charm dissolves apace,
And as the morning steals upon the night,
Melting the darkness, so their rising senses
Begin to chase the ignorant fumes that mantle
Their clearer reason.

Shakespeare, The Tempest *(Act 5, Scene 1)*

The issues of persuasion and convincing without shiftiness bring along with them nuances of *illusion* and *deceiving*, which seem to be both necessary (as Aristotle implies) and dangerous, as we shall now see. The "confounding of the imagination" from which mixed metaphor, that "unnatural medley" as Parker calls it, is said to emerge (and which it is said to produce) is often experienced as a suspicion that the author of the mixed metaphor is not quite honest. He or she means to pull the wool over our eyes. Of course, the question of whether these metaphors are in the context of a poem, a political speech, a scientific treatise, a sermon, or an ethnography matters; but, surprisingly, suspicion about the professional integrity and/or moral character of the author appears in all of these contexts. Adam Smith, for example, evaluates metaphors in terms of their "justice" (1971: 26–27). In the case of rhetoric, one argument concerning the danger of using metaphor in general is that

the unthinking majority are content with the crudest generalizations and *will accept a picture for an argument.* Counting on this, the mob orator . . . will tacitly assume that such and such a resemblance or analogy is complete *in all points* and will begin to draw arguments therefrom. All opposing facts and differences are quietly ignored. Moreover, the appeal is not really to reason, even unreasonable reason, but rather to passion. (Brown 1966: 238; emphasis mine)

This idea of the kinds of metaphoric pictures that make for acceptable argument raises philosophical questions. No one has addressed these more directly than Stephen Pepper.

In *World Hypotheses*, Pepper explicitly proposes that, at certain points in theoretical thought, just such an assumption that "the analogy is complete" is *necessary*, exactly *because of* the incorrectness of mixing root metaphors. Since, Pepper argues, all facts are not explicable by any one hypothesis, *some* major facts about the world are tested according to a potentially useful hypothesis, and then if it seems to be a powerful one, the assumption is made for the rest of the facts (1942: 97–98). Each "world hypothesis" (based on one "root metaphor") is *autonomous*, and, Pepper says, the interpretations of each make such a convincing picture that, if one hasn't compared them with parallel interpretations of rival hypotheses, one will inevitably accept them as indubitable and self-evident (ibid.: 101). There are two ways of acknowledging other theories, in Pepper's view. On the one hand, "we need *all* world hypotheses, so far as they are adequate, for mutual comparison and correction of interpretive bias" (ibid.: 101; emphasis mine). On the other hand, "eclecticism is confusing"; "if world hypotheses are autonomous, they are mutually exclusive" (ibid.: 104).

Although Pepper says that this last is a *cognitive* distinction, rather than a *practical* one, and that practical matters "often entail other than cognitive considerations" (ibid.), he does not follow up on this important distinction. He raises the question of whether a more adequate world theory can be developed by selecting "the best" in each theory and organizing these bits with a synthetic set of categories, as he claims Alfred North Whitehead and other philosophers do. But he answers that "the eclectic method is mistaken *in principle* in that it adds no factual content and confuses the *structures of fact* which are clearly spread out in the *pure* root-metaphor theories; such mixing is almost inevitably *sterile* and confusing" (ibid.: 106; emphasis mine). We are deposited back where we began, with the usual objections: that mixed metaphor is confusing and, in addition, sterile (as mating snakes and doves, in Horace's words, must be). Monstrous imagery is invoked:

But why do it? As a flight of fancy it may be amusing, as men have fancied fauns, centaurs, angels, and dragons. But it can hardly be a genuinely creative cognitive achievement. If a man is to be creative in his construction of a new world theory, he must dig among the crevices of common sense. There he may find the pupa of a new moth or butterfly. This will be alive and grow, and propagate. But *no synthetic combination of the legs of one specimen and the wings of another will ever move except as their fabricator pushes them about with his tweezers.* Moreover, what happens at the joints? What happens under the skin between the centaur's neck and body? How do the wings of angels fit into their shoulders? Either the eclectic glosses these difficulties over or we perceive confusion. (ibid.: 112; emphasis mine)

This argument is based on an ideal of an *organic sense or life* felt to reside only in *whole, unbroken models.* Thus the trace of the organic metaphor in concepts of culture and society implied by words like "system." The definitive "picturing" test for mixed metaphor shows quite clearly what sort of image is considered incorrect; we as a culture seem to need to deny that we have use for these mythological beasts, except to classify them as marginal beings which, like medieval and age-of-exploration conceptions of creatures at the unimaginable fringes of the world, are in need of civilization. Not only "the unthinking majority" accepts pictures for arguments.

Here Pepper treats the *deliberate* mixing of models, yet the monsters he uses to speak of contrivance are the same as the products of impassioned or sloppy, inept mixtures, and the same sort as Spencer's organic metaphor, outlined in footnote 3 above, suggests. Pepper says that ultimately, the strength of world hypotheses comes from *structural corroboration* and that we find them credible because their "scope is unlimited"; eclectic efforts limit the scopes of the contributing metaphors, have no root metaphor, and therefore do not move cognition forward at all (ibid.: 112). I am not clear on what kind of cognition this is. It seems to be the same kind that Thomas Kuhn assumes to be involved in the business of "normal science," which precludes the mixing of paradigms.

This part of Pepper's argument is quite similar to Kuhn's descriptions of the incompatibility and actual impossibility of two or more paradigms coexisting during any given period of productive "normal science"; both writers take this into account as an inevitable radical narrowing-down of the world to fit into the conceptual categories indicated or established by the reigning metaphor or paradigm. Kuhn writes that "the enterprise seems an attempt to force nature into the preformed and relatively inflexible box that the (learned) paradigm supplies. No part of the aim of normal science is to call forth new sorts of phenomena" (1970: 24). Novelties subversive of the basic commitments of the present paradigm are suppressed. Changing paradigms is considered a waste of scientific energy: "As in manufacture so in science—retooling is an extravagance to be reserved for the occasion that demands it." Kuhn's relativist claim is that once students learn their paradigm's language, that paradigm is a gestalt-like absolute and that a shift "must occur all at once . . . or not at all" (ibid.: 150). Thus, as in Pepper's model, worldviews are incommensurable and do not mix.

Shiftiness and the "Reality" of Social Science

When a man says he promises anything, he in effect expresses a resolution of performing it; and along with that by making use of this form of words, subjects himself to the penalty of never being trusted again in case of failure.

David Hume, A Treatise of Human Nature

According to both Pepper's and Kuhn's theories, mixed metaphor inevitably appears, but it is not normal. In general, the fear is that the "black art of metaphor" not only can confine our outlook and conceal evidence, but can also seduce us by changing models midstream, thereby convincing us of virtually anything (assuming that we are completely seduced).

The shiftinesses of metaphor and particularly of mixed metaphor slide inevitably into shiftiness of the author's character; anyone who displays more than one single "own vision of things" must be shifty, the type liable to "engender snakes with doves." "The experience seems quite impossible. The metaphor does not ring true. *The writer is convicted of falsehood to his own vision of things*" (Buck 1899: 64). Again, this points to the conclusion that *one image used in an argument is experienced as a promise*, a commitment to control the future, to synchrony; *two images vio-*

late that promise, for they suggest the imminence of other "more promising" arrangements.

If certain relations (or even communications) between people are *constituted* by a promise (as in a sense marriage is, going back to our metaphor), then, as Peter Wilson observes, breaking such a promise "results in the self-destruction of the relations. . . . If the failure of promises amounts to the disintegration of structure, then this failure must be regulated" (1980: 101)—that is, there must be a taboo.

An additional "problem" with eclecticism is revealed by another class of major complaints about mixed metaphor. On the one hand, mixed metaphor can cause unclarity and muddled confusion: "If the terms of the comparison become too soft and indefinite, the poetry disappears into a shimmering incoherence, . . . the relation between terms dissolves into a vague emotional blur" (Brooks 1965: 321–23). On the other hand, this confusion from mixed metaphor can be portrayed as a much more abrupt thing: an enigma, riddle, or mystery (Aristotle 1951: 83). Either way, perusal of it becomes "fatiguing" (Quintilian 1891: 127). Work is needed— and one may feel that no amount of work or "words supplied by the mind of the reader" (Bett 1932: 243) will help attain the desired end point, which seems to be *coherence, integration, a unitary "finished understanding."* If closure is the goal, mixed metaphors only "tease."

As Elliott Coleman has noted, Aristotle and Quintilian also said that metaphor itself "names the nameless" (1965: 151) and so fills semantic gaps, indeed says more than single words. Yet by thus pointing to complex relationships and images rather than to already known "kinds," metaphor must *necessarily* tend to ask the reader to do some work. Keith Basso writes that "metaphorical concepts must be attained on one's own through private acts of discovery and recognition. . . . Such acts are *creative* in the fullest and most genuine sense, for they presuppose and exemplify an ability to arrange familiar semantic features into unfamiliar combinations, to form fresh categorizations" (1976: 110). "T.D." writes that "moderating the intellect" may be even more dangerous than to attempt the more challenging broken metaphor: "Nothing can be more nauseous than a long drawn-out simile, crawling upon as many legs as a centipede" (1825: 722). There is an implied ideal in many of the "confusion" complaints, also implicit in the stipulation that rhetoric should not be noticed. This is the ideal that the *truth* of a (scientific) matter should be brought to us and deposited at our feet, so that we need do nothing but passively absorb it, as opposed to some supposed license of "art" to impressionistically allude to things or to "refer" to them "symbolically."

Tompkins writes that "On the one hand, the Metaphor, though shorter than the Simile, usually makes the mind do *more work*; on the other hand, the mind is rendered *more able to do work*— not, however, because it is gratified, but because it is *stimulated* to exertion" (1897: 310; emphasis mine). Let us then look at the way social scientists, especially anthropologists, work with metaphor, for they cannot, given the complexity of human relationships and human expressivity, simply lay the truth at our feet.

Gilbert Lewis, in his ethnography of the Gnau of New Guinea, uses concepts from Ernst Gombrich in his discussion of the "framing" of ritual symbols and of the way in which ordinary images and actions may thus "gain mystery" and ultimately additional meaning. Informants may explain a detail; there may be a straightforward explanation or an ordinary object involved; yet, in situations that strike us as "mysterious," we are nevertheless strangely "alerted" to the presence of the symbolic. Something is inappropriate, out of place; it must be a symbol. "Thus we become confused, speculation is invited" (Lewis 1980: 30). By violating convention, ordinary practice, or common knowledge, one can call attention to mystery—to complicated issues in all their complexity—by isolating elements usually known in other contexts. Alternatively, one may, if clarity is the goal, set the object or action round with clues to its meaning. The anthropologist, like the connoisseur, becomes sensitized to such stylistic cues and "learns to seek or judge whether what is aimed at is clear, unambiguous representation; or whether he, *just like those within the society*, is being asked to speculate and perceive something familiar in a new light. Isolation and cognitive dissonance may be recognizable as techniques at work in ritual" (ibid.; emphasis mine).

Of course, Lewis continues, the anthropologist is not free to assume that everything he does not understand aims at mystery in this way—yet "there are suggestive indications when the spectator is invited to 'ungate' through the isolation and situational oddity of some object or action or ritual" (ibid.: 31).

One marginally appropriate use of mixed metaphor which several sources grudgingly allow is when it is expressive of a *mood* we are to attribute to the utterer or the situation. This, of course, in a poem or a sermon, not in a scientific context, where it is expected that what cannot be given explicitly ought not be given. George Whalley argues against "common-sense 18th-century advice" prohibiting the promiscuity of "making two inconsistent metaphors on one object." He asserts: "A successful 'mixed metaphor' seems not so much to clarify the single image as to establish a certain 'tone.' . . . Hamlet's violent desperation is conveyed by a wretched incongruity" (1967: 150). And Bett writes that in a speech of Macbeth, "the metaphors are outrageous. . . . But despite this there is here a real justification of a psychological kind. . . . We feel that [the murderer's] insincerity is reflected in these strained and artificial metaphors" (1932: 244–45). Note that these sanctions of the mixing of metaphor when it expresses or generates a mood imply that the internal organization of the metaphorical domain *may* be "unrealistic" if (and only if) it is to be experienced *as incongruously organized*, that is, experienced *formally*, as representative of the kind of order or disorder it exists in—or, as Foucault says, the sort of "site" it could occur on.

The discovery of mixed metaphors in the work of "learned writers" also gets a different, more approving response. Those mixtures found in Shakespeare and Milton caused a great deal of debate and searching for justification over the years. Although Hamlet's line on taking arms against a sea of troubles was more than once, in the eighteenth century, actually pronounced some sort of misprint, originally written by Shakespeare as "assail of troubles" or other inoffensive version, John Ruskin found what he called "compressed significance" (Bett 1932: 242) in a mixed metaphor from Milton's *Lycidas*; and Gibbons finds some strings of metaphors to be "actually distinct sentences" (1969: 32). This interpretation of mixed metaphor as an acceptable or at least comprehensible "ellipsis," which I mentioned earlier (Bett 1932: 243), is invoked in such circumstances.

In "Edification by Puzzlement," Fernandez discusses the sermons of the Bwiti syncretist religious movement of the Fang. By using many "likenesses" in the sermons, Fernandez says, the Bwiti leader tries to "knit the world together," a world that is supposed to be "one thing, but the witches try to isolate men from each other so they can eat them" (1986: 179). Above, I quoted, Wallace Stevens that "reality is the indispensable element of each metaphor." The Bwiti sermon with its endlessly mixed metaphors, says Fernandez,

> sends us elsewhere to obtain our answers. They are rich in images which must, however, be contextualized by extension into the various domains of Fang culture. The interpretive task is therefore to move back and forth between text and context. . . . These sermons are examples of what Vygotsky . . . has called "thinking in complex." The sequence of images— the body images, the forest images, the vital liquids images, the suspended things images, the food images—put forth are not dominated by any overall conceived and stated purpose or by any dominant image. . . . New materials from various domains of Fang experience are introduced on the basis of association by similarity or contiguity, contrast, or complementarity with this sequence. But then again, abruptly, new elements with all their alternatives are allowed to enter the thought process and raise new thematic preoccupations—and to suggest new possible nuclei of attention. By any standard of administered intellectuality, such sermons seem diffuse and spontaneous in the extreme. (ibid.: 181–82)

This use of mixed metaphor in preaching in a distinctly different culture reminds us that there are text writers who admit the uses of mixed metaphors; yet this has been done close to home as well. Gibbons quotes Longinus and Demosthenes in making a general exception to the rule "no mixing": he says "we may on the same subject and in a manner in the same breath, introduce very different Metaphors . . . two or three at the most. . . . The time of using them is when the passions rush like a torrent, and bear along with them a multitude of Metaphors as necessary for the occasion" (1969: 30). Gibbons describes the way

> the sacred indignation of the Apostle blazes out and ceases, blazes out and ceases again, till he has finished his account of those most profligate wretches whose characters he was representing. . . . I aver that seasonable and vehement passions, and a noble sublimity, are a sufficient apology for the number and boldness of Metaphors; *for it is natural for the passions . . .*

by their own impetuous violence, to seize and carry all before them, and therefore as by an absolute necessity they challenge the boldest Metaphors; nor will they give leisure for the hearer to cavil against their number, as they inspire him with all the ardor of the Speaker. (ibid.: 33; emphasis mine)

Mixing metaphor for the creation of "mood" calls attention to incongruity and so is excused. Passionate, seductive mixing moves us through *not* calling attention to the device. The above arguments concerning the passionate mixing of metaphor go well with what Fernandez writes concerning the "mission of metaphor" in Bwiti sermons, "to turn inchoate objects of religious attention into something graspable and then to turn them into each other, to reconcile them, . . . suggesting an overarching integrity of things, a cosmology, by a convincing form of argument: the argument of images" (1982: 546). In general, it seems that the rhetoric of mixed metaphor has a home in religious contexts because of the performative implications, as well as because of a general acceptance that it is a *legitimate* purpose of sermons to seduce their listeners. It is a Durkheimian vision of a profane and broken-up world made sacred through a contagion of collective, often mixed-up imagery. "By forcing contextualization on the auditor, the cultural experience he is obliged to extend his interpretations to and consult is revitalized . . . cosmogony of an important kind" (Fernandez 1986: 181).

The important point is that cosmogony emerges out of mixing or "ill-formedness." Basso argues against Noam Chomsky's limitation of creative possibility in language use to "the unfolding of existing structures." "Wise words are prime examples of *appropriately ill-formed* utterances," he writes, citing Clifford Geertz in attributing the power of metaphor to generate what Basso calls *novel semantic categories* to "the interplay between discordant meanings" (Basso 1976: 111). The gifted maker of metaphor, who speaks in semantic contradictions, says Basso, is not "consistently obedient to the strictly grammatical rules of language" and *violates* rules rather than unfolding them when he produces and understands novel utterances (1976: 116). Harries notes how

Challenging Aristotle's claim that "a good metaphor implies an intuitive perception of the similarity in dissimilars," recent discussions have often insisted that, in poetry at least, metaphor joins dissimilars not so much to let us perceive in them some previously hidden similarity but to create something altogether new. As C. Day Lewis claims, "we find poetic truth struck out by the *collision* rather than the *collusion* of images." (1978: 73)

We have seen that the eclectic, colliding, mixing use of metaphor is excused if it happens to be done by great writers or speakers who are given the benefit of this doubt; it is often seen as a side effect of some higher level of functioning. Even Pepper writes that though eclecticism "does not move cognition forward at all, . . . all (or nearly all) the great philosophers were in various degrees eclectic." His three reasons for the occurrence of eclecticism are: (1) "undue faith in self-evidence and the indubitability of fact"; (2) "the desire to give credit to all good intuitions with the idea that these all have to be put inside *one* theory"; and (3) the recognition that "the great philosophers were not so much systematizers as seekers of fact, men who were *working their way into new root metaphors and had not yet worked their way out of old ones*. The eclecticism of these writers is, therefore, *cognitively accidental* and not deliberate, though psychologically unavoidable" (1942: 106; emphasis mine).

All three of these situations are familiar from our discussions of mixed metaphor and its perpetrators, the inspired, the impassioned, the unifiers of the world, the people in confused states of mind. "Confused" has negative connotations, whereas Pepper describes "exceptional" people in transitional states, looking around, in process. Are these "great philosophers" related to the "learned writers" who, we assume, have some "higher" reason to break metaphors, that we should try to interpret? Kuhn says that a multiplicity of paradigms appears at two stages in the scientific process. The first is in early developmental stages of most sciences, when many views of nature are competing and being tried out and there is no common body of belief (1970: 4). He adds, by the way, that "It remains an open question" what parts of social science have yet gotten beyond this stage and reached the point where one paradigm, "which emphasizes only some part of the too sizable and inchoate pool of information," triumphs (ibid.: 14, 20). The second stage—at which we see the rules for normal research loosened and "numerous partial solutions" appearing, along with a "proliferation of competing articulations, a willingness to try anything, the expression of explicit discontent, the recourse of philosophy and debate over fundamentals" (ibid.: 91)—is during a transitional crisis or "scientific revolution." These crises are characterized by ad hoc adjustments of theories with other theories, blurring of models, and in general, "a world out of joint," as described by Copernicus: "It is as though an artist were to gather the hands, feet, head and other members for his images from diverse models, each part excellently drawn, but not related to a single body, and since they in no way match each other, the result would be monster rather than man"; and by Einstein: "It was as if the ground had been pulled out from under one, with no firm foundation to be seen anywhere, upon which one could have built" (both from Kuhn 1970. 83).

Pepper insists that the "great [eclectic] philosophers" intuit a new root metaphor, but the intuitions are yet primitive, lack a technical vocabulary, and so are enmeshed in the categories of a former metaphor. We should honor their "keen sense for the facts," he says, not their "confusing eclecticism"; the cognitive value of the work of these men "comes not from the eclectic factor (which is entirely obstructive), but from the creative factor" (1942: 107).

Despite this, or perhaps because of it, what we are seeing emerge is a general, rigorous, and absolute sanction against mixed metaphor and an indictment of its creators in all domains of our culture, yet at the same time a general sanctioning of it, or at least a certain forgiveness, in the case of either great men, authorities, innovators, and geniuses or the subjects of anthropological inquiry. We allow these (however we determine who they are) to break the very rules which, according to Kuhn, are *necessary* for *normal* science to move on.[4]

The struggle over understanding how worlds are to be con-

---

[4] Mary Douglas, in her 1966 work on taboo, posits a structural analogy between pollution and sacredness. *Purity and Danger* could be read as an extended essay on the abhorrence of mixed metaphor: "though we seek to create order, we do not simply condemn disorder. We recognize that it is destructive to existing patterns; also that it has potentiality. It symbolizes both danger and power" (1966: 114).

structed is seen in microcosm in the struggle to understand how
the "small world" of the person is to be constructed. Here too we
find the same authority of ideas of unity, coherence, wholeness.
And the matter is not irrelevant to our topic, particularly if we
understand that we "build" ourselves metaphorically by predicat-
ing various metaphors on ourselves or on others (Coleman 1965;
Fernandez 1972).

Robert Barrett describes schizophrenia as a concept that per-
tains to failure to achieve our culture's ideal of personhood, as the
"quintessential disease category which absorbed and epitomized"
the images of a central nineteenth-century debate within psychi-
atric thought, a debate that "revolved around two concepts of
personhood in tension—on the one hand the person as a unified
indivisible ego and on the other as a divided ego" (1987: 21). As the
description of failure, in effect, to be a social person, the concept
of schizophrenia reveals negatively valued images (Barrett says
"symbols") that imply by opposition Western ideological expectations of individualistic "personhood."

The central features of this individualistic concept, Barrett
writes, quoting Paul Hirst and Penny Wooley, are

those of boundedness, autonomy and indivisibility. It is the conception
of the person as centered in a unitary consciousness, a subject "self-
possessed" in its conducts, experiences and thoughts, all of which flow
from a single and continuous origin. Consistency in conduct, self-
originated action, and unity of memory and experience are all criteria of
normality of this subject as conscious origin of itself. (ibid.: 7)

This "autonomous, integrated, atomistic, indivisible individual
characterized by reflective self-consciousness" (ibid.: 3) is the
ideal type, says Barrett, of "person" in our culture, "person" defined (following Donald Pollock) as "a being to whom members of
a culture attribute the capacity to be an agent of meaningful action" (ibid.: 6). In this "undivided totality in relation to God"
(ibid.: 21), of course, we recognize the Platonic ideal.

The concept of "ego splitting," on the other hand, appears

in the empirical ego psychology of the early nineteenth century, encapsu-
lated most clearly in the realist philosophy of Herbart. . . . In common
with anthropological psychiatry this tradition located personhood in con-

sciousness. . . . However the commitment to realism also led to a view of the person as an aggregate of multiple egos. Since consciousness changes depending on changing situations and relations, the ego is constantly changing—a heterogeneous ego. (ibid.: 22)

The ideology of split personhood that derived from this tradition "found clearest enunciation by Janet, whose concept of 'dissociation' referred to a weakening of the highest integrative functions, leading to a loss of the reality functions" (ibid.: 23). Thus we see here again the same clustering of the same terms—reality, unity, integration, autonomy, etc.

Conclusion: Purity and Opportunity

We never arrive intellectually. But emotionally we arrive constantly.

Wallace Stevens, Opus Posthumous

Mixed metaphor, besides being "untrue" and "unreal," is an *impure* union: Rudolf Flesch says that "clearly, if we want to avoid any misunderstanding, the best thing is not to use any rhetoric whatsoever. In other words, we must try *not* to play any games with our words or ideas" (1946: 104). Flesch offers a list of "plain talk" rules such as "Do not use metaphors without an explanation"; "Do not use periodic sentences"; and "Do not use irony (half the people won't get it)." Well. Enough said. Except that, as Rudolf Arnheim notes, "If simplicity were the one overriding goal of art, evenly stained canvases or perfect cubes would be the most desirable art objects." In art, "the simplicity principle rules unopposed only in closed systems" (1974: 410–11). One aspect of such closed systems is their autonomy, which I have touched on above. Autonomy is apparently an important part of the ideal that I am discussing and that mixed metaphor challenges. Another aspect is what Goodman calls the "touchstone of realism," the *ease* with which information issues from a work of art. This ease depends, he says, on "how stereotyped the mode of representation is" (1976: 36). The nature of the "realism" of metaphorical domains is too shifty—it ultimately refers back to "what is conventional" or persuasive, an ideal of a "living" coherence. As we have

242   *Metaphor and Coherence of Culture*

seen, however, neither the etiquette of metaphor nor the ideology
behind it is consistent; mixed metaphor is criticized for being un-
persuasive, yet feared and allowed for its persuasive power.

Harries writes that there is a tension in our expectations of art
in that, although we judge works of art by their unity, if metaphor
opens a work of art to a dimension that transcends it, refers to
things outside of it, then "it destroys our experience of the work
of art as a self-sufficient whole." But unity is not necessarily as
simple a thing as Flesch might maintain. Harries says that a demand for unity has not traditionally

> denied complexity, tension and incongruity, but order should triumph so
> that what may at first appear to be discordant elements are in the end rec-
> ognized to have been absolutely necessary. In a successful work of art
> [traditionally] nothing is superfluous, while it is impossible to add any-
> thing without weakening or destroying the aesthetic whole. The task of
> the observer or the reader is only to open himself to the artist's creation.
> Emphasis on the unity of the aesthetic object thus implies aesthetic dis-
> tance, separation of art from life. (1968: 74; bracketed comment mine)

As we have seen, truth seems to imply knowledge of some
whole, knowledge only possible from outside that integrated,
structured, distanced whole. Thus the "pure knowing subject," as
Harries calls him, must be imagined in the place of God—that is,
sharing with God the quality of being one's own foundation. The
autonomy of the ideal objective observer and the autonomy of
which he has this objective knowledge seem inherently linked—
which presents paradoxes. We expect works of art and other
"wholes" both to point beyond themselves, have meaning, be open,
and also to be closed, finished, with the presence of things of
nature.

> *More and more we tend to make our ability to comprehend the measure
> of reality.* Our commitment to objectivity and transparence forces us to
> see the world that moves us with its sights and sounds as no more than the
> perspectival appearance of a reality that yields its secrets only to the dis-
> located spirit. *So understood, reality leaves no room for genuine myster-
> ies.* (Harries 1978: 87–88, emphasis mine)

Such is the predicament involved in one debate over mixed
metaphor which satisfies emotionally but irritates intellectually.

But as the epigraph from Stevens makes clear, it is one thing to arrive emotionally and quite another to arrive intellectually. And it may just be that it is this emotional world of constant arrivals that anthropologists and poets are obliged to live in—as at least their first world. And it may be for that reason that they—unlike their more formal colleagues in the academy—are prepared to admit the creative power for both world and person of mixed metaphor.

Perhaps consciousness *cannot* leave room for "genuine mysteries." What is called mixed metaphor, as we have seen above, is the coming into consciousness of a mixing that goes on all the time, a consciousness that offends our sensibilities because it "calls attention to the device" and perhaps might reveal the inexplicable bases of our worldview.

The Japanese Tea Ceremony:

Coherence Theory and Metaphor in Social Adaptation

Benjamin N. Colby

> *In my own hands I hold a bowl of tea: I see all of nature repre-*
> *sented in its green color. Closing my eyes I find green mountains*
> *and pure water within my own heart. Silently sitting alone and*
> *drinking tea, I feel these become part of me.*
>
> Soshitsu Sen, Tea Life, Tea Mind

The tea ceremony is often regarded as the quintessence of things Japanese. "No student of Japanese culture," Okakura wrote, "could ever ignore its presence" (1964: 2). Sadler described the ceremony as "an epitome of Japanese civilization" (1963: vii). Most people will agree that tea masters have had an influential role in setting artistic standards for flower arrangement, painting, lacquer, and pottery in Japan. Many see these standards extending to art and taste in Japanese daily life—the manner of arranging and serving food and the use of muted earth-toned colors in decoration. Still others have said that simplicity and humility in the ceremony have influenced the general conduct of life in Japan. While statements like these are common, they fail to answer the deeper questions about why the ceremony exists or what psychocultural function it may fulfill for its participants.

In the tea ceremony, the social act of serving tea is given an artistic and literary quality by transforming the experience to ritual and symbols. It may be compared to the same effect created in a Japanese garden where nature is molded and manicured to highlight its more dramatic features. Similarly, a haiku celebrates the feelings of a perceived moment captured from time and replayed, distilled, and savored in harmony with a mood of impassioned contemplation. Seen as a literary process, the tea ceremony and statements about it yield interesting clues through metaphor and synecdoche. Symbolic representations form a web of meanings that jump across and link different domains of attention. At the center is the green tea itself as a representation of nature—green mountains and pure water.

Now there are two paths an anthropologist might take toward decoding this ceremony and the numerous Japanese writings about it. One path reaches toward the goal of the emic solution, which is to say, the description of the culture in its own terms so as to get at the meaning of experience and the "springs of action" in local parlance. This, though, is a difficult goal, because the elements in distribution are unclear and unbounded and the anthropologist constantly has to make decisions of interpretation that are questionably local, which is to say emic, in nature (if we use the term "emic" loosely; for a rigorous emic solution, see Colby 1973, Colby and Colby 1982). They might well be the anthropologist's own decisions. Further, emic solutions are descriptive rather than functional or causative. Today's pace of culture change and the demands for relevance in a dangerous age press, in my view, for predictive rather than descriptive theory. More feasible, then, is a second, more socially relevant, approach in which culture theory accounts for culture dynamics and transmission. Such a theory would necessarily be anchored in processes of natural selection—selection both of culture patterns and of individuals. Let us see what such a theory might amount to, taking into account the coherence in culture achieved by metaphoric associations and extensions.

The tea ceremony, like any other culture pattern, has evolved over a number of centuries. Earliest records of the use of tea itself are in China, where it was thought by Taoists to be a life-prolonging elixir. When it was brought to Japan by Buddhist monks, it was used in a religious context. The secular form of the ceremony as we know it today did not take shape until the fifteenth century under the patronage of the shogun Ashikaga Yoshimasa.

Shoguns had tea masters who were often influential figures— sometimes too much so in the eyes of their patrons. The great tea master Sen Rikyu was ordered by the shogun Toyotomi Hideyoshi to commit ceremonial suicide, which he did after holding a last ceremony. The day of his self-immolation has been romanticized in a manner that brings to mind writings on the death of Socrates— the contrasts, however, dramatically highlight differences between East and West. In the Japanese instance, emphasis is put on the politics of maintaining one's proper place and on taste, dignity, and procedure. In Greece, the issue centered on the relation of political rights and obligations to questions of individual human freedom and autonomy. Before his suicide, Rikyu arranged the flowers and decorations of his tea room and held his last ceremony, after which he gave away kettle, tea bowl, and other implements, and composed two poems. He then removed his tea clothes, revealing underneath the white clothes of ceremonial self-immolation. The principal guest remained during the final act, and Rikyu died by his own hand.

There are conflicting accounts of the motivation for Hideyoshi's order, but underlying most of them is a variation on one theme: Hideyoshi was angered by a growing presumptuousness on the part of Rikyu. Keeping one's proper place, as Ruth Benedict indicated long ago, is very important in Japan. Following this rule in everyday life, but even more in political life, is fraught with dangers, for each interpersonal relationship and situation is different, and the participants may not always agree on what one's proper place might be relative to others or whether one's behavior is appropriate to that place.

How might a culture theory sensitive to metaphor and yet based on the idea of natural selection and biocultural success be applied to these interpersonal anxieties and to the tea ceremony? Natural selection of patterns and people is best seen over the short run in terms of adaptive potential and such indicators of biocultural success as health and longevity.

Three Worlds of Human Concern

In one formulation of adaptive potential theory, there are three cognitive systems concerning worlds of human concern that organize analysis: the ecological (natural/material), the social, and the interpretive (Colby 1987b). We can begin with an observation concerning two of the three: the ceremony combines an idealization of the natural world with an extraordinary control over the social one. The idealization of nature centers on certain synecdochic relations engendered by a series of contextualizations that bring a natural world into being. The ceremony is first contextualized by its location, a tea hut in a garden. The approach to the hut, the waiting, and the entrance are all done in a manner designed to establish a mind-state that is receptive to the idealization of nature. The garden approach is described by the tea master Soshitsu Sen XV: "Quiet and unpretentious, modeled after a mountain trail, the simple stone pathway leads the guests through the compactly arranged trees, shrubs, and moss. The function of the garden is only to lead guests to the tea hut. In so doing the guests leave the mundane world and have an opportunity to relax and free their minds from worldly matters" (1979: 27).

Nature is thus enhanced in the garden through which guests pass on their way to the tea hut. The garden and path have been freshly watered, pathways not to be taken are blocked by a small stone wrapped with cord. There is a small spring or washing place where guests use bamboo cups to wash their hands and rinse out their mouths. Even the man-made objects, including the tea hut itself, are designed to accentuate the natural setting: "As the garden suggests a mountain trail, the tea hut suggests a simple mountain hermitage. Everyday materials, unpainted wooden posts and lintels, wattle walls, and thatched or bark roofs allow the structure to blend unobtrusively into the surroundings" (ibid.: 27).

As participants in the tea ceremony enter the hut, an ambience is created that sets the proper mood, bringing certain feelings and ideas to the fore. Each guest has his or her own image of the natural world—of forests, mountains, pathways, gardens—and of the state of mind associated with that world—a feeling of relaxation, of refuge from working life. The garden experience brings these feelings into play, so that they are readily attached to whatever experiences are to follow.

Inside the tea room there is silence, save for the sound of boiling water in the tea kettle: "The kettle sings well, for pieces of iron are so arranged in the bottom as to produce a peculiar melody in which one may hear the echoes of a cataract muffled by clouds, of a distant sea breaking among the rocks, a rainstorm sweeping through a bamboo forest, or of the soughing of pines on some far-away hill" (Okakura 1964: 35).

On entering, each guest goes to the *tokonoma* (an alcove in the tea room), places his fan on the mat, and bows in the direction of the scroll that hangs on the wall in the *tokonoma*. The guest silently admires the scroll and the flower arrangement, bows again, and proceeds, in turn, to observe and admire the charcoal fire, the kettle, and the brazier. Emphasis is on feeling the overall atmosphere that the tea master has studiously created—the view of the garden through an open door, the smell of incense in the charcoal fire, the flower arrangement.

The ecology, or setting, of the ceremony brings two analytical categories to the fore: diversity of culture patterns and efficacy of their production or use. Diversity is seen in the special selection of utensils, the subtle differences that mark the tea master's individuality and stamp: "In the tea-room the fear of repetition is a constant presence. The various objects for the decoration of a room should be so selected that no colour or design shall be repeated. If you have a living flower, a painting of flowers is not allowable. If you are using a round kettle, the water pitcher should be angular. A cup with a black glaze should not be associated with a tea-caddy of black lacquer" (ibid.: 40).

Efficacy in the serving of tea is emphasized by its performative nature in full view of the guests. After the period of silent appreciation, the guests take their places. Once seated, the first or principal guest invites the host (who has been waiting for this cue in the preparation room) to enter the tea room. On doing this, formal greetings are exchanged with each guest. The first guest then asks about the garden, the decorations, and other matters on behalf of the others.

Once these initial exchanges have been made, the tea making begins. Momentary pauses, positioning the tea container, examining the edges of the silk wiping cloth, purifying the tea scoop, positioning the tea whisk, wiping the lacquered container lid, picking up the water ladle, using special movements (each with its own terminology), and many other actions are carefully done with the greatest of attention given to the smallest detail.

Nearly every aspect of the ceremony, including the verbal exchanges, is highly scripted. Since the ecological world is characterized precisely by procedure and success is measured in terms of efficacy, the primary attention given to the process involves the ecological system. One looks in vain for the modality (modes of behavior) indicators that are important to recognize and code in the cognitive system of the social world to which we are ordinarily adapted.

In adaptive potential theory, these interpersonal modalities are defined by positive or negative degrees of autonomy or dependence in one dimension and by affection or intimacy in the other. Thus interactions involving a respect for the autonomy of all parties (i.e., tolerance and an absence of both power-seeking and dependency relations) and a positive affection toward them can be described as an egalitarian modality and are conducive of altruistic behavior. On the other hand, affection with dependency or low autonomy is typical of a paternalistic modality. Lack of affection (or, more negatively, presence of hostility) with dependency or dominance is typical of an authoritarian modality of behavior.

Here is precisely where the tea ceremony is so unusual to the Western mind, for it suppresses these modalities in every dimensional configuration. This contrasts starkly with everyday life. In Japan social interactions are so caught up with subtle distinctions in social position that they extend even to the language itself. It is for this reason that ritualized patterns of interaction are so prevalent, though unlike the tea ceremony, the ritualized etiquette of everyday life accentuates the modalities of social behavior rather than mutes them. The very rigor of this etiquette with bowing and ritualized apologies suggests a high need for regularity and predictability in social relations even though it brings in patterns of dominance and inferiority. In the tea ceremony, however, the dominance patterns are suppressed or changed, and the etiquette is brought to a pure form. The emphasis on procedure dampens the agential quality of interpersonal interaction and reduces the anxiety that may arise from differential perceptions of one's proper place—proper, that is, either in terms of the interacting situation or in terms of the broader social system.

At the tea ceremony, guests are present for only one explicit purpose, to ceremonially drink tea. Differential relations of social power among the guests have no way of being expressed. There is no sitting furniture where some chairs might be higher or more comfortable or impressive than others. Everyone sits in a kneeling position on a floor of tatami mats. Further, to enter the place of the ceremony in the most formal ceremonies requires that guests crawl through a narrow space, a symbolic stripping of social rank. While the first guest has a different position from the other guests in that he must initiate some of the interaction and perform his part in a slightly different way from the others, the first-guest position is a recognition of skill and familiarity with the ritual process as much as an act of hospitality. The first-guest position is not usually a recognition of social power or rank. This principle is illustrated with a story about Rikyu, who hosted a ceremony in which a merchant was to be the first guest. Just before the ceremony a powerful lord visited Rikyu, learned of the ceremony, and asked to be a guest. He happily took the last place, not being at all concerned that a lower-status person was the first guest (Sen 1979: 39).

Even the Zen background of the ceremony inhibits the expression of interpersonal modality, because in the obliteration of distinctions between small and great, mundane and spiritual, or trivial and ponderous, as occurs in Zen philosophy, persons as well as the material world are included. It is a material egalitarianism with far-reaching implications.

This attention to the smallest detail is one of the most remarkable aspects of the tea ceremony. The actions already mentioned are just a few in a long sequence of specified procedures. Another example is the prescriptions for exactly where on the mat the bowl is to be set (to the server's right) when the tea is served. This is then the cue for the first guest to slide forward, pick up the bowl, and return to his place. He places the bowl between himself and the second guest, and all bow. The first guest then picks it up with his right hand and turns the bowl twice in a clockwise direction so that when drinking his lips will not touch the front of the bowl (the part facing him when first set down by the host) and so on through the remainder of the ritual.

The way food and drink are served is generally a universal

touchstone of human relations in a society. Here we have seen how the offering of hospitality and food has been mechanized, stripped of all spontaneity and emotional reactivity. In so doing, a condition of concern in the ecological world, efficacy of procedure, has been extended to cover the social world as well. What can be made of this effacing of social modality? Studies by John Roberts suggest an answer.

The Use of Anxiety-Free Models

All societies, according to Roberts (Roberts and Sutton-Smith 1962; Roberts 1987), have certain areas of behavior in which cognitive conflict among individuals is more likely to occur than it is in others. Those who are conflicted in these areas are drawn to activities in the society that are associated with an anxiety-free model for behavior in the conflicted area. Involvement in these models allows anxiety-free learning of necessary skills that can be carried over to the conflicted area. They also assuage emotions that arise out of that conflict. All this is possible because the models are sufficiently disguised or removed from the reality being modeled. For example, the game of hide-and-seek models the negotiation of traffic.[1] The skills needed to cross a busy street (in horse-and-buggy days as well as today) involve the tracking of moving objects with respect to some goal (gaining the other side of the street or avoiding collision). They also require continuous vigilance in all directions. At the street corner, a young child may detect his mother's concern in these activities, or he may have been instructed to watch out for horses or cars, so that some anxiety and a heightened concern is associated with both the situation and the requisite skills required in the situation. Hide-and-seek requires the same skills: estimating how close other children may be to the home base requires the same skill as deciding if oncoming cars are still sufficiently distant to cross the street safely. Keeping a sharp lookout for someone suddenly emerging from a hiding place to race toward home base is the same as being alert for the

[1] This example remains unstudied and unconfirmed. Less intuitively obvious examples can be found in various studies by John Roberts (e.g., Roberts 1987; Roberts and Sutton-Smith 1962).

sudden appearance of new vehicles emerging from around a corner. These reasons for a child's attraction to the game are probably not conscious, but they are a subliminal recognition that the skills in the two activities are the same.

If the tea ceremony assuages anxieties in the sphere of social relationships, one would expect to find disguise or suppression of explicit representation in that area. Indeed, we find it in the absence of human figures in the paintings or the scrolls that are displayed on the wall in the tea room. We find it in the emphasis on nature itself, in which human presence is indicated only by artifacts or material things. In the tea ceremony this attention to the material aspects of the natural world shifts to the material aspects of the man-made world in the ritual appreciation shown toward the instruments of the tea-making process. After the tea drinking is finished, the tea bowls themselves are turned over and, in a reversal of Western etiquette, the artist's name or stamp on the bottom (if there is one) is noted with much ostentation and audible admiration.

The valuing of the material over the social is found in other cultural models in Japan. Favorite Japanese dramas depict the loss, or threatened loss, of a famous artifact or masterpiece. Early in this century, Kakuzo Okakura in his writing on the tea ceremony cited the story of a samurai who rushed into a burning building to save a religious painting. Upon reaching the painting, he found himself cut off from all means of escape. To save the picture, he wrapped the painting with his torn sleeve, then seizing his sword, he slashed open his body and plunged the wrapped painting into the gaping wound of his body. After the building burned to the ground, the half-consumed corpse yielded up the painting undamaged by the fire.

It has been argued here that the tea ceremony removes agential threats or anxiety arising out of interpersonal modality conflicts by the ritualization of social interaction and by a heightened emphasis on the ecological world, both in its natural (the garden) and material (utensils and process) aspects. In the light of Roberts's (1987) theory of expressive models and adaptive potential theory, the evidence suggests that anxiety in Japanese social interaction is diminished by materializing social behavior and reducing it to procedures that are stylized and predictable, as in the tea ceremony.

In the absence of sampling procedures and conflict measures, one can only speculate about the source of this anxiety and conflict. One can, however, mention the half-humorous observation noted by Matsudaira Sadanobu, a critic of the late eighteenth and early nineteenth centuries: "Tea people are liable to a number of complaints such as blindness, a slandering tongue, curio-mania, garden-mania, building-mania, swelled head, sycophancy, argumentativeness, over-eating and drinking, obsession with technique and cleanliness, stinginess, introversion, covetousness and dilettantism" (quoted in Sadler 1963: 84).

Except for blindness, dilettantism, and overeating, the terms in this list are traits likely to generate social conflict, given the behavioral logic that prevails in Japanese culture.[2]

Achieving Coherence in the Interpretation of the World

If predictability and harmony in Japanese social relations are problematic, if their achievement requires special effort and concentration to avoid anxiety and conflict, we can look to the third world of concern in adaptive potential theory, the interpretive world, for additional clues about how the tea ceremony assuages this anxiety. The interpretive world is touched most strongly by the need for coherence, which might be negatively defined as the absence of cognitive conflict. Coherence in the interpretive world concerns both oneself and one's circumstances. There must be meaning for the self, and this must connect to meaning for human existence generally.

Coherence in this respect takes on a special role in culture the-

[2]This does not necessarily mean, however, that people who characteristically generate social conflict provide the clientele for tea ceremonies. While such people are likely to be on the receiving end of reciprocal negative social behavior (and thus have need for learning more socially harmonious procedures such as are modeled in the tea ceremony), correlational studies should be directed at conflict rather than at personality traits. Conflicted personalities may be behaviorally suppressed but still be passed on from one generation to the next. Perhaps even the anxiety associated with conflict may be passed on, without the behaviors generating that anxiety.

ory. Since Ruth Benedict's configuration approach and Bronislaw
Malinowski's dimensional and systemic approach, there really has
not been anything like a fully integrative theory of cultural process that might be linked to the fundamental needs of individuals.
But coherence needs constitute a central, all-reaching force for the
individual, and it is precisely this force that underlies the creation
of culture (Colby 1987a).

Indeed this new role for coherence as a fundamental force is
well developed in James Fernandez's Bwiti (1982). Fernandez speaks
about returning to the whole through a series of metaphoric predications and ritual experiences in the Bwiti cult. In this process,
there is a "growth of human identity" and a transformation or
transcendence of a state where previous inadequacies were felt or
perceived. Fernandez speaks both of specific instances of metaphoric predication, and the resulting coherence created at this specific level, and of a larger sense of coherence created through many
metaphoric predications and expressive events in religious situations. The first kind of coherence is the familiar type discussed by
George Lakoff and Mark Johnson (1980b). The second, rarely explicitly discussed, concerns both sociological and psychological
coherence. It is a major concern, for example, in ethnomethodology,
which looks at how people reason to typify and normalize their
circumstances. As Harold Garfinkel explains, ethnomethodologi-
cal studies "show for ordinary society's substantive events, in material contents, that and just how members concert their activities
to produce and exhibit the coherence, cogency, order, meaning,
reason, methods, i.e., the orderliness, in and as of their ordinary
lives together, in detail" (1987: 9).

Constructing coherent patterns in social interaction involves
the second kind of high-level coherence that Fernandez refers to, a
psychological coherence. Another contribution to an integrative
theory in this area can be found in the work of Aaron Antonovsky,
which links mind and body. Just as Johnson (1987) emphasizes the
bodily basis of meaning and imagination, so Antonovsky (1987)
emphasizes a physiological basis for validating his measure of
coherence; people high in his Sense-of-Coherence measure are
physically healthier. Antonovsky defines sense of coherence as

a cognitive concept with three components: comprehensibility, manageability, and meaningfulness.

Comprehensibility is similar to Clyde Kluckhohn's (1956) binary value categories, Determinate–Indeterminate and Unitary–Pluralistic, except that Kluckhohn never linked his categories to a causal theory as Antonovsky does. In Kluckhohn's Determinate–Indeterminate definition, the world is seen as ordered, consistent, structured, and clear rather than chaotic, disordered, random, or accidental. In the Unitary–Pluralistic definition, the distinction is whether the world is seen as a single manifold of phenomena or whether things and forces operate under a plurality of different principles and systems.

Antonovsky's second component is manageability, or a feeling of control over the world, either through resources available to the individual or through a sense of being part of a social world populated by those one can count on or trust. The third component, meaningfulness, is described as "the extent to which one feels that life makes sense emotionally" (1987: 18).

In Antonovsky's words, coherence then involves "a global orientation that expresses the extent to which one has a pervasive, enduring though dynamic feeling of confidence that (1) the stimuli deriving from one's internal and external environments in the course of living are structured, predictable, and explicable; (2) the resources are available to one to meet the demands posed by these stimuli; and (3) these demands are challenges, worthy of investment and engagement" (ibid.: 19). The idea of coherence has created interest in behavioral medicine because it is predictive of health.

Fernandez, in referring to a similar coherence, has also linked coherence to stress on a broad scale. Bwiti ritual is "a process of 'tying together' (atsinge) that which witches and sorcerers and the agents of the colonial world and simply modern times have rent asunder into that anxious, isolated condition where men and women, bereft of the solidarity of the group, the strength of the whole, are, like the doomed Mba Muswi, preyed upon" (1982: 562). This higher type of coherence may be seen by empiricists as a literary conceit rather than as an observable and measurable concept that can facilitate the building of cumulative knowledge and understanding. But Antonovsky's work has clearly demonstrated that this is not so. The more abstract, higher-level coherence can indeed be measured, albeit indirectly, and shown to be valid and useful in behavioral medicine.

The Meaning of Coherence

One may first be inclined to object that coherence at a high level of conceptualization is very different from lower-level coherence, especially in its linguistic aspect. But this response is likely to arise from what Lakoff and Johnson would describe as an objectivist position. For Johnson, meaning applies to all levels: "Meaning is a matter of human understanding, regardless of whether we are talking about the meaning of someone's life, the meaning of a historical happening, or the meaning of a word or sentence" (1987: 176). If meaning applies to all levels, so also does coherence. And if this is so, one asks what these different levels of coherence have in common.

To begin with, there can be no sense of coherence without a prior sense of conceptual integrity of the component parts involved. That is, one has to start with two or more separate notions that are initially perceived as having separate existences. In metaphor, this relates to the idea of core meaning, but may also link to different notions of totality described by Edward Sapir (1930).

However described, conceptual entities that are distinguishable, that have conceptual boundaries such as exist in a metaphor, are necessary for establishing a coherence relation. That is, (1) there must be a sense of focused conceptual integrity that includes a boundary and (2) that boundary must be crossed. These are the essential characteristics of a coherence relation no matter what type or level.

How does one establish boundaries of ideas or topics of focused conceptual concern? There are two primary ways. One is to determine boundaries of syntagmatic cohesion between events or processes through time, especially narrative events and topics, particularly as they cluster or cohere in larger units, usually marked in English written texts as paragraphs. A method for doing this has already been worked out in a preliminary set of rules for measuring quanta in cohesion ties and salience indicators (Colby 1988).[3]

The other is to establish a focus of conceptual integrity through the identification of gestalts and core meanings. There are already several procedures for doing this analytically, but these have been limited mostly to material objects and have not been related to metaphoric relations. New work, however, has added some important theoretical changes and methodological techniques. In theory, David Kronenfeld has extended the core meaning approach in several sociosemantic studies that exemplify an extensionist theory of "central or core exemplars (schemas—in a sense, Gestalten)" (1988: 44).

The main function of metaphor, in Fernandez's theory, is to give what is here called focus and conceptual integrity to some inchoate feeling or notion through a metaphoric linkage or predication. Metaphor and other forms of analogy operate by pattern matching. Simply put, two concepts—source, or vehicle, and target, or tenor—are linked through the intersection of common attributes. This process can be represented in terms of metaphoric templates in an intersection frame. A template is not a complex pattern that precludes flexibility. The emphasis in metaphoric predication is rather on micro-sized templates that can join together in a variety of cognitive tasks, just as in the immune system antigens are recognized by antibodies. Templates match minimal meaning units or semantic attributes. Thus, in metaphoric predication, two separate concepts are linked by templates at one or more attribute points. So it is convenient to think of these templates as constituting an intersection frame in which these template-matched points are given special salience through association with the imagistically stronger or source element.

---

[3] The different kinds of cohesion ties have been described by Halliday and Hasan (1976). See also Greenberg's 1966 work on marked and unmarked categories. Some of the salience indicators at a higher level (Colby 1988) are: changes in scene, time, characters; particularization or narrowing of focus (often through metaphor); existentials; modality changes; valence and potency changes. Through a set of rules using these indicators, quantitative indices are assigned that represent conceptual integrity or syntagmatic coherence and story junctures by means of salience quanta.

Translating Theory into Analysis

How can all this be translated in an actual analysis? Let us take the tea ceremony. In the synecdochic relation of tea to nature, the tea has several attributes: (1) it is a frothy green; (2) it is made from pure water; and (3) it has a special, herbal smell. The garden outside has similar attributes that can be seen as coincidental to the tea in the cup. There is first the green of the garden, with its green plants, trees, and moss-covered ground. This links to the green froth of the tea, attribute (1). Next is the spring or water element in the garden for washing the hands and mouth which links with attribute (2). Finally, the smell of the garden, wet leaves, and earth (brought out more by sprinkling water around the garden path just before the ceremony) links with attribute (3). These three garden elements, in turn, can be linked at one more remove to the natural world beyond the garden.

But an intersection frame is not all that must be considered. Equally important is how the context of situation shapes or limits the semantic attributes in the intersection. Indeed, the context may have an even more profound influence than that of simply shaping or modifying attributes. As Kronenfeld points out, "if the context is common enough and stable enough for people to have standard or canonical expectations about it, secondary or context-specific cores can develop which, in that context, temporarily override the general core" (1988: 14). Whether minor modification or profound change in core meaning, the contextual influence requires another kind of frame, a contextual frame that links to the intersection frame. This more general frame is provided first by the garden and tea hut as a whole, and second, by the ritual itself. Thus the tea in the bowl, which already has a natural objectivity and saliency, is enhanced by the physical setting and by the ceremony that revolves around it.

Once having established this high degree of salience and meaning, the second process begins: the linking of coherence relations to achieve a symbolic controlling of the world, a restoring of the outer regions in the life space to a sense of coherence that is rarely to be found in the bustle of crowded subways, public work spaces, and all the stresses and hassles of modern urban life.

This, then, is a two-step process. First is metaphoric predication, the establishment of a source-to-target or vehicle-to-tenor linkage. Often this involves the imposition of a focused and conceptually integrated concept on what Fernandez speaks of as inchoate ideas. Then, after establishing a salient and focused idea through metaphor, one goes on to make the coherence linkage between that idea and some other.

In the tea ceremony control, serenity, and coherence are the conditions that are established in the interpretive system through a dual process: (1) moving from the inchoate to the focused through symbolic manipulations and contextualizations and (2) establishing cohesive ties and meaningful coherence.

Summarizing so far, in the social world, the confusions and uncertainties of interpersonal behavior are diminished by materializing social relations through the ecological world and reinterpreting and bringing them into a set of coherence relations in the interpretive world. The interpretive world includes art, science, and religion—the world of high culture, which is, of course, what most Japanese think of when they recognize the importance of the tea ceremony. The setting of standards for high culture in style and taste has indeed influenced Japanese artistry.

Conclusion: Toward Coherent Interdisciplinary Dialogue

In the modern world art for art's sake is a position often taken, but neither art nor high culture more generally considered can develop out of a vacuum. Religiosity, status distinctions, economics, and other strong forces are background for high culture (E. Sapir 1951; Bourdieu 1984). These forces give impetus and sustenance to high culture. There are, however, other forces at a deeper level of relevance, without which high culture cannot develop or exist. These concern the interpretive system in the most fundamental way: through a biocultural bonding noted by Victor Turner in his Notre Dame lecture, "Body, Brain, and Culture" (1987), in which he called for "a dialogue between neurology and culturology," suggesting that culture involves more than the external world and the physical accommodations that humans must make in that world. There is also the internal cognitive or neurophysiological world to consider. Turner suggested that a major function of ritual is to enable different parts of the brain, some more primitive or primordial than others, to come to terms with each other.

Turner's focus on coherence of cognitive functions is the first step. We then must proceed from this linkage between mind and culture, and between different components of the mind, to the one existing between mind and body. This last linkage has become more significant with the new knowledge that neurotransmitters and humoral communicators move in both directions, from mind to body and from body to mind.

Tea's first use was as a medicine, and what has developed since that time in Japan, it is argued here, has been a symbolic creation and contextualization of tea that, in itself, can benefit health through the reduction of stress and conflict arising out of social situations. This conflict is reduced via a therapeutic ritualistic involvement in the tea ceremony.

Anthropology, with its emphasis on the whole person and the whole cultural system, on the biological as well as the cultural person, is in a unique position to provide the insight so sorely needed for these studies as new data on psychoneuroimmunology emerge. Without coherence, adaptive potential is low.[4] With adaptive potential low, the modalities of human interpersonal behavior will be authoritarian rather than egalitarian, hostile and self-serving rather than friendly and life-supportive.

In the tea ceremony, the focus is on the tea as the nodal intersection of the symbolic network. As a mood-inducing substance, tea is ideal. There is high salience in its physical attributes and physiological effect. It is whipped to a frothy green drink with a special taste and smell. The consuming of this liquid then becomes the final act in the crossing of boundaries. The symbolic matrix of externally observed circumstances is crossed by incorporating the natural world and the controlled and materialized social world into the body.

---

[4] On the other hand, because high coherence can also exist with low adaptive potential this relationship does not work in the reverse direction.

Reference Matter

Bibliography

Addison, Joseph
　　1859 [1711–14] *The Works of Joseph Addison.* New York: Harper and Bros.
Albisetti, C., and A. J. Venturelli
　　1962 *Enciclopedia Bororo,* vol. 1. Campo Grande, Brazil: Museu Regional Dom Bosco.
Alvarez-Pereyre, J.
　　1984 *The Poetry of Commitment in South Africa.* London: Heinemann Educational Books.
Antonovsky, Aaron
　　1987 *Unraveling the Mystery of Health: How People Manage Stress and Stay Well.* San Francisco: Jossey-Bass.
Aristotle
　　1951 *Poetics.* Trans. S. H. Butcher. New York: Dover.
　　1960 [1932] *The Rhetoric of Aristotle.* Trans. L. Cooper. New York: Appleton-Century Crofts.
Armstrong, R. P.
　　1975 *Wellspring: On the Myth and Source of Culture.* Berkeley: University of California Press.
Arnheim, Rudolf
　　1974 *Art and Visual Perception.* Berkeley: University of California Press.
Attinasi, John, and Paul Friedrich
　　1990 "Dialogic Breakthrough: Catalysis and Synthesis in Life-Changing Dialogue." In Bruce Mannheim and Dennis Tedlock, eds., *The Dialogic Emergence of Culture.* Philadelphia: University of Pennsylvania Press.
Bakhtin, Mikhail
　　1981 *The Dialogic Imagination: Four Essays by M. M. Bakhtin.* Ed. Michael Holquist; trans. Caryl Emerson and Michael Holquist. Austin: University of Texas Press.

1984a *Problems of Dostoevsky's Poetics*. Ed. and trans. Caryl Emerson. Minneapolis: Minneapolis University Press.
1984b *Rabelais and His World*. Trans. Helen Iswolsky. Bloomington: Indiana University Press.

Barrett, Robert
1987 "Schizophrenia and Personhood." Manuscript.
1988 "Interpretations of Schizophrenia." *Culture, Medicine, and Psychiatry* 12 (3, Sept.): 357–88.

Barthes, Roland
1964 *Elements of Semiology*. London: Weston.

Bartlett, F. C.
1932 *Remembering*. Cambridge, Eng.: Cambridge University Press.

Basso, Keith
1976 "'Wise Words' of the Western Apache: Metaphor and Semantic Theory." In Keith H. Basso and Henry A. Selby, eds., *Meaning in Anthropology*. Albuquerque: University of New Mexico Press.

Bastien, Adolph
1895 *Ethnische Elementargedanken in der Lehre von Menschen*. Berlin: Weidmanische Buchhandlung.

Bastien, Joseph
1978 *Mountain of the Condor: Metaphor and Ritual in an Andean Ayllu*. St. Paul, Minn.: American Ethnological Society.

Beidelman, T. O.
1968 "Some Nuer Notions of Nakedness, Nudity, and Sexuality." *Africa* 38: 113–67.

Benjamin, Walter
1979 *Charles Baudelaire: A Lyric Poet in the Era of High Capitalism*. Trans. Harry Zohn. London: New Left Books.
1986 *Reflections*. New York: Schocken Books.

Berlin, Brent
1968 *Tzeltal Numeral Classifiers*. The Hague: Mouton.

Berlin, Brent, Dennis Breedlove, and Peter Raven
1974 *Principles of Tzeltal Plant Classification*. New York: Academic Press.

Berlin, Brent, and Paul Kay
1969 *Basic Color Terms: Their Universality and Evolution*. Berkeley: University of California Press.

Bett, Henry
1932 *Some Secrets of Style*. Port Washington, N.Y.: Kennikat Press.

Bicchieri, Cristina
1988 "Should a Scientist Abstain from Metaphor?" In A. Klamer, D.

McCloskey, R. Solow, eds., *The Consequences of Economic Rhetoric*. Cambridge, Eng.: Cambridge University Press.

Black, Max
1962 *Models and Metaphors*. Ithaca, N.Y.: Cornell University Press.

Blair, Hugh
1854 *Lectures on Rhetoric and Belles Lettres*. Philadelphia: Hayes & Zell.

Boas, Franz
1914 *The Handbook of American Indian Languages*. Washington, D.C.: Bureau of American Ethnology, Bulletin No. 40.
1982 "Metaphorical Expression in the Language of the Kwakiutl Indians." In *Race, Language, and Culture*. Chicago: University of Chicago Press.

Bolinger, Dwight
1980 *The Melody of Language*. Ed. Linda Waugh and C. H. van Schooneveld. Baltimore: The Johns Hopkins University Press.

Booth, Wayne
1978 "Metaphor as Rhetoric: The Problem of Evaluation." *Critical Inquiry* 5 (1), special issue.
1983 *The Rhetoric of Fiction*, 2nd ed. Chicago: University of Chicago Press.

Bourdieu, Pierre
1984 *Distinction: A Social Critique of the Judgment of Taste*. Trans. R. Nice. Cambridge, Mass.: Harvard University Press.

Brooks, Cleanth
1949 *The Well Wrought Urn: Studies in the Structure of Poetry*. London: Harcourt Brace Jovanovich.
1965 "Metaphor, Paradox, and Stereotype." *British Journal of Aesthetics* 5 (4): 315–28.

Brown, Stephen J.
1966 *The World of Imagery: Metaphor and Kindred Imagery*. New York: Russell and Russell.

Brugman, Claudia
1981 "Story of Over." M.A. thesis, University of California, Berkeley.

Buck, Gertrude
1899 "Pathological Forms of Metaphor." In *The Metaphor: A Study of the Psychology of Rhetoric*. Ann Arbor, Mich.: Inland Press.

Bühler, Karl
1982 [1934] *Sprachtheorie*. Stuttgart: Fischer.

Burke, Kenneth
1955 *A Grammar of Motives*. New York: George Braziller.

1957 *The Philosophy of Literary Form: Studies in Symbolic Action.*
      New York: Vintage Books.
1966 *Language as Symbolic Action.* Berkeley: University of California
      Press.
Bynner, Witter, and Kiang Kang-Hu
1957 [1929] *The Jade Mountain.* New York: Knopf.
Carnap, Rudolf
1956 *Meaning and Necessity.* Chicago: University of Chicago Press.
Carrithers, Michael
1985 "An Alternative Social History of the Self." In M. Carrithers,
      S. Collins, and S. Lukes, eds., *The Category of the Person.* Cam-
      bridge, Eng.: Cambridge University Press.
Carrithers, Michael, Steven Collins, and Steven Lukes, eds.
1985 *The Category of the Person.* Cambridge, Eng.: Cambridge Univer-
      sity Press.
Caton, Steven C.
1987 "Contributions of Roman Jakobson." *Annual Review of Anthro-
      pology* 16: 223–60.
Cheng, François
1982 *Chinese Poetic Writing: With an Anthology of T'ang Poetry.*
      Trans. Donald A. L. Riggs and Jerome P. Seaton. Bloomington: In-
      diana University Press.
Chomsky, Noam
1966 *Cartesian Linguistics.* New York: Harper and Row.
1972 *Language and Mind.* New York: Harcourt Brace Jovanovich.
Clifford, James
1983 "On Ethnographic Authority." *Representations* 1 (2): 118–46.
Cohen, Theodore
1979 "Metaphor and the Cultivation of Intimacy." In S. Sacks, ed., *On
      Metaphor.* Chicago: University of Chicago Press.
Colby, B. N.
1973 "A Partial Grammar of Eskimo Folktales." *American Anthropolo-
      gist* 75 (3): 645–62.
1987a "Coherence in Language and Culture." In Ross Steele and Terry
      Threadgold, eds., *Language Topics.* Amsterdam: John Benjamins.
1987b "Well-Being: A Theoretical Program." *American Anthropologist*
      89 (4): 879–95.
1988 "Mapping Plot Junctures in Traditional Narrative." To appear in a
      Festschrift for John M. Roberts, Ralph Bolton, ed. New Haven,
      Conn.: HRAF Press.

Colby, B. N., and Lore M. Colby
    1982 *The Daykeeper: The Life and Discourse of an Ixil Diviner.* Cambridge, Mass.: Harvard University Press.
Colby, B. N., J. W. Fernandez, and David Kronenfeld
    1981 "Towards a Convergence of Cognitive and Symbolic Anthropology." *American Ethnologist* 8 (3): 442–50 (special issue on Symbolism and Cognition, ed. J. Doherty and J. W. Fernandez).
Coleman, Elliott
    1965 "The Meaning of Metaphor." *Gordon Review* 8 (4): 151–63.
Coleridge, Samuel T.
    1973 "Kubla Khan" and "Biographia Literaria" (Selections). In Harold Bloom and Lionel Trilling, eds., *Romantic Poetry and Prose.* Oxford: Oxford University Press.
Collins, A., M. Collins, and Ross Quillian
    1969 "Retrieval Time from Semantic Memory." *Journal of Verbal Learning and Verbal Behavior* 8: 240–47.
Constable, John
    1731 *Reflections Upon Accuracy of Style.* London.
Crafts, Wilbur F., and H. F. Fisk
    1884 *Rhetoric Made Racy or Laugh and Learn.* Chicago: Geo. Sherwood and Co.
Crocker, J. Christopher
    1977 "The Social Functions of Rhetorical Forms." In J. David Sapir and J. Christopher Crocker, eds., *The Social Use of Metaphor.* Philadelphia: University of Pennsylvania Press.
    1985 "My Brother the Parrot." In Gary Urton, ed., *Animal Myths and Metaphors in South America.* Salt Lake City: University of Utah Press.
Culler, Jonathan
    1981 *The Pursuit of Signs: Semiotics, Literature, Deconstruction.* Ithaca, N.Y.: Cornell University Press.
D., H. [Hilda Doolittle]
    1957 "Epitaph." *Selected Poems of H. D.* New York: New Directions.
"D., T."
    1825 "On the Use of Metaphors." *Blackwood's Edinburgh Magazine* 18: 719–23.
D'Andrade, Roy
    1982 "Reason versus Logic." Paper presented at a symposium on "The Ecology of Cognition: Biological, Cultural, and Historical Perspectives," Greensboro, N.C., Apr.

1989 "Cultural Cognition." In Michael I. Posner, ed., *Foundations of Cognitive Science*. Cambridge, Mass.: MIT Press.

n.d. "Culturally Based Reasoning." Manuscript. Department of Anthropology, University of California, San Diego.

de Man, Paul

1979 *Allegories of Reading*. New Haven, Conn.: Yale University Press.

Douglas, Mary

1966 *Purity and Danger: An Analysis of Concepts of Pollution and Taboo*. Harmondsworth: Penguin.

Duncan, Robert

1973 [1961] "Ideas of the Meaning of Form." In Donald M. Allen and Warren Tallman, eds., *The Poetics of the New American Poetry*. New York: Grove Press.

Eliot, T. S.

1975 "Tradition and the Individual Talent." In Frank Kermode, ed., *Selected Prose of T. S. Eliot*. New York: Farrar, Strauss, and Giroux.

Errington, Joseph J.

1985 "On the Nature of the Sociolinguistic Sign: Describing Javanese Speech Levels." In E. Mertz and R. Parmentier, eds., *Semiotic Mediation: Sociocultural and Psychological Perspectives*. Orlando, Fla.: Academic Press.

Evans-Pritchard, E. E.

1956 *Nuer Religion*. Oxford: Oxford University Press.

Fernandez, James W.

1969 *Microcosmogony and Modernization in African Religious Movements*. Montreal: McGill University Center for Developing Area Studies.

1972 "Persuasions and Performances: Of The Beast in Every Body and the Metaphors of Everyman." *Daedalus* 101 (1): 39–80.

1974 "The Mission of Metaphor in Expressive Culture." *Current Anthropology* 15 (2): 119–45.

1982 *Bwiti: An Ethnography of the Religious Imagination in Africa*. Princeton, N.J.: Princeton University Press.

1985 "The Argument of Images and the Experience of Returning to the Whole." In V. Turner and E. Bruner, eds., *The Anthropology of Experience*. Champaign: University of Illinois Press.

1986 *Persuasions and Performances: The Play of Tropes in Culture*. Bloomington: Indiana University Press.

Flesch, Rudolf

1946 *The Art of Plain Talk*. New York: Harper and Bros.

Fodor, Jerry A.
   1975 *The Language of Thought.* New York: Crowell.
   1983 *The Modularity of Mind: An Essay in Faculty Psychology.* Cambridge, Mass.: MIT Press.
Fogelin, Robert
   1988 *Figuratively Speaking.* New Haven, Conn.: Yale University Press.
Foucault, Michel
   1970 *The Order of Things: An Archeology of the Human Sciences.* New York: Random House.
Fox, James J.
   1971 "Sister's Child as Plant: Metaphors in an Idiom of Consanguinity." In R. T. Needham, ed., *Rethinking Kinship and Marriage.* London: Tavistock.
   1977 "Roman Jakobson and the Comparative Study of Parallelism." In D. Armstrong and C. Van Schooneveld, eds., *Roman Jakobson: Echoes of His Scholarship.* Lisse, Neth.: Peter de Ridder Press.
Frazer, J. G.
   1927 *Man, Gods, and Immortality.* New York: Macmillan.
   1935 *The Golden Bough,* 2-vol. ed. New York: Macmillan.
Freedman, Maurice
   1969 "Geomancy." In *Proceedings of the Royal Anthropological Institute of Great Britain and Ireland for 1968.* London: Royal Anthropological Institute of Great Britain and Ireland.
Frege, Gottlob
   1952 "On Sense and Reference." In P. Geach and M. Black, eds., *Translations from the Philosophical Writings of Gottlob Frege.* Oxford: Blackwell.
Friedrich, Paul
   1978 *The Tarascan Suffixes of Locative Space: Meaning and Morphotactics.* Bloomington: Indiana University Press.
   1979 *Language, Context, and the Imagination: Essays by Paul Friedrich.* Ed. Anwar S. Dil. Stanford, Calif.: Stanford University Press.
   1986 *The Language Parallax.* Austin: University of Texas Press.
   1988 "Eerie Chaos and Eerier Order." Review of *Chaos: Making a New Science,* by James Gleick. *Journal of Anthropological Research* 44 (4): 435–44.
   1989 "Language, Ideology, and Political Economy." *American Anthropologist* 91 (2): 295–312.
Frost, Robert
   1974 "Out, Out—." In *Poetry of Robert Frost.* Ed. Connery Lathem. New York: Holt, Rinehart and Winston.

Garfinkel, Harold
   1987 "A Reflection." *The Discourse Analysis Research Group News-letter* 3 (2).
Geertz, Clifford
   1973 *The Interpretation of Cultures*. New York: Basic Books.
Gennette, Gerard
   1972 *Metonymie chez Proust*, Figures III. Paris: Seuil.
Gentner, Dedre, and Donald R. Gentner
   1983 "Flowing Waters or Teeming Crowds: Mental Models of Electricity." In D. Gentner and A. L. Stevens, eds., *Mental Models*. Hillsdale, N.J.: Lawrence Erlbaum Associates.
Gibbons, Thomas
   1969 [1767] *Rhetoric; or a view of its principal tropes and figures*. Menston, Eng.: Scolar Press.
Gilmore, J. H.
   1891 *Outlines of Rhetoric for Schools and Colleges*. Boston: Leach, Shewell, and Sanborn.
Gleick, James
   1988 *Chaos: Making a New Science*. New York: Viking.
Goldman, Alvin I.
   1986 *Epistemology and Cognition*. Cambridge, Mass.: Harvard University Press.
Gombrich, Ernst H.
   1963 "Visual Metaphors of Value in Art." In *Meditations on a Hobby Horse*. Chicago: University of Chicago Press.
Goodman, Nelson
   1976 *Languages of Art*. Indianapolis: Hackett.
   1978 *Ways of Worldmaking*. Indianapolis: Hackett.
Gordimer, Nadine
   1973 *The Black Interpreters*. Johannesburg: Raven Press.
Granet, Marcel
   1977 [1922] *The Religion of the Chinese People*. Trans. Maurice Freedman. New York: Harper and Row.
Greenberg, Joseph H.
   1966 *Language Universals with Special Reference to Feature Hierarchies*. The Hague: Mouton (Janua Linguarum No. 59).
Halliday, M. A. K., and Ruqaiya Hasan
   1976 *Cohesion in English*. London: Longman.
Hanks, William F.
   1990 *Referential Practice: Language and Lived Space*. Chicago: University of Chicago Press.

Hardy, Thomas
  1986 [1901] "The Ruined Man." In X. J. Kennedy, ed., *An Introduction to Poetry*, 6th ed. New York: Little, Brown.
Harries, Karsten
  1968 *The Meaning of Modern Art: A Philosophical Interpretation*. Evanston, Ill.: Northwestern University Press.
  1978 "Metaphor and Transcendence." In Sheldon Sacks, ed., *On Metaphor*. Chicago: University of Chicago Press.
Hawkes, David
  1967 *A Little Primer of Tu Fu*. Oxford: Oxford University Press.
Hegel, G. W. F.
  1977 [1807] *Phenomenology of Spirit*. Trans. A. V. Miller, with analysis of the text and foreword by J. N. Findlay. Oxford: Oxford University Press.
Henderson, Harold G.
  1958 *An Introduction to Haiku. An Anthology of Poems and Poets from Basho to Shiki*. Garden City, N.Y.: Anchor.
Herrick, Marvin T.
  1974 "Catachresis." In Alex Preminger, Frank J. Warnke, and O. B. Hardison, eds., *Encyclopedia of Poetry and Poetics*. Princeton, N.J.: Princeton University Press.
Herzfeld, Michael
  1987 *Anthropology Through the Looking Glass: Critical Ethnography in the Margins of Europe*. Cambridge, Eng.: Cambridge University Press.
Hesse, M. B.
  1976 "Models versus Paradigms in the Natural Sciences." In L. Collins, ed., *The Use of Models in the Social Sciences*. London: Tavistock.
Hirson, B.
  1979 *Year of Fire, Year of Ash. The Soweto Revolt: Roots of a Revolution?* London: Zed Press.
Holland, Dorothy, and Naomi Quinn, eds.
  1987 *Cultural Models in Language and Thought*. Cambridge, Eng.: Cambridge University Press.
Hollis, Martin
  1985 *Of Masks and Men*. In M. Carrithers, S. Collins, and S. Lukes, eds., *The Category of the Person*. Cambridge, Eng.: Cambridge University Press.
Hume, David
  1888 [1739] *A Treatise of Human Nature*. Ed. L. A. Selby-Bilgge. Oxford: Clarendon Press.

272 Bibliography

1927 [1739–40] "A Treatise of Human Nature." In Charles W. Hendel, Jr., ed., *Hume Selections*. New York: Charles Scribner's Sons.

Humphrey, Caroline
1988 "Material Objectifications of the Self in Mongolian Ritual of Death." Paper presented at a conference on "The Representation of Complex Cultural Categories," King's College, Cambridge University, Mar. 21–25.

Hung, William
1952 *Tu Fu, China's Greatest Poet*. Cambridge, Mass.: Harvard University Press.

Hunt, Theodore W.
1891 *The Principles of Written Discourse*. New York: A. C. Armstrong and Son.

Iida, Michio
1973 *Saru Yomoyama Banashi—Saru to Nihon no Minzoku* (Tales about monkeys—the monkey and Japanese folkways). Tokyo: Hyōgensha.

Inada, Kōji, and Tatehiko Ōshima
1977 *Nihon Mukashibanashi Jiten* (Dictionary of Japanese folktales). Tokyo: Kōbundō.

Ingold, Tim
1986 *Evolution and Social Life*. Cambridge, Eng.: Cambridge University Press.
1988 *What Is an Animal?* London: Unwin Hyman.

Jackendoff, Ray
1983 *Semantics and Cognition*. Cambridge, Mass.: MIT Press.

Jakobson, Roman
1956 "Two Aspects of Language and Two Types of Aphasic Disturbances." In R. Jakobson and M. Halle, *Fundamentals of Language*. The Hague: Mouton.
1957 "Shifters, Verbal Categories, and the Russian Verb." In *Selected Writings of Roman Jakobson*, vol. 11. The Hague: Mouton.
1960 "Concluding Statement: Linguistics and Poetics." In T. A. Sebeok, ed., *Style in Language*. Cambridge, Mass.: MIT Press.

Jakobson, Roman, C. Fant, and M. Halle
1952 *Preliminaries to Speech Analysis*. Massachusetts Institute of Technology Acoustics Laboratory, Technical Report No. 13, 2nd ed.

Jakobson, Roman, and Morris Halle
1956 *Fundamentals of Language*. The Hague: Mouton.

Jardine, Nick
  1980 "The Possibility of Absolutism." In D. H. Mellor, ed., *Science, Belief, and Behaviour: Essays in Honour of R. B. Braithwait*. Cambridge, Eng.: Cambridge University Press.
Johnson, Mark
  1987 *The Body in the Mind: The Bodily Basis of Meaning, Imagination, and Reason*. Chicago: University of Chicago Press.
Karsten, Rafael
  1926 *The Civilisation of the South American Indians*. London: Kegan Paul.
Katz, Jerrold
  1972 *Semantic Theory*. New York: Harper and Row.
Kay, Paul
  1979 *The Role of Cognitive Schemata in Word Meaning: Hedges Revisited*. Department of Linguistics, University of California, Berkeley.
Kay, Paul, and Chad McDaniel
  1978 "The Linguistic Significance of the Meanings of Basic Color Terms." *Language* 54 (3): 610–46.
Kellogg, Brainerd
  1895 *A Text-Book on Rhetoric*. New York: Maynard, Merrill, and Co.
Kempton, Willett
  1981 *The Folk Classification of Ceramics: A Study of Cognitive Prototypes*. New York: Academic Press.
Kluckhohn, Clyde
  1956 "Toward a Comparison of Value-Emphases in Different Cultures." In Leonard D. White, ed., *The State of the Social Sciences*. Chicago: University of Chicago Press.
Kokot, Waltraud
  1982 *Perceived Control and the Origins of Misfortune: A Case Study in Cognitive Anthropology*. Berlin: Dietrich Reimer Verlag.
Kokot, Waltraud, Harmut Lang, and Eike Hinz
  1982 "Current Trends in Cognitive Anthropology." *Anthropos* 77: 329–50.
Kovecses, Zoltan
  1986 *Metaphors of Anger, Pride, and Love: A Lexical Approach to the Study of Concepts*. Philadelphia: J. Benjamins.
Kripke, S.
  1972 "Naming and Necessity." In Donald Davidson and Gilbert Harman, eds., *Semantics of Natural Language*. Dordrecht, Neth.: Reidel.

Kristeva, Julia
    1984 *Revolution in Poetic Language.* Introduction by Leon S. Roudiez.
        New York: Columbia University Press.
Kroeber, Karl
    1983 "The Wolf Comes In: Indian Poetry and Linguistic Criticism." In
        Brian Swann, ed., *Smoothing the Ground: Essays on Native Ameri-
        can Oral Literature.* Berkeley: University of California Press.
Kronenfeld, David B.
    1988 "Full Bloods and Protestants: Extensionist Semantics in Complex
        Domains." Paper presented at a conference on "The Representa-
        tion of Complex Cultural Categories," King's College, Cambridge
        University, Mar. 21–25.
Kuhn, Thomas
    1970 *The Structure of Scientific Revolutions.* Chicago: University of
        Chicago Press.
Kurano, Kenji, and Yūkichi Takeda, eds.
    1958 *Kojiki Norito* (Kojiki and Norito). Tokyo: Iwanami Shoten.
LaFleur, William R.
    1983 *The Karma of Words.* Berkeley: University of California Press.
Lakoff, George
    1986 "A Figure of Thought." *Metaphor and Symbolic Activity* 1 (3):
        215–25.
    1987a "Foreword" to Mark Turner, *Death Is the Mother of Beauty.*
        Chicago: University of Chicago Press.
    1987b *Women, Fire, and Dangerous Things: What Categories Reveal
        About the Mind.* Chicago: University of Chicago Press.
Lakoff, George, and Mark Johnson
    1980a "Conceptual Metaphors in Everyday Life." *Journal of Philosophy*
        77 (8): 453–86.
    1980b *Metaphors We Live By.* Chicago: University of Chicago Press.
Langer, Susanne K.
    1980 [1942] *Philosophy in a New Key.* Cambridge, Mass.: Harvard Uni-
        versity Press.
Leach, Edmund
    1964 "Anthropological Aspects of Language: Animal Categories and
        Verbal Abuse." In E. H. Lenneberg, ed., *New Directions in the
        Study of Language.* Cambridge, Mass.: MIT Press.
    1976 *Culture and Communication.* Cambridge, Eng.: Cambridge Uni-
        versity Press.
Levin, Samuel
    1977 *The Semantics of Metaphor.* Baltimore: The Johns Hopkins Uni-
        versity Press.

Lévi-Strauss, Claude
1963 [1962] *Totemism*. Boston: Beacon Press.
1964 *Le Cru et le Cuit*. Paris: Plon.
1966 [1962] *The Savage Mind*. Trans. George Weidenfeld and Nicolson Ltd. Chicago: University of Chicago Press.
1967 [1958] *Structural Anthropology*. New York: Doubleday & Co.
Levy-Bruhl, Lucien
1910 *Les Fonctions mentales dans les sociétés inférieures*. Paris: Librairies Alcan et Guillaumin.
Lewis, Gilbert
1980 *Day of Shining Red*. Cambridge, Eng.: Cambridge University Press.
Lincoln, Bruce
1987 "Ritual, Rebellion, Resistance: Once More on the Swazi Newala." *Man* 22 (1): 132–56.
Linde, Charlotte
1987 "Explanatory Systems in Oral Life Stories." In D. Holland and N. Quinn, eds., *Cultural Models in Language and Thought*. Cambridge, Eng.: Cambridge University Press.
Liu, James
1983 [1962] *The Art of Chinese Poetry*. Chicago: University of Chicago Press.
Lord, Albert B.
1965 *Singer of Tales*. New York: Atheneum.
Mandler, J. M., and N. S. Johnson
1977 "Remembrance of Things Parsed: Story Structure and Recall." *Cognitive Psychology* 9: 111–51.
Mandler, J. M., S. Scribner, M. Cole, and M. DeForest
1980 "Cross-Cultural Invariance in Story Recall." *Child Development* 51: 267–76.
Marcus, G., and D. Cushman
1982 "Ethnographies as Texts." *Annual Review of Anthropology* 11: 25–69.
Mauss, Marcel
1985 [1938] "A Category of the Human Mind: The Notion of Person; the Notion of Self." In M. Carrithers, S. Collins, and S. Lukes, eds., *The Category of the Person*. Cambridge, Eng.: Cambridge University Press.
McClintock, Anne
1987 "'Azikwelwa' (We Will Not Ride): Politics and Value in Black South African Poetry." *Critical Inquiry* 13: 597–623.

276

Bibliography

Miller, Daniel
1987 *Material Culture and Mass Consumption*. Oxford: Basil Blackwell.
Minakata, Kumakusu
1972 [1971] *Minakata Kumakusu Zenshū* (Collected essays by Minakata Kumakusu), vol. 1. Tokyo: Heibonsha.
Mitchell, W. J. T.
1986 *Iconology: Image, Text, Ideology*. Chicago: University of Chicago Press.
Montague, R.
1973 "The Proper Treatment of Quantification." In R. Thomason, ed., *Formal Philosophy*. New Haven, Conn.: Yale University Press.
Müller, Friedrich Max
1873 *Introduction to the Science of Religion*. London: Longmans.
Nakamura, Teiri
1984 *Nihonjin no Dōbutsukan—Henshintan no Rekishi* (Japanese views of animals—history of tales about metamorphoses). Tokyo: Kaimeisha.
Ndebele, Njabulo
1987 "The English Language and Social Change in South Africa." In David Bunn and Jane Taylor, eds., *From South Africa* (*TriQuarterly* 69: 217–35). Reprinted in Bunn and Taylor, eds., *From South Africa: New Writing, Photographs, and Art*. Chicago: University of Chicago Press, 1988.
Needham, Rodney
1985 "Psalmanaazaar, Confidence-Man." In *Exemplars*. Berkeley: University of California Press.
Neruda, Pablo
1971 [1962] "Brussels." In Neruda and Vallejo, *Selected Poems*. Trans. and ed. Robert Bly. Boston: Beacon Press.
Niane, D. T.
1965 *Sundiata: An Epic of Old Mali*. Trans. F. D. Pickett. London: Longman Group.
Noppen, Jean-Pierre, S. J. Knapp, and R. Jongen
1985 *Metaphor: A Bibliography of Post-1970 Publications*. Amsterdam: John Benjamins.
Northrup, F. S. C.
1947 *The Logic of the Sciences and the Logic of the Humanities*. New York: Macmillan.
Ohnuki-Tierney, Emiko
1973 "Sakhalin Ainu Time Reckoning." *Man* 8 (2): 285–99.

1981 "Phases in Human Perception/Cognition/Symbolization Processes: Cognitive Anthropology and Symbolic Classification." *American Ethnologist* 8 (3): 451–67.

1984 *Illness and Culture in Contemporary Japan.* Cambridge, Eng.: Cambridge University Press.

1987 *The Monkey as Mirror: Symbolic Transformations in Japanese History and Ritual.* Princeton, N.J.: Princeton University Press.

1988 "Emergent Meanings and Transforming Categories." Paper presented at a conference on "The Representation of Complex Cultural Categories," King's College, Cambridge University, Mar. 21–25.

1990a "The Ambivalent Self of the Contemporary Japanese." *Cultural Anthropology* 5: 197–216.

1990b "The Monkey as Self in Japanese Culture." In E. Ohnuki-Tierney, ed., *Culture Through Time: Anthropological Approaches.* Stanford, Calif.: Stanford University Press.

n.d. a "The Emperor as *Kami*: The Japanese Imperial System in Historical Perspective." Completed ms.

n.d. b *Rice as Self.* Manuscript in preparation.

Okakura, Kakuzo

1964 [1906] *The Book of Tea.* New York: Dover.

Ollman, Bertell

1976 *Alienation,* 2nd ed. Cambridge, Eng.: Cambridge University Press.

Ortner, Sherry

1973 "On Key Symbols." *American Anthropologist* 75 (6): 1338–46.

Ortony, Andrew, ed.

1979 *Metaphor and Thought.* Cambridge, Eng.: Cambridge University Press.

Ouspensky, Boris

1973 *A Poetics of Composition: The Structure of the Artistic Text and Typology of Compositional Form.* Trans. V. Zavarin and S. Wittig. Berkeley: University of California Press.

Parker, Richard G.

1852 *Aids to English Composition.* New York: Harper and Brother.

Parra, Nícanor

1960 *Poems and Anti-Poems.* Trans. Lawrence Ferlinghetti, Allen Ginsberg, et al. San Francisco: City Lights.

Peirce, Charles S.

1940 *Selected Writings.* Ed. Justus Buchler. New York: Dover Press.

Pepper, Stephen C.

1942 *World Hypotheses.* Berkeley: University of California Press.

Philippi, Donald, trans.
    1969 *Kojiki*. Princeton, N.J.: Princeton University Press. Tokyo: University of Tokyo Press.
Piaget, Jean
    1968 *Le Structuralisme*, "Que sais-je?" 1311. Paris: P.U.F.
Poe, Edgar Allan
    1968 *The Complete Poetry and Selected Criticism of Edgar Allan Poe*. Ed. and with Intro. by Allen Tate. New York: New American Library.
Porkert, Manfred
    1974 *The Theoretical Foundations of Chinese Medicine: Systems of Correspondence*. Cambridge, Mass.: MIT Press.
Putzar, Edward D.
    1963 *The Tale of Monkey Genji, Sarugenji-zoshi. Monumenta Nipponica* 1–4: 286–312.
Quine, W. V. O.
    1960 *Word and Object*. Cambridge, Mass.: MIT Press.
Quinn, Naomi
    1981a "Commitment in American Marriage: A Cultural Analysis." *American Ethnologist* 9 (4): 299–311.
    1981b "Marriage Is a Do-It-Yourself Project: The Organization of Marital Goals." In *Proceedings of the Third Annual Conference of the Cognitive Science Society*. Berkeley: University of California Press.
    1987 "Convergent Evidence for a Cultural Model of American Marriage." In D. Holland and N. Quinn, eds., *Cultural Models in Language and Thought*. Cambridge, Eng.: Cambridge University Press.
    1988 "Love and the Experiential Basis of American Marriage." Paper presented at a conference on "Love in Social and Historical Perspective." Charlottesville, Va., Apr.
    in progress *American Marriage: A Cultural Analysis*.
Quinn, Naomi, and Dorothy Holland
    1987 "Culture and cognition." Introduction to D. Holland and N. Quinn, eds., *Cultural Models in Language and Thought*. Cambridge, Eng.: Cambridge University Press.
Quintilian
    1891 *Institutes of Oratory*, vol. 2. Trans. George Bell. London.
Radcliffe-Brown, A. R.
    1952 *Structure and Function in Primitive Societies*. Glencoe, Ill.: Free Press.

Radin, Paul
 1945 *The Road of Life and Death: A Ritual Drama of the American Indians*. New York: Pantheon Press.
 1949 *The Culture of the Winnebago as Described by Themselves*. Special Memoir, *International Journal of American Indian Languages*.
Restle, F., and E. Brown
 1970 "Organization of Serial Pattern Learning." In K. W. Spence and J. T. Spence, eds., *The Psychology of Learning and Motivation: Advances in Research and Theory*, vol. 4. New York: Academic Press.
Ribs, L. J., E. J. Shoben, and E. E. Smith
 1973 "Semantic Distance and the Verification of Semantic Relations." *Journal of Verbal Learning and Verbal Behavior* 12: 1–20.
Rice, G. Elizabeth
 1980 "On Cultural Schemata." *American Ethnologist* 7 (1): 152–71.
Richards, I. A.
 1950 [1936] *The Philosophy of Rhetoric*. New York: Oxford University Press.
Ricoeur, Paul
 1987 [1975] *The Rule of Metaphor*. Toronto: University of Toronto Press.
Roberts, John M.
 1987 "Within Culture Variation." *American Behavioral Scientist* 31 (2): 266–79.
Roberts, John M., and Brian Sutton-Smith
 1962 "Child Training and Game Involvement." *Ethnology* 1: 166–85.
Rorty, Richard
 1978 *Philosophy and the Mirror of Nature*. Princeton, N.J.: Princeton University Press.
Rosaldo, Michelle
 1972 "Metaphor and Folk Classification." *Southwestern Journal of Anthropology* 28 (1): 83–99.
Rosaldo, Renato
 1968 "Metaphors of Hierarchy in a Mayan Ritual." *American Anthropologist* 70 (3): 524–36.
Rosch, Eleanor
 1973 "Natural Categories." *Cognitive Psychology* 4: 328–50.
 1975 "Cognitive Representations of Natural Categories." *Journal of Experimental Psychology* 104: 192–233.
 1977 "Human Categorization." In N. Warren, ed., *Studies in Cross-Cultural Psychology*. New York: Academic Press.

1978 "Principles of Categorization." In E. Rosch and B. B. Lloyd, eds., *Cognition and Categorization*. New York: Halsted.

1981 "Prototype Classification and Logical Classification: The Two Systems." In E. Scholnik, ed., *New Trends in Cognitive Representation: Challenges to Piaget's Theory*. Hillsdale, N.J.: Lawrence Erlbaum Associates.

Sacks, Sheldon, ed.

1979 [1978] *On Metaphor*. Chicago: University of Chicago Press.

Sadler, A. L.

1963 *Cha-No-Yu: The Japanese Tea Ceremony*. Rutland, Vt., and Tokyo: Charles E. Tuttle Co.

Saigō, Nobutsuna

1967 *Kojikino Sekai* (The world of the *Kojiki*). Tokyo: Iwanami Shoten.

Sakamoto, Tarō, Saburō Ienaga, Mitsusada Inoue, and Susumu Ōno, eds.

1967 *Nihon Shoki*, vol. 1. Tokyo: Iwanami Shoten.

Sapir, J. David

1977 "The Anatomy of Metaphor." In J. D. Sapir and J. C. Crocker, eds., *The Social Use of Metaphor*. Philadelphia: University of Pennsylvania Press.

Sapir, J. David, and J. Christopher Crocker, eds.

1977 *The Social Use of Metaphor: Essays on the Anthropology of Rhetoric*. Philadelphia: University of Pennsylvania Press.

Sapir, Edward

1930 *Totality*. Language Monograph No. 6.

1951 "Culture, Genuine and Spurious." In David G. Mandelbaum, ed., *Selected Writings of Edward Sapir in Language, Culture and Personality*. Berkeley: University of California Press.

Saussure, F. de

1966 *Course in General Linguistics*. New York: McGraw-Hill.

Searle, John R.

1975 "A Taxonomy of Illocutionary Acts." In J. Gunderson, ed., *Language, Mind, and Knowledge*. Minnesota Studies in the Philosophy of Science, no. 6.

1983a *Intentionality: An Essay in the Philosophy of Mind*. Berkeley: University of California Press.

1983b [1969] *Speech Acts: An Essay in the Philosophy of Language*. Cambridge, Eng.: Cambridge University Press.

Sen, Soshitsu, XV

1979 *Tea Life, Tea Mind*. New York: Weatherhill.

Shapiro, Michael, and Marianne Shapiro

1976 *Hierarchy and the Structure of Tropes*. Bloomington: Indiana University Publications, Studies in Semiotics, vol. 8.

1988 *Figuration in Verbal Art*. Princeton, N.J.: Princeton University Press.

Shimonaka, Yasaburō, ed.
  1941 *Shintō Daijiten* (Encyclopedia of Shintō), vol. 2. Tokyo: Heibonsha.

Silverstein, Michael
  1976 "Shifters, Linguistic Categories, and Cultural Description." In K. Basso and H. A. Selby, eds., *Meaning in Anthropology*. Albuquerque: University of New Mexico Press.

Smith, Adam
  1971 [1762–63] *Lectures on Rhetoric and Belles Lettres*. Carbondale: Southern Illinois University Press.

Smith, Jonathan Z.
  1972 "I Am a Parrot (Red)." *History of Religions* 2 (4): 391–413.

Smith, Robert J.
  1983 *The Japanese Society*. Cambridge, Eng.: Cambridge University Press

Snyder, Gary
  1978 [1960] "Hunting 13." In *Myths and Texts*. New York: New Directions.
  1980 *The Real Work. Interviews and Talks, 1964–79*. New York: New Directions.

Spencer, Herbert
  1967 *The Evolution of Society*. Ed. Robert L. Carneiro. Chicago: University of Chicago Press.
  1981 [1860] "The Social Organism." In *Man Versus the State*. Indianapolis: Liberty Fund Classics.

Stankiewicz, Edward
  1964 "Problems of Emotive Language." In Thomas A. Sebeok, ed., *Approaches to Semiotics*. The Hague: Mouton.
  1978 "Poetics and Literary Art." In Thomas A. Sebeok, ed., *A Perfusion of Signs*. The Hague: Mouton.

Stevens, Wallace
  1951 *The Necessary Angel: Essays on Reality and the Imagination*. New York: Knopf.
  1954 "The Idea of Order at Key West" and "The Planet on the Table." In *The Collected Poems of Wallace Stevens*, pp. 128–30, 532. New York: Knopf.
  1969 *Opus Posthumous: Poems, Prose, Plays*. New York: Knopf.

Sweetser, Eve
  1990 *From Etymology to Pragmatics: Metaphorical and Cultural Aspects of Semantic Structure*. Cambridge, Eng.: Cambridge University Press.

Tambiah, S. J.
  1968 "The Magical Power of Words." *Man* (n.s.) 3 (2): 175–208.
  1969 "Animals Are Good to Think and Good to Prohibit." *Ethnology* 8 (4): 423–59.
Tannen, Deborah
  1987 "Repetition as Spontaneous Formulacity." *Text* 7 (3): 215–43.
Tarski, A.
  1952 "The Semantic Conception of Truth." In L. Linsky, ed., *Semantics and the Philosophy of Language*. Urbana: University of Illinois Press.
Tedlock, Barbara, and Dennis Tedlock
  1985 "Text and Textile: Language and Technology in the Arts of the Quiche Maya." *Journal of Anthropological Research* 41 (2): 121–46.
Todorov, Tzvetan
  1970 "Synecdoques." *Communications* 16: 26–35.
  1982 *Symbolism and Interpretation*. Ithaca, N.Y.: Cornell University Press.
  1987 [1977] *Theories of the Symbol*. Ithaca, N.Y.: Cornell University Press.
Tompkins, Arnold
  1897 *The Science of Discourse*. Boston: Ginn and Co.
Tsvetaeva, Marina
  1968 "Popytka revnosti" (Attempt at jealousy). In *Marina Tsvetaeva*. Trans. Elsa Triolet. Paris: Gallimard.
Turco, Lewis
  1973 *Poetry: An Introduction Through Writing*. Reston, Va.: Reston Publishing Company.
Turner, Mark
  1987 *Death is the Mother of Beauty*. Chicago: University of Chicago Press.
Turner, Terence
  1973 "Piaget's Structuralism." *American Anthropologist* 25 (2): 351–73.
  1977a "Narrative Structure and Mythopoeisis: A Critique and Reformulation of Structuralist Approaches to Myth and Poetics." *Arethusa* 10 (1): 103–63.
  1977b "Transformation, Hierarchy, and Transcendence: A Reformulation of Van Gennep's Model of the Structure of Rites de Passage." In Sally F. Moore and Barbara Meyerhoff, eds., *Secular Ritual*. Assen, Neth.: Van Gorcum.
  1985 "Animal Symbolism, Totemism, and the Structure of Myth." In

Gary Urton, ed., *Animal Myths and Metaphors in South America*. Salt Lake City: University of Utah Press.

Turner, Victor
1967 *The Forest of Symbols*. Ithaca, N.Y.: Cornell University Press.
1974 *Dramas, Fields and Metaphors*. Ithaca, N.Y.: Cornell University Press.
1987 "Body, Brain, and Culture." In *Waymarks: The Notre Dame Inaugural Lectures in Anthropology*. Notre Dame, Ind.: University of Notre Dame Press.

Tyler, Stephen A.
1978 *The Said and the Unsaid*. New York: Academic Press.

Tylor, E. B.
1877 *Primitive Culture: Researches into the Development of Mythology, Philosophy, Religion, Language, Art, and Custom*. New York: Macmillan.

Ullmann, Stephen
1964 *Language and Style*. Oxford: Blackwell.

Urciuoli, Bonnie
1985 "The Cultural Construction of Linguistic Variation." Ph.D. diss., University of Chicago.

Van Baaren, Th. P.
1969 "Are the Bororo Parrots or Are We." *Liber Amicorum: Studies in Honor of Professor Dr. C. J. Bleeker*. Leiden.

Vaughan, M.
1985 "Literature and Populism in South Africa." In G. M. Gugelberger, ed., *Marxism and African Literature*. Trenton, N.J.: Africa World Press.

Vico, Giambattista
1976 [1948; 1961] *New Science of Giambattista Vico*. Ed. T. Bergin and M. Fisch. Ithaca, N.Y.: Cornell University Press.

Voloshinov, V. N.
1986 [1973] *Marxism and the Philosophy of Language*. Trans. Ladislav Matejka and I. R. Titunik. Cambridge, Mass.: Harvard University Press.

Voltaire
1835 "Remarques sur le Cid." *Oeuvres Completes*, vol. 31. Paris: Chez Furne.

von den Steinen, Karl
1894 *Unter den Naturvölkern Zentral-Brasiliens*. Berlin.

Wagner, Roy
1975 *Invention of Culture*. Chicago: University of Chicago Press.
1986 *Symbols That Stand for Themselves*. Chicago: University of Chicago Press.

Watsuji, Tetsurō
  1959 *Rinrigaku* (Ethics), vol. 1. Tokyo: Iwanami Shoten.
Weller, Susan, and A. Kimball Romney
  1988 *Structured Interviewing and Data Collection Techniques*. Beverly Hills, Calif.: Sage Publications.
Werner, Oswald, and G. Mark Schoepfle
  1987 *Systematic Fieldwork: Foundations of Ethnography and Interviewing*, 2 vols. Beverly Hills, Calif.: Sage Publications.
Whalley, George
  1967 *Poetic Process*. Cleveland: World Publishing Co.
Wheelwright, Philip
  1962 *Metaphor and Reality*. Bloomington: Indiana University Press.
White, Hayden
  1983 [1973] *Metahistory: The Historical Imagination in Nineteenth-Century Europe*. Baltimore: The Johns Hopkins University Press.
  1978 *Tropics of Discourse: Essays in Cultural Criticism*. Baltimore: The Johns Hopkins University Press.
Whitman, Cedric
  1965 *Homer and the Homeric Tradition*. New York: Norton.
Whorf, Benjamin Lee
  1956 "The Relation of Habitual Thought and Behavior to Language." In *Language, Thought, and Reality*. Cambridge, Mass.: MIT Press.
Willemse, Hein
  1987 "Poem." In David Bunn and Jane Taylor, eds., *From South Africa* (*TriQuarterly* 69: 180–81). Reprinted in Bunn and Taylor, eds., *From South Africa: New Writing, Photographs, and Art*. Chicago: University of Chicago Press, 1988.
Williams, Raymond
  1985 [1977] *Marxism and Literature*. Oxford: Oxford University Press.
Williams, William Carlos
  1979 "Projective Verse *and* The Practice." In Reginald Gibbons, ed., *The Poet's Work*. Boston: Houghton Mifflin.
Wilson, Peter
  1980 *Man, the Promising Primate: The Conditions of Human Evolution*. New Haven, Conn.: Yale University Press.
Wimsatt, W. K.
  1954 *The Verbal Icon: Studies in the Meaning of Poetry*. Lexington: University Press of Kentucky.
Wimsatt, William
  1986 "Developmental Constraints, Generative Entrenchment, and the Innate/Acquired Distinction." In W. Bechtel, ed., *Integrating Scientific Disciplines*. Dordrecht, Neth.: Martinus Nijhoff.

Witherspoon, Gary
  1977 *Language and Art in the Navajo Universe.* Ann Arbor: University of Michigan Press.
Wittgenstein, L.
  1953 *Philosophical Investigations.* Oxford: Oxford University Press.
Yamaguchiken Kyōiku Iinkai Bunkaka (Cultural Section, Kyōiku Iinkai, Yamaguchi Prefecture), ed.
  1980 *Suō Sarumawashi Kinkyū Chōsa Hōkokusho.* Yamaguchi Prefecture: Board of Education, Yamaguchi Prefecture.
Yanagita, Kunio, ed.
  1951 *Minzokugaku Jiten* (Ethnographic dictionary). Tokyo: Tōkyōdō.
Yokoi, Kiyoshi
  1980 *Gekokujō no Bunka* (Literature of the Gekokujō [The below conquering the above]). Tokyo: Tokyo Daigaku Shuppankai.
Yoshino, Hiroko
  1984 [1983] *Inyō Gogyō to Nihon no Minzoku* (Yin-Yang and the Five Elements—their presence in the lives of the Japanese). Kyoto: Jinbun Shoin.

Index

In this index "f" after a number indicates a separate reference on the next page, and "ff" indicates separate references on the next two pages. A continuous discussion over two or more pages is indicated by a span of numbers. *Passim* is used for a cluster of references in close but not consecutive sequence.

Library of Congress Cataloging-in-Publication Data

Beyond metaphor : the theory of tropes in anthropology / edited by
    James W. Fernandez.
      p.   cm.
    Includes bibliographical references and index.
    ISBN 0-8047-1870-9 (cl.) ISBN 0-8047-1940-3 (pbk.)
      I. Symbolism.   2. Metaphor—Cross-cultural studies.   3. Cognition
and culture.   4. Ethnology—Philosophy.   I. Fernandez, James W.
GN452.5.B48   1991
306—dc20   90-21170
                                                              CIP

⊗ This book is printed on acid-free paper.